RENNER
A TO Z

**Comments and Quotes by Rick Renner
on 400 Bible Topics A to Z!**

Unless otherwise indicated, all scriptural quotations are from the *King James Version* of the Bible.

Renner A to Z —
Comments and Quotes by Rick Renner on 400 Bible Topics A to Z!
ISBN: 978-1-6675-0584-8
Ebook ISBN: 978-1-6675-0585-5
Copyright © 2024 by Rick Renner
1814 W. Tacoma St.
Broken Arrow, OK 74012

Published by Harrison House
Shippensburg, PA 17257
www.harrisonhouse.com

1 2 3 4 5 6 / 28 27 26 25 24
1st printing

Editorial Consultants: Veronica Bagby and Rebecca L. Gilbert
Cover Design: Lisa Moore
Text Design: Lisa Simpson, www.SimpsonProductions.net

DEDICATION

This book is filled with 1,780 comments and quotes from books I have written over many decades of ministry. Throughout the years during which I've written these books, it has been our partners who have supported every aspect of our ministry as we've ministered God's Word all over the world through every available means.

According to First Corinthians 3:6, three components are required for anything to grow in ministry. *First*, someone must be willing to do the job of planting. *Second*, someone must be willing to water what has been planted. And *third*, the correct atmospheric conditions must be present so that what has been planted and watered can grow.

When I think of these three components, I see this principle at work in our own ministry. *First*, I see how Denise and I, our sons, and our team have done our part in planting the message of the Gospel, the teaching of God's Word, and the establishing of the Church around the world. *Second*, I see how He has brought faithful partners to us whose agreement, finances, and prayers have been used to strategically water what we have planted by His grace. *Third*, I see how God — the most important part of it all — is the One who has supplied the environment required to make it all grow.

I am thankful that the Lord has allowed Denise and me and our family to do what He has assigned us to do. But I am also profoundly thankful to every one of our precious partners who has sown his or her agreement, faith, finances, and prayers over what we have planted by God's grace. And, of course, I am most of all thankful to God for faithfully and supernaturally doing His part to make it all grow and bear fruit.

I am so aware, and I'm sure you know it's true, that even if we each do our part of planting and watering, nothing can grow unless God does His part. That's why I am so grateful to Him, our Ultimate Partner, to whom all glory is due for what has been accomplished in this ministry by His grace, strength, ability, and power. But because of our ministry partners' role over the years to faithfully water what we have planted, I desire to dedicate this book to *them*.

To you, partner of RENNER Ministries: My family and I are eternally grateful for your belief in us and in what God has called us to do. For every prayer of agreement you've prayed and every gift you have sown to help us fulfill the ministry He has given us, we say *thank you*. We have done our part, God has done His part — and you have done your part!

For all this, I dedicate this book to you.

CONTENTS

D

E

W

X

Y

Z

A

Abortion

Make no mistake — this present generation is tainted with the blood of innocent children. And one could argue that this generation as a whole is largely guilty of the most heinous and barbaric behavior perhaps in the entire history of mankind because of the murder of these 2 billion unborn children worldwide in the past 100 years.

Fallen Angels, Giants, Monsters,
and the World Before the Flood

Although we may think the mass killings that occurred at the hands of Nero, Domitian, Hitler, Stalin, or other cruel leaders were barbaric and cruel — a fact that no one would argue with — those barbaric times do not come close to the magnitude of the horrific cost of lives that abortion providers as a whole are responsible for.

Last-Days Survival Guide —
A Scriptural Handbook To Prepare You
for These Perilous Times

Absolute Truth

Despite the immense external pressures on Christians to water down their message of absolute moral truth in order to make the Gospel seem more inclusive, Christ calls on believers to refuse to compromise their rock-solid commitment to Him and to the unwavering truth of Scripture.

No Room for Compromise —
Christ's Message to Today's Church, Volume Two —
Seven Messages to the Seven Churches

Unfortunately, many Christians are gravitating toward a more pluralistic, inclusive position. In fact, the trend toward such thinking is increasing so rapidly among young people *in churches* that many are even wavering on the very basic tenets of the Christian faith. Foundational beliefs — such as the virgin birth, the sinlessness of Christ, the need to repent, moral rights and wrongs, and a literal Heaven and hell — are all on the table with the younger generation. Recent statistical analyses clearly show that the belief in absolute truth has already regressed to such a point that the younger generation generally sees no need to convert acquaintances or friends of a different faith to Christ.

No Room for Compromise

If today's Church and its leadership don't stand up for *the faith* — regardless of the price required to proclaim it in its purest form — it will be only a matter of time until Christianity is reduced to nothing more than another life-less religion or philosophy among a cast of many others.

Fallen Angels, Giants, Monsters,
and the World Before the Flood

Accountability

There are times we all need someone to speak into our lives who will watch out for our souls — trustworthy individuals who will pray with us, speak the Word to us, be honest and forthright with us, and hold us accountable.

Last-Days Survival Guide

Accountability to godly people that the Lord places around you is part of His design for protecting your divine calling and your life, and it is just a fact that it is difficult to maintain long-term spiritual and emotional health without people in your life who know you and who can help strengthen and fortify you in your Christian walk.

Signs You'll See Just Before Jesus Comes

Having a measure of accountability helps one to correct his or her mistakes, but if there are no authoritative voices in one's life to bring mistakes to his or her awareness, the possibility for a person to float further and further off track with grave consequences grows more probable and more dangerous — and it is not only dangerous for the one who is adrift, but also for those who listen to and who follow his or her ministry.

Apostles and Prophets — Their Roles in the Past,
the Present, and the Last Days

Rather than try to "go it alone" in a world where morals have been thrown to the wind, why not join a support system of friends who can hold you accountable to your commitment to maintain a godly life? Providing yourself with this kind of accountability can save you from serious mistakes, but it could also guard you from mistakes with long-term consequences. A network of godly friends can help you stay on track with the Lord and assist you as you move forward to fulfill your divine destiny and calling.

Signs You'll See Just Before Jesus Comes

Addiction

As a result of the widespread consumption of alcohol and misuse of prescription drugs and illegal drugs in today's society, thousands of families have suffered greatly from the havoc wreaked by addicted family members, and this has contributed to a deepening disintegration of the family unit because of the confusion and disconnection these addictions produce in relationships.

Last-Days Survival Guide

Research shows that children who grow up in environments of addiction struggle deeply within themselves with brokenness. If the children don't succumb to addiction themselves, they often isolate themselves from others as a form of self-protection.

Last-Days Survival Guide

Frequently, an addict slides into deeper poverty, with a host of other problems propelling the decline — such as marital troubles, divorce, loss of job, and possibly arrest and criminal charges. In short, the impact of addiction creates a never-ending, losing battle for financial survival that often leads to financial ruin.

Last-Days Survival Guide

Adventure

Pick up your feet and take that first step into the unknown! That's where your faith will explode and the adventure will take off. You'll never know the joy of truly serving God in a life of faith by sitting at home, watching television, avoiding new challenges in life, or ignoring what you know the Holy Spirit is asking you to do!

The Point of No Return —
Tackling Your Next New Assignment
With Courage and Common Sense

I can personally testify that neither Denise, nor I, nor our sons, ever really lost anything by saying *yes* to Jesus' call on our lives and by committing ourselves completely, 100 percent, to doing whatever He has asked us to do. Our family learned that when you obey what Jesus asks you to do, it never *takes away* from you — it *adds* to you, leading you into an unlikely and amazing life full of adventure!

Unlikely — Our Faith-Filled Journey
to the Ends of the Earth

Adventure and excitement lie *on the other side of the river!* When you first step off the bank and put your foot into the waters, you'll experience a surge of faith and excitement like you've never before known in your life — and when those waters part for you, you'll know a dimension of faith that can only be known by the bravest and most daring men and women of God.

The Point of No Return

Agreement

When you find yourself in a dilemma and need help from Heaven, find another believer who can get into prayerful agreement with you. Take turns praying, and pray together in the Spirit, letting your spirits mix and mingle and harmonize as they ascend to the throne of God to produce a symphony of prayer. When God hears this, it's only a matter of time until He begins to move Heaven and earth to answer your prayers!

Sparkling Gems From the Greek, Volume 2

Creative power is released when the heart and mouth get into agreement! That is why you must be careful about what you believe in your heart and say with your mouth, because when your heart and mouth get "in sync" with each other, it literally makes things come to pass!

Sparkling Gems From the Greek, Volume 1

The biblical meaning of being in "agreement" is having a cooperative attitude and learning to play one's part — to carry out one's assignment and fulfill one's role alongside others and in submission to the appointed authority in any sphere of life.

A Life Ablaze — Ten Simple Keys
To Living on Fire for God

You are standing on solid ground when you pray in agreement with the revealed will of God, the Bible. Since your request is in agreement with what God has already revealed in His Word, you know you can be bold when you make your request! And there is no need for you to pray out of fear and anxiety either. Just quiet down, let the Word of God fill you, and ask in faith.

Sparkling Gems From the Greek, Volume 1

Alternative Lifestyles

There is currently a global public-relations campaign to endorse sin and to encourage the unrestrained acceptance of every immoral lifestyle, regardless of how it conflicts with the time-tested, authoritative voice of God's Word.

Last-Days Survival Guide

Those who participate in alternative sexual lifestyles project it to be a more advanced, liberal way of living. Even the Sodomites viewed themselves as progressives who were unshackled by moral restraints of the past. But what they were doing was not taking them forward — it was a moral reversion that produced a cesspool of moral depravity.

Fallen Angels, Giants, Monsters,
and the World Before the Flood

It's true that every person is loved by God. Mankind was so loved that God sent His Son Jesus to die as the ultimate Sacrifice for sin in order to reconcile us to Himself and purchase our eternal freedom (*see* John 3:16). But equally true is Ephesians 5:5, which tells us that fornicators, unclean persons, and idolaters have no inheritance in the Kingdom of Christ and of God. Ephesians 5:12 stresses that it is a "shame" to even speak of such things among God's people, let alone to bring those sinful ideas and lifestyles in as an accepted part of the church.

Last-Days Survival Guide

Angels

Divine protection is activated in those of us who *believe* that God's promise of protection will work for us. When we enter dangerous territory in fear, doubt, and unbelief, we are likely to get in trouble. But if we will go into that space believing and claiming that God's protection is ours and that the enemy can't do anything to hurt us, our faith in this promise will activate it and cause it to be manifested in our lives — it will even activate the ministry of angels to keep us safe!

Unlikely

Anger

When we act rashly, we usually end up later loathing the stupidity of our words and actions.

Paid in Full — An In-Depth Look at the Defining Moments of Christ's Passion

You may have suffered a hurt or offense in the past that harmed you terribly. In fact, it may have robbed you of something that can never be returned or restored. But if you refuse to forgive — to let go of anger, animosity, and bitterness — that offense will continue to work its destruction in your life. A past-tense problem will become a present-tense issue when you refuse to let go of your bitterness. If you don't get over that past offense, you will give it the power to damage and even destroy your future as you drag it along like a bag of garbage or toxic waste. At some point, you have to just let it go and get over it for your own benefit and for the benefit of those around you.

Sparkling Gems From the Greek, Volume 2

Hotheaded moments rarely produce good fruit.

Paid in Full

I'm sure you've been in situations when you've been railed at because you failed to meet someone's demands. Can you think of a time when something like this happened to you? How did you respond? Did you yell and scream back at that person when he vented his anger at you, or were you able to remain quiet and controlled as Jesus did when He was tried before Pilate, Herod Antipas, and the chief priests and elders?

Paid in Full

Anointing

When you hear the Scripture expounded by the anointing of the Holy Spirit and take it by faith into your heart, its supernatural power is *unleashed.* When that happens, every part of your being — your heart, will, thoughts, emotions, and memories — are all touched by God's power.

Last-Days Survival Guide

God Himself — the Great Anointer — fills His hands with the essence of the Spirit and lays His mighty hands upon our lives, pressing the Spirit's power and anointing ever deeper into us! If we would like a fresh anointing of the Holy Spirit upon our life, we must come before the Great Anointer to receive it!

Sparkling Gems From the Greek, Volume 1

You are anointed to help others who are struggling with what seems to be a sinking world all around them. You are called to be a part of a company of faithful, fearless believers in Jesus Christ who will act as His "hands and feet" and His voice in the earth. You can reach out to those who need strength and guidance in these perilous times — and you can be a source of deliverance and great comfort to all those around you.

Last-Days Survival Guide

You must fortify yourself and your family by sitting under the anointed preaching and teaching of the Word that encourages you, confronts you, and helps you conform to the likeness of Jesus Christ. If you are currently attending a church where the Word of God is *not* taught in power, or where a weakened and watered-down version of the Bible is preached, I urge you to begin looking for a pastor who will feed you the Bible in a way that leads to personal transformation.

Last-Days Survival Guide

Remind yourself every day that the same power that raised Jesus from the dead now resides within you and is at your disposal 24 hours a day. Then the next time you're faced with a situation that needs to be turned around with supernatural power, open your heart and let that power flow — because the anointing that rested on Jesus when He walked this earth now lives inside *you!*

Paid in Full

Answers

God is not the God of a clenched fist, but the God of an open hand — and He is willing and ready to give you the answer you need right now!

How To Receive Answers From Heaven —
What To Do When Your Prayers Go Unanswered

God will *not* rebuke you or reprove you for asking for answers. You are His child, and He wants you to have the answers you need for life. You'll find God to be open-hearted and ready to answer any question you ever put to Him. His answer may not always be what you want to hear, but if you'll really listen, He will answer your questions marvelously!

Sparkling Gems From the Greek, Volume 1

The Bible is jam-packed with the answers you need — and that includes the answers you desperately need for tricky problems that are rampant in a last-days society. God's Word provides answers to even life's most difficult problems — as long as you are willing to search them out and then walk in obedience once the answers are found.

Last-Days Survival Guide

There will undoubtedly be times in your life when the answers to your prayers won't come quickly. However, God requires you to stay spiritually strong — pushing forward and continuously engaging in robust prayer until you see what you are believing Him for come to fruition. If you are tenaciously determined to *continue* in prayer, you *will* receive the answers you seek!

Sparkling Gems From the Greek, Volume 2

Antichrist

Current society did not accidentally arrive at its present sad state of affairs. Its downward trend has been strategically orchestrated step by step, year by year, and century by century by a devious satanic plan designed to prepare the way for the man of lawlessness called the Antichrist.

Last-Days Survival Guide

The Antichrist will throw out all previously agreed-upon moral standards and rise as an aggressive proponent of departing from God's well-established laws. He will not be just a person with a lawless attitude, he will be *the* man of lawlessness — the epitome of one who has fully discarded God's well-established laws to become Satan's perfect candidate to lead a mutinous world that has likewise rejected the voice of God and of Scripture as its internal compass.

Last-Days Survival Guide

Although the Antichrist will claim to lead the world into a more "progressive" future, what he will actually bring to the world is *doom, destruction, rot, ruin,* and *decay,* and there will be absolutely no redeeming values in anything produced by his rule. He will be *brazenly against* every previous godly way of thinking, and he will lead a lawless world in an effort to bulldoze former dogmas and established codes of morality out of the way. His goal will be to construct a new world order — one that is utterly free of God's influence.

Last-Days Survival Guide

The sole reason the Antichrist and his accompanying evil has not already been fully unleashed into the world is because the Church is *a restraining force* holding back the manifestation of this satanic agenda — and this restraining force is *stalling, delaying,* and *postponing* this end-time evil.

Last-Days Survival Guide

Apostasy

The apostle Paul declared that at the end of the age, apostasy would emerge inside the Church and dress itself in the guise of the Christian faith. But like a mannequin that looks real, yet is lifeless, the apostate church will contain no life and no power.

How To Keep Your Head on Straight
in a World Gone Crazy —
Developing Discernment in These Last Days

In pulpits and congregations around the world, truth is being altered to reflect the inclusive values of a changing culture, and a major shift has occurred as pure, sound doctrine has been completely replaced over a period of years by "feel-good" messages. As a result, many people sitting in church pews today are ignorant of even the most elementary tenets of the faith.

How To Keep Your Head on Straight
in a World Gone Crazy

When a church or denomination departs from the truth, eventually it becomes little more than a humanistic good-will organization that lacks the power of God and endorses only the portions of Scripture that society finds comfortable. As a result, people stream into hell, having not been confronted with the truth they need in order to repent and be transformed by the power of the Holy Spirit.

How To Keep Your Head on Straight
in a World Gone Crazy

Once a person has erroneously concluded there is no absolute truth, that person will reach another conclusion by default — that no one has the moral authority to bring correction to someone else regarding faith, truth, and belief. This is a refashioned camouflage for an ancient sin issue called *rebellion to authority*, one that enables people to escape correction, at least temporarily, in the name of open-mindedness.

How To Keep Your Head on Straight
in a World Gone Crazy

Apostles

Apostles are *real* and *powerful* as a fivefold ministry gift, but only a *handful* of those who claim to be apostles today are real apostles — that is, compared to an ever-growing list of those who claim to be apostles or who are incorrectly called apostles by others. I want to be *kind* to those who incorrectly call themselves apostles or who incorrectly call others apostles today because I believe the misuse of this term is largely due to *unclear teaching* on the subject of apostleship.

Apostles and Prophets

The term "apostle" has become wrongly used as a badge of respect to endorse a minister's hard work and ground-breaking, pioneering efforts, but this is an incorrect use of the word "apostle" and it has created confusion. A person may be a real innovator and be good at successfully pioneering and starting things — but that alone does not qualify a person to be an apostle.

Apostles and Prophets

Apostolic ministry is real front-line ministry — it is a spiritual military expedition to push into new territory, to fight against the powers of darkness, and then to bulldoze demonic opposition out of the way so the foundation of the Church can be established where it never existed before.

Apostles and Prophets

If we count all those in the New Testament to whom the word "apostle" is specifically applied, there are *at least* 26 people who are described as apostles and who did apostolic work — and I say "at least" because there are actually a few more who could potentially be added to this list.

Apostles and Prophets

I will tell you that I personally know authentic apostles, and it is my observation that they *thrive* in territories that others find difficult or nearly impossible to even penetrate. I am not implying that their task is easy. Frontline, apostolic work can be very difficult. But an apostle is especially anointed to supernaturally cross into new territory. Once there, he becomes like a divine bulldozer to clear demonic rubbish out of the way so the process can begin for the establishing of the Church where it has never existed before.

Apostles and Prophets

Ask

If you have a specific request, you need to be *specific* when you ask God to bring about His will in the matter you're bringing before Him. You'll only experience discernible answers to prayer if you get specific when you pray.

Sparkling Gems From the Greek, Volume 2

Have you ever had the experience of asking God for the right thing in the wrong way and then never receiving what you asked for because you prayed in fear? Praying scripturally and in faith is essential if you want your requests to be answered positively. Knowing both *what* to pray and *how* to pray is vitally important.

How To Receive Answers From Heaven

Forget about the idea that you can only ask God for spiritual blessings, for the principal meaning of the Greek word for "ask" means to ask for material blessings, such as food, clothes, shelter, etc. Study the scriptures to find out exactly what God is willing to do for you and then boldly ask Him for that.

How To Receive Answers From Heaven

God isn't offended when you ask Him for clarification, and He *encourages* you to ask! When He answers, you may not enjoy what He has to tell you, or you may not be mature enough to really understand it yet, but God *likes* it when you ask Him for His wisdom. So ask in faith to receive a *bountiful, liberal, extravagant* dose of *divine insight and guidance* for the path right up ahead!

Sparkling Gems From the Greek, Volume 2

Assignment

When you look at the immensity of the assignment God is asking you to do, you may feel very small and ill-equipped for the task. But that isn't entirely bad! As long as your feelings of inadequacy don't prevent you from accepting God's new assignment, those same insecure feelings may ultimately be very beneficial to you. It's actually good to realize your dependence upon God as you initiate a major new step in your life. It's only when you become cocky and arrogant — so reliant upon yourself that you forget your need for God's strength — that you can fail.

The Point of No Return

You must face the fact that if God has called you to do something — no matter what the assignment is — there will be times when hell's forces come against you. Settle it within yourself right now that you will *always* encounter some form of opposition as you serve the Lord. It simply goes with the territory for those who are advancing God's Kingdom!

Life in the Combat Zone —
How To Survive, Thrive, and Overcome
in the Midst of Difficult Situations

When God has called you to do something important, you must be willing to do whatever is required to complete that task. This may mean that if there is no one else to do the job, you will have to sweep the floor, lick and seal envelopes, take out the trash, or answer the telephone. When someone else is raised up to do these smaller tasks, you will be freed to concentrate more fully on your larger vision. But until then, you must have a willing heart to do whatever is required to keep things functioning well on the road to fulfilling your assignment.

Sparkling Gems From the Greek, Volume 1

To ensure that we're really ready for our next big assignment, sometimes it takes a little longer than we might like before God promotes us. It's hard on the flesh while we wait, yet it is actually the mercy of God at work. You see, during that time of waiting, the imperfections that could potentially ruin us are exposed so that God can remove them. Then He can move us up into the new position with no concern that a hidden flaw will cause us to fall flat on our faces. By taking time to make sure you're ready, when God finally does promote you, you'll have what you need both naturally and spiritually to stay in that God-ordained position as you fulfill your assignment with excellence!

Unlikely

Attacks

If you're under attack, *be encouraged!* You must be right on track, because the devil is terribly concerned about what will happen if you act on what God has revealed to you. Don't back down and don't surrender to the enemy's attack! Don't surrender to the enemy's vicious lies in your mind, his attacks against your body, his challenges to your finances, or his assaults on your relationships. Regardless of how much resistance he tries to bring against you, don't you dare back up on that word God gave you!

Sparkling Gems From the Greek, Volume 1

None of Satan's attacks to destroy the Church has ever succeeded. By studying Church history, it becomes evident very quickly that each attack the enemy has waged against the Church has ultimately helped further the cause of Jesus Christ. Two thousand years of experience emphatically tell us that the devil has absolutely no winning strategies. He simply does not know how to win!

Dressed To Kill — A Biblical Approach
to Spiritual Warfare and Armor

You need to know that when you're finally positioned in the will of God, the devil will do his best to find a way to push you off course. He doesn't want you to stay on God's path for your life, so he will try to muster an attack against you to scare you away, to knock you off track, or to convince you to abandon God's direction for your life.

The Will of God — The Key to Your Success:
Positioning Yourself To Live in God's
Supernatural Power, Provision, and Protection

If an unprepared believer is hit hard by one of Satan's attacks, it has the potential to remove him or her permanently from the fight, and history has shown time and time again that some believers are unwilling to do what is necessary to withstand the enemy's onslaughts. Instead of standing their ground and tenaciously fighting back, they crumble under the pressure and retreat, seceding the front lines of battle that God has called them to protect.

Life in the Combat Zone

When thoughts of failure and feelings of depression assail your mind, you need to recognize them as an attack of the devil to make you believe you are less than who you are. You are a threat to the devil and his works because of the divine power that is at your disposal. Think about what that power will do when released into a situation — and then expect it to flow through you!

Paid in Full

Believe me when I tell you that our family has experienced some of Satan's unfair tactics as he has tried to create impasses for us to stop us from fulfilling our mission. Some of these attacks have taken us by surprise and some were self-inflicted. But we learned that if the devil tries to create an impasse to stop us — those moments can become opportunities to use our faith to slap the wits out of him and to get back on track if we've veered from the course!

Unlikely

It doesn't matter what the devil does — God is able to turn it around and make it work for your good even though

God did not authorize the assault waged against you and would never do such things to you. But by the time God is done using that attack as a steppingstone to get you to a place of greater victory, the devil will be sorry he ever attacked you!

The Will of God — The Key to Your Success

Attitude

A person's attitude is like the sap of a tree. It comes directly from inside him. And just as the sap of a tree produces good or bad fruit, a person's inner thoughts and attitudes will be manifested in his outward attitudes and actions. If you want to know what's deep inside a person, observe his attitudes and watch how he relates to other people. His fruit will tell you the truth about who he really is.

Ten Guidelines To Help You Achieve Your Long-Awaited Promotion!

We're not able to control what others do or say to us, but we *are* able to control what goes on inside of us, and it's that "inside" part — *the part we control* — that God will hold us responsible for.

You Can Get Over It — How To Confront, Forgive, and Move On

Just as you wouldn't go to bed in dirty clothes at night, neither should you go to bed with wrong attitudes. You must deal with them like an old set of filthy clothes. *You have to decide to get rid of those bad attitudes!* And it's important to realize that dirty clothes don't fall off your body by accident! To get them off, you have to push the buttons through the buttonholes, unzip the zipper, and slip the clothes off your arms and legs one piece at a time. Dirty clothes don't automatically come off just because you realize they are dirty. They will come off only if you do something to remove them! You must start taking steps to remove those negative things from your life — to lay them down and push them so far away that you'll never be able to reach them again!

Sparkling Gems From the Greek, Volume 1

When we harbor wrong attitudes in our hearts, those attitudes restrict us from moving up into higher realms of God's presence and glory, and we are unable to enter into the full dimension of God that's available to us because those negative attitudes will block us from experiencing His anointing.

You Can Get Over It

If you'd just decide to smile all day and act as though you were totally fulfilled and content with life, you'd be amazed at how that one decision can affect your attitude and your life in general. Scientists have proven that the configuration of your mouth can affect the attitude of your mind. Tests have shown that people who frown are always sad and those who smile have a more positive outlook on life.

Dream Thieves — Overcoming Obstacles
To Fulfill Your Dreams

Authority

How a person relates to authority — or how a person does *not* relate to authority — will eventually be one of the determining factors to gauge how high or low that person will go in life.

A Life Ablaze

Christ respects and honors those whom He has set in authority, and He doesn't bypass the divine order He has established in the church. Even if a God-appointed messenger, such as a pastor, refuses to hear, Jesus will nevertheless speak to him *first* by His Spirit; then the pastor has the opportunity to accept, ignore, or reject what the Holy Spirit is saying. But even if Christ knows that the pastor doesn't have ears to hear, He will not circumvent the chain of authority in the local church.

A Light in Darkness, Volume One —
Seven Messages to the Seven Churches

We are not puny, struggling believers who are somehow trying to learn how to cope with the devil's attacks against us. We're not merely trying to learn how to scrape by or survive. Jesus' death and resurrection gave us the legal authority to keep Satan under our feet!

Sparkling Gems From the Greek, Volume 1

Those who are in positions of authority today are under assault, and we must undergird them with prayer. From the highest to the lowest levels of authority — from the President, to our congressmen and senators, state governors, city mayors, police, schoolteachers, parents, and pastors — uncivil behavior is being unleashed in these end times on a ferocious scale.

A Life Ablaze

B

Backslidden Believers

It is entirely possible to lead a large, thriving ministry and yet be backslidden and no longer enraptured with the Lord. Spiritual backsliding occurs when believers lose their focus on Jesus and become preoccupied with other things — *including the work of the ministry.*

A Light in Darkness

Society is composed of individuals who are being negatively affected by the unrelenting mental bombardments of evil influences. This includes believers who have allowed themselves to drift so far from God's ways that they lie, steal, cheat, fornicate, live as couples outside of marriage, explore other types of sexuality outside the confines of God's Word, and watch movies that once would have grieved their hearts.

How To Keep Your Head on Straight in a World Gone Crazy

When someone we know and love — perhaps even someone we have trusted in the past — falls into error or sin, we may be tempted to feel betrayed and angry toward that person. We may wonder how that person could have ever veered off track into such deep moral or spiritual foolishness. But holding a hostile attitude against those who are walking in doctrinal error or living in blatant sin will not set them free — and it won't help our heart condition either.

How To Keep Your Head on Straight
in a World Gone Crazy

Never forget that the Holy Spirit is a Divine Lover. He is preoccupied with you. He wants to possess you totally, and He desires that your affection be set wholly on Him. That's why the Holy Spirit feels like a lover who has been robbed if you walk and talk like an unbeliever or give your life to the things of this world. He jealously desires His relationship with you to be restored. He has divine malice toward the worldliness that has usurped His role in your life.

Sparkling Gems From the Greek, Volume 1

Balaam

Balaam — one of history's most famous sorcerers — was absolutely unable to penetrate God's protective shield that held fast and secure around His people. Although there are some today who allege that people involved in the occult have the power to curse believers, Scripture clearly teaches that *no one* has the power to curse what God has blessed, and the story of Balaam serves as a perpetual reminder that what God has blessed is *blessed*, and that fact cannot be reversed.

Sparkling Gems From the Greek, Volume 2

In ancient rabbinic literature, Balaam is commonly referred to as "the wicked one" and depicted as blind in one eye and lame in one foot. He was essentially viewed as being the pagan equivalent to Moses, widely known for his abilities to interpret dreams, practice witchcraft, and foresee the future. Ancient commentary also asserts that Balaam's followers were known for possessing an evil eye and a haughty spirit and for being greedy and morally corrupt.

No Room for Compromise

Despite Balaam's reputation, there is not a single biblical record that confirms he actually possessed the ability to bless *or* curse anyone, much less the entire nation of Israel. People may have *believed* he had these powers, but there is no biblical evidence to support this claim.

No Room for Compromise

The story of Balaam serves as a perpetual reminder to God's people through the centuries that although Satan may be the god of the unbelieving world and may exert a measure of control over it, he does *not* have the ultimate power to control, defeat, or curse God's people — for what God has blessed is blessed, and this fact simply cannot be reversed!

No Room for Compromise

Baptism (Water)

In the Early Church, although water baptism was *not* essential for salvation, it *was* considered essential for one to walk as a serious disciple. That's why from the beginning to the end of the book of Acts, we find this divine pattern: People were water baptized immediately after they were saved.

Build Your Foundation —
Six Must-Have Beliefs for Constructing
an Unshakable Christian Life

Scripture commands all who repent and who receive Jesus Christ as Lord to be water-baptized — and in this act, Christians declare to the world that they have died with Christ and have been raised with Him to walk in the newness of life. Although water baptism is not a requirement for salvation, it is a required step for every Christian to embark on a life of obedience.

How To Keep Your Head on Straight
in a World Gone Crazy

The spiritual action taking place through the act of water baptism is so powerful that people can emerge from the baptismal waters delivered, healed, and set free from the shackles that clung to them through the old man.

Build Your Foundation

I've seen over the years that Christians who skip or disregard this step of water baptism in the building of their spiritual foundation often fall out of fellowship and eventually fall back into sin. Or they struggle with being obedient in many other areas of their lives. That would make sense, because they argued with the Lord at the very first point of obedience to be baptized. Their decision — perhaps even innocently — to disregard this foundational step forms a pattern of disobedience in their lives.

Build Your Foundation

Baptism in the Holy Spirit

The baptism in the Holy Spirit is a promise offered to all believers that is distinct from the new birth — and with it comes power for life, power for service, and the bestowment of the gifts of the Holy Spirit.

How To Keep Your Head on Straight
in a World Gone Crazy

Eventually, every hungry Christian reaches this turning point — a time when the heart is no longer satisfied and seeks for more. That is when God's Spirit beckons that person and draws him or her closer — to enter a deeper relationship with Him. The season of spiritual hunger and thirst that precedes this infilling can be one of the most uncomfortable, unsatisfying periods a person can ever experience. Amazingly, it is in this state of spiritual misery that a person is driven to a position where God can reveal Himself to him or her in a more meaningful, personal, and powerful way.

Unlikely

The baptism in the Holy Spirit opens the door for a person to operate in the power of God and in the supernatural workings of the Holy Spirit's gifts. The baptism in the Holy Spirit unleashes a flood of divine power to empower and enable a believer to operate mightily in spiritual gifts for the benefit of man and the furtherance of God's Kingdom.

Why We Need the Gifts of the Holy Spirit

Belief

With God *all* things are possible; therefore, *it's up to you and me* to get our thinking in line with God's Word. And as we build up our faith to the level it needs to be for the new challenge ahead of us, we will experience an explosion of supernatural power in us that literally carries us over into the realm where impossible things become possible!

Sparkling Gems From the Greek, Volume 2

God is a good God who gives good things to people, and He is *not* the one who sends bad things into people's lives. It is important that we settle this in our hearts, for it helps us know what to receive and what to reject in our lives. Remember, *what we believe ultimately determines what we receive.*

The Will of God — The Key to Your Success

It's crucial to realize Satan can't force you to do anything! You are the final authority when it comes to what you choose to believe, the attitudes you choose to develop, the company you choose to keep, the way you choose to behave, and the works you choose to accomplish. Ultimately, you decide whether or not you will do what you or what God wants you to do — whether you will do things your way or God's way.

Dream Thieves

We are living in a time when people exalt their personal beliefs — founded on compromise, family of origin, environment, emotions, and so forth — over the truth of the Bible.

How To Keep Your Head on Straight
in a World Gone Crazy

If God has told me to do something — regardless of how big or how impossible it seems to the natural mind — I begin to tell myself that I can do it and that my eyes will see it come to pass. *After all, if it couldn't be done, why would He ask me to do it?*

Sparkling Gems From the Greek, Volume 2

Betrayal

We've all been burned at least once in life, but if we allow the fear of being hurt again to take root in our hearts, it could cause us to step backward into isolation, never again to develop close relationships, to receive a supply from others, or to make deposits into others' lives. And if you allow this to occur in your life, you will become "fatally wounded." *Satan's plan will have worked!* It simply isn't possible for you to live and fight in the spiritual combat zone — and *win* — without the assistance of others.

Life in the Combat Zone

When you have been through a hurtful experience, letting your emotions get the best of you by telling yourself to go on alone is not the right answer. You need to get up, brush off the dirt, learn from your mistakes, and go for it again with all your heart. Rather than blame someone else for what has happened, just accept responsibility for where *you* may have failed. Stop moaning about the bump in the road you've hit and allow that ordeal to become a learning experience.

Sparkling Gems From the Greek, Volume 1

The number-one reason we get hurt in relationships is not that we let people get close to us; it's that we let the *wrong* people come alongside us in life.

Life in the Combat Zone

It is painful to feel betrayed by someone that is close to you, but if you'll allow this experience to work for you and not against you, it will make you a stronger and better person. Then when you come out on the other side of this experience, you'll be in a position to understand what others are going through who have been hurt by betrayal so you can be a help and a blessing to them.

Paid in Full

The Bible

The Bible *itself* is fire — infused with the fiery presence of the Holy Spirit who inspired men to write it.

A Life Ablaze

God didn't just breathe *on* the Scriptures — He breathed *into* them. And God is *in* the Bible! You need to understand that the very Presence of *God Himself* is contained in the pages of the Bible.

Last-Days Survival Guide

The Bible contains the saving and delivering power of God. If you'll believe it, embrace it, and act upon it, the latent power in His words will be released to cause you to progressively experience more and more deliverance, healing, and wholeness in every area of your life!

Last-Days Survival Guide

There has never been a more important time in history for Christian believers to read, study, and meditate on the Word of God — the *Bible*. The way to circumvent spiritual seduction and deception is by knowing, understanding, and being rooted in the truth of God's Word.

Signs You'll See Just Before Jesus Comes

If we'll silence our minds and let the words of the Bible enter our spiritual ears and hearts, those words will come *alive* inside us in the same way the Scriptures were ignited and burned in the hearts of the disciples who walked with Jesus on the road to Emmaus (*see* Luke 24:13-32).

A Life Ablaze

When God breathed out the Scriptures, every word, every paragraph — *every part of it* — was infused with His divine presence, and there's not a word in the Bible that is void of the presence and power of God. And by meditating on and studying God's Word, you will begin to release the presence of God that is in the Bible directly into your life.

Last-Days Survival Guide

The Bible is the only piece of spiritual armor that is tangible to hold and visible to the eye, which means it was so important for us to have the Word of God in our possession that God permitted this divine Word to pass from the spirit realm into our world so we could hold it in our hands. It is the only weapon in our full arsenal of weaponry that we can actually physically hold and see!

Dressed To Kill

Satan knows the life-transforming power that is locked inside the Bible. That's why he fights so hard to get believers and churches to back away from it. He lures them to water it down, modify it, or even eliminate it.

A Life Ablaze

Right there in your home or apartment is a source of power beyond your wildest imagination. It's probably sitting on a shelf, situated nicely on a table, or perhaps even kept in the magazine rack in the bathroom. Or maybe you keep this source of power in the drawer of your desk at work or on the back seat of your car. You may have guessed by now that I'm talking about your Bible, which is one of the greatest sources of power on earth!

Sparkling Gems From the Greek, Volume 1

We have to open our Bible like we would open a treasure and allow *Who* is inside it to permeate every part of our being — and as we do, the Bible has the power to put us on our feet again, secure our foundation, heal us, restore us, make us whole, protect us, and set our marriages and families on the right course.

Last-Days Survival Guide

Bible Education

The most basic tenets of faith are today not largely known by churchgoers. Basic Bible doctrines such as the virgin birth, the sinlessness of Christ, man's sin, salvation, holiness, and eternal judgment are either unknown, seldom taught, or considered optional.

How To Keep Your Head on Straight
in a World Gone Crazy

So many are hungry for the pure teaching of God's Word, but they're not receiving it because much of the solid teaching that was taught to earlier generations has been replaced by motivational sermons — or *teaching of a different kind.* But when the Bible is taught correctly, it has a sobering effect on people. It helps them keep their own heads on straight, it helps them win in the circumstances of life, and it stabilizes them in times of instability and uncertainty.

Sparkling Gems From the Greek, Volume 2

In some churches today, there is very little Bible teaching to awaken people's hearts and clear their obscured thinking. As a result, people are becoming biblically illiterate and spiritually numb — completely uninformed of what the Bible says concerning very serious issues. This is certainly not true of all churches, but it is a disturbing and growing trend.

Signs You'll See Just Before Jesus Comes

When the emphasis of the Bible is diminished on a wide scale, many within the Church have historically lost their ability to discern what is and isn't a true move of the Holy Spirit. In those times, movements have drifted into nonsense that is presented as a move of the Spirit, which has frequently led to incorrect perceptions about the Holy Spirit.

How To Keep Your Head on Straight
in a World Gone Crazy

Many people are regrettably unable to intelligently explain what they believe from the Bible. But it is important that each of us studies to be able to provide *biblical answers* for any person who is sincerely seeking God and His Word. So I must ask you — can *you* defend what you biblically believe?

Unlikely

Bitterness

Most people "chew" on their feelings of bitterness and unforgiveness for a long time. They nibble on the offense for a while, then they pause to digest what they've eaten, and then they start nibbling on it again — taking one little bite, then another. As they think and meditate on the perceived offense, they internalize their bitter feelings toward the person or persons who offended them, and in the end, the sour, bitter fruit of unforgiveness makes *them* sour and bitter as well.

You Can Get Over It

Bitterness grows a little here and a little there until it finally becomes a huge, ugly growth that defiles our entire lives. It usually starts peeking up out of the depths of our souls in the form of negative thoughts about another person or a sour, sharp, distrusting, cynical attitude toward someone who has offended us. If the root is not quickly uprooted and removed, that bitterness will eventually become a full-blown tree that produces *bitter, wounding, hurtful,* and *scornful* fruit for everyone who eats of it.

Sparkling Gems From the Greek, Volume 1

The devil knows that if he can get you to spend a little time meditating on a wrong that was done to you, that perceived wrong will be blown out of proportion until you finally become ensnared in bitterness, resentment, and unforgiveness.

You Can Get Over It

Blame-Shifting

When people don't want to face the consequences of their own failure, they often look for someone else to blame. They point the finger at others and say, *"They are the reason we are in this mess!"* By pointing their fingers away from themselves and shifting the blame to someone else, they attempt to deflect the punishment they deserve themselves. But shifting blame to someone else started all the way back in the Garden of Eden when Adam pointed his finger at Eve and blamed her for his failure to obey God. When sin entered the human race, one of the first manifestations of sinful nature was Adam's refusal to accept responsibility for his choices and for his attempt to blame his wife for his failure.

Sparkling Gems From the Greek, Volume 2

When God confronted Adam and Eve, they had the opportunity to accept responsibility for their sinful failure, but Adam failed to accept responsibility and instead attempted to shift the blame for their disobedience entirely to Eve. Then Eve tried to shift the blame to the serpent for beguiling her. Thus, Adam and Eve played the first "blame game" as they both ardently tried to convince God that someone other than themselves should be blamed for their own personal failures. With this first act of disobedience, blame-shifting was introduced to the human race as one of the earliest symptoms of sin, and it has remained one of sin's chief characteristics ever since the inexcusable failure that occurred in the Garden of Eden.

A Light in Darkness

Blasphemy

The Holy Spirit prophesied that blasphemy would become commonplace as we approached the end of the age.

Last-Days Survival Guide

The Greek word for "blasphemy" means *to slander, to accuse, to speak against,* or *to speak derogatory words for the purpose of injuring or harming someone's reputation.* It also signifies profane, foul, unclean language, but in general, it refers to any derogatory speech intended to defame, injure, or harm another's reputation.

The Will of God — The Key to Your Success

So much of what was once considered obscene, indecent, or profane is no longer included in the profanity category. Society has descended into such a moral abyss that blasphemous language in private life and in public forums goes nearly unnoticed.

Last-Days Survival Guide

Scientific study has revealed that the use of profanity generally produces profane behaviors, and this tells us that when the bar is lowered regarding what comes out of the mouth, the bar is also lowered concerning other people's behaviors or actions. It should also be noted that there is a proven scientific correlation between profanity and dishonesty.

Last-Days Survival Guide

Shocking is the only word I can think of to describe the embarrassing public behavior of politicians that displays such a sharp descent from respectful disagreement to an ugly mess of intolerance and blasphemous mudslinging. And a widespread weaponizing of the media is being used to perpetuate this indecent assault.

Last-Days Survival Guide

Blessing

God wants you to eat and enjoy the fruit of your labors, just as a hard-working farmer does after giving his life to see his crops grow in his field. Your part is to work your land and labor strenuously to see your dream come to pass; then God promises that you will eventually eat the fruit of your hard work! As you focus on doing your job well, you can expect to be blessed, recognized, rewarded, and remunerated for your efforts, for God says that anyone who works hard and sticks with his project to the end deserves to eat the fruit!

Sparkling Gems From the Greek, Volume 1

You may be tempted to resist being a blessing or to do nothing for someone you feel has done wrong to you. But it is *never* your job to pay someone back for what he or she did to you or to withhold a blessing when you are able to give it.

Sparkling Gems From the Greek, Volume 2

Church should be a place where everyone is committed to being a blessing to one another. If each member of a local church family took this approach, observing and contemplating each other's needs this thoroughly, it would be very hard for discouragement to find its way into the family of God!

Sparkling Gems From the Greek, Volume 1

The Blood of Jesus

If you have been forgiven and washed in the precious blood of Christ, you are forgiven — *period*. The devil may try to hassle you in your mind and torment you with past memories that God Himself doesn't remember. But since Christ's blood has been applied to your life, He finds you completely blameless and free from shame.

Sparkling Gems From the Greek, Volume 2

Jesus' blood was poured out for *you*. Think about the kind of love that would compel Jesus to pour out His life so you could have mercy instead of judgment and your debt could be paid in full.

Paid in Full

The price Jesus paid for us was the highest price ever paid for a slave in the history of mankind. It was the shedding of Jesus' own blood that guaranteed our deliverance and lasting freedom from demonic powers that previously held us captive.

Dressed To Kill

Don't let your heart become hard by allowing unconfessed sin to build in your soul. *Quickly* confess sin and submit it to the cleansing power of Jesus' blood. As you do, you'll immediately receive forgiveness and mercy as the blood of Jesus cleanses you from any act or thought that has grieved the Spirit of God. Once your sin is placed under the blood of Jesus, *it is under the blood of Jesus forever*, and God will never deal with you about it in eternity, because that sin has become nonexistent in the mind of God.

Build Your Foundation

You don't have to keep being negative about yourself all the time, and you don't have to beat yourself over the head, constantly telling yourself how unworthy you are. In fact, you actually insult the power of the redemptive work of Jesus when you do that, for Jesus Christ *made* you worthy when He went to the Cross on your behalf and shed His own precious blood. He *made* you righteous! He *made* you a new creation in Him.

The Holy Spirit and You —
Working Together as Heaven's Dynamic Duo

A day is coming in the near future when all those who have been washed in the blood of the Lamb will join around His majestic throne to worship and give honor to Jesus Christ.

A Light in Darkness

Body

The human body is fragile. A wrong diet can kill it; working too hard can break it; too much pressure can damage it, and even after caring tenderly for it our whole lifetime, it still dies. The greatest minds, the most creative inventors, the highest intellects, the most colorful writers, and the most talented politicians all die. Eventually the human body breaks under the stress of age, and the vessel that carried such incredible talent and potential is reduced to unrecognizable dust, totally devoid of value. Some human vessels break earlier and some last longer, but eventually they all break, they all collapse, and they all return to dust.

The Holy Spirit and You

We decorate our exteriors with beautiful clothing and cosmetics; nevertheless, our bodies remain *fragile, inferior, low-grade, mediocre, shoddy, second-rate, substandard,* and *flawed.* Yet God chose to place the inexhaustible treasure of His Spirit in us, and He turned us into a vessel that is designed to carry this divine treasure wherever we go.

Apostles and Prophets

Consider how valuable you and your body must be to God that He would allow His Son to be scourged for you to be healed!

Paid in Full

By mastering his body and keeping it under his control, Paul made his flesh an instrument through which he preached the Gospel. His feet became his tool to take the Gospel to places that had never heard the Good News. His eyes became instruments through which he was able to identify needs that God's power could meet. His voice became the voice of salvation, healing, and deliverance to those who heard him preach. His hands became the hands of God that brought a healing and compassionate touch to those in need. Paul's body, which he determined to make his slave and his instrument, was never allowed to have its own way. Rather, Paul kept it under his command and made it his slave for the purpose of accomplishing his God-given dreams.

Sparkling Gems From the Greek, Volume 1

If you continue going the way you are going right now, is your physical body going to be a fine-tuned instrument that God can use, or is it going to be the very tool the devil uses to bring you into discredit and shame? Who is running your life today — you or your flesh? Don't join the ranks of those who were once used by the Lord but are now set aside and ruined because they refused to bring their bodies into subjection!

Sparkling Gems From the Greek, Volume 1

Boldness

You are anointed to help others who are struggling with what seems to be a sinking world all around them. You are called to be a part of a company of faithful, fearless believers in Jesus Christ who will act as His "hands and feet" and His "voice" in the earth. You can reach out to those who need strength and guidance in these perilous times, and you can be a source of deliverance and great comfort to them.

Last-Days Survival Guide

As representatives of God, we have a responsibility to raise the standard of His truth in every situation — being willing to stand at odds with every law that is opposed to Scripture, to dig our heels into scriptural truth, and to *refuse* to bend with the times — no matter what everyone else around us is doing.

*How To Keep Your Head on Straight
in a World Gone Crazy*

Although the religious people of Jesus' day often took offense at His blunt words of truth, the common folk were not offended by His message — and, in fact, they were *drawn* to Him because they knew that they could depend on Him to tell them the truth.

*How To Keep Your Head on Straight
in a World Gone Crazy*

When we go to the Lord, He *wants* to hear exactly what we have to say! God is not bothered when we're honest with Him. He may correct us or take us to the Word to help fix our wrong thinking and believing, but He is always glad when we go to Him and speak freely from our hearts.

How To Keep Your Head on Straight
in a World Gone Crazy

Jesus didn't change His behavior or His message to fit the doubters in the crowds of people He taught. In fact, knowing that they were present, Jesus poured it on even more strongly — and as a result, they eventually left Him and, for that time at least, bothered Him no more. Just like Jesus, we are not to change the way we present ourselves or our message simply because of who is in the audience or because of whom we're talking to at the moment. We have no need to apologize for what we believe or for the power of God that works through us. If we shrink in fear, observers will perceive it as weakness, but if we stand forth boldly and pour out what we really believe with the convicting power of the Holy Spirit, it will silence our critics.

Sparkling Gems From the Greek, Volume 2

We are called to come out from the catacombs of intimidation, as well as from the defilement of the world — and to stand as beacons of God's truth, regardless of opposition or backlash.

How To Keep Your Head on Straight
in a World Gone Crazy

Born Again

When you gave your life to Christ, in that exact same instant, the will of God was deposited into your spirit and you received His divine plan for your life. You may not have comprehended it yet, but it's there, deep inside you.

The Will of God — The Key to Your Success

Christ's work on the Cross literally put our old man in the grave! In God's mind, that old man — that is, who we used to be — is just as dead as any corpse in a morgue or any dead body being buried in a cemetery. Its life is gone, and it is nothing more than a hull. Nothing can resuscitate it; no one can breathe life back into it; and there is nothing that can stimulate it into action again — because it's *dead*. The life of that old man has been *terminated for good* — *PERMANENTLY*.

Unlikely

A genuinely born-again person cannot continue habitually in his past sinful patterns. His new nature will compel him to be different, to be holy, to be like God. His born-again spirit will grieve and be sorrowful if sins are committed, because such actions violate the new nature that has been implanted in his spirit. If a person continues in sin as though nothing happened inside him, then *nothing* is probably exactly what did happen. More than likely, he was never really born again, for if he had been born again, that new nature of God within him would not permit him to continue living habitually in sin.

Sparkling Gems From the Greek, Volume 1

I don't know about you, but I am personally convicted by the lack of excitement I see in church when a sinner gets saved. People yawn and cover their mouth, as if it is just routine activity — when, in fact, it is the greatest miracle that can occur on planet Earth! It is worth our shouting, yelling, and jumping up and down in joy, for there is no greater miracle than the new birth!

Sparkling Gems From the Greek, Volume 2

Breastplate of Righteousness

When you know that God has made you righteous — and you have your breastplate of righteousness fixed firmly in place — it doesn't matter how many arrows the enemy shoots against you, because not one arrow will penetrate. No word of condemnation, no false allegation, and no guilty thought will penetrate your heart or lodge in your mind when you are walking in your breastplate of righteousness.

Dressed To Kill

When you understand that God has freely imparted righteousness to you and that this God-given righteousness now serves you as a gorgeous breastplate, it affects your attitude profoundly, as you move into a new level of confidence and authority.

Dressed To Kill

Brokenhearted

The word "brokenhearted" in Luke 4:18 is translated from a Greek word that depicts *a person who has been shattered or fractured by life*. It is the picture of those whose lives have been continually split up and fragmented. If you are from a divided family, or have been shattered by relationships, this word could describe you and the shattered emotions you may deal with as an aftermath of the broken relationships you've experienced.

Sparkling Gems From the Greek, Volume 2

Brokenhearted people usually need someone's arms wrapped about them. They also need to feel like they're not all alone. And sometimes they need a shoulder to cry on — not because that will make everything better, but simply because they need a tender touch in that moment of crisis. This is why Paul said we need to "...weep with them that weep" (Romans 12:15).

Sparkling Gems From the Greek, Volume 1

Calling

When God calls you, His intent is to fully equip and prepare you to effectively complete your assignment. He will use every aspect of who you are and where you came from to bring about His will in your life. He uses your background, your level of education, your past occupations, and everything else you've accumulated from your life experiences, and many times He will also lead you into new territory where you are surrounded by unfamiliar faces in order to teach you lessons that you couldn't learn any other way.

The Will of God — The Key to Your Success

The Holy Spirit has come to teach us everything we need to know, and an unlimited supply of wisdom and revelation is available regarding God's plan for our lives and how we fit into His greater plan for man — *if* we'll listen to the Holy Spirit, cooperate with Him, and allow Him to do what He was sent to do for us.

The Holy Spirit and You

Very few whom God has called have been the "cream of the crop" when He called them. Again and again, Scripture shows that God chose those who were ill-esteemed in the eyes of the world when He needed a candidate or a group of people to do a special job. God has always used "common people" to build His Kingdom. In other words, He doesn't primarily choose famous movie stars or the royalty and nobility of the world to fulfill His plans and purposes.

Unlikely

The call of God rarely comes at a convenient moment. Rather, it usually comes when you are in the middle of doing something else or when you've already made other plans. Then suddenly God speaks to your heart, and you are jarred into facing the reality that He is asking you to do something you hadn't previously considered or thought about. From that moment forward, you start trying to figure out how to get from where you are to where you need to be in order to accomplish what God is asking you to do!

Dream Thieves

Regardless of where you live or what you believe God has asked you to do, it is important that you give your whole heart and soul to your divine assignment. Even if it is difficult sometimes, you must keep pressing forward toward your God-given goal in obedience to the Lord. And whenever the way of obedience seems difficult, you need to remind yourself once again of His promise that "your labor is not in vain in the Lord" (*see* 1 Corinthians 15:58).

Sparkling Gems From the Greek, Volume 2

Callousness

If you see that your tolerance level for violence and blood-shed — even in entertainment — is greater than it once was, it is entirely possible that your soul has become calloused in this area of your life. That is not a small thing. The calloused soul is a serious condition, because the person who possesses such a soul finds it more difficult to hear the tender voice of the Holy Spirit.

Last-Days Survival Guide

The results of spiritual callousness can be seen in Lot, who was so spiritually calloused by living for an extended period of time in the midst of the negative environment of Sodom that he didn't want to leave the city, even when the angels informed him that judgment was coming.

How To Keep Your Head on Straight
in a World Gone Crazy

When I read about the crucifixion of Jesus, it makes me want to repent for the callousness with which the world looks upon the Cross today. In our society, the cross has become a fashion item, decorated with gems, rhinestones, gold, and silver. Beautiful crosses of jewelry adorn women's ears and dangle at the bottom of gold chains and neck-laces, and they are even tattooed on people's flesh — and in beautifying the Cross to make it pleasing to look upon, people have forgotten that it wasn't beautiful or lavishly decorated at all. The Cross of Jesus Christ was *shocking* and *appalling*.

Paid in Full

Carnality

Today Jesus is still crying out for the Church to repent of worldliness and carnality. As is true in each generation, we have a choice to harden our hearts and turn a deaf ear to the Holy Spirit or to allow Him to deal deeply with us and produce true repentance in our hearts and souls. Although Christ is always ready to transform His Church, no transformation can occur unless we are willing to hear what His Spirit is saying to us. And once we do hear that divine message, we must be willing to respond with humble obedience.

A Light in Darkness

The gifts of the Holy Spirit operated so powerfully in Corinth that sin, wrong attitudes, and carnality were supernaturally brought to the surface. Through these demonstrations of the Spirit, whatever needed to be addressed was exposed and dealt with *God's* way. The sin that might stay hidden below the surface in other churches could not remain hidden in Corinth, because the abundant flow of the revelatory gifts of the Spirit at that church ensured that it *would* become exposed. It was the gifts of the Holy Spirit that *brought these sinful issues to light* so God could *purge* the sin from their midst.

Why We Need the Gifts of the Holy Spirit

When we are tempted to feel dismayed about the carnality and powerlessness that sometimes seem so pervasive in the contemporary Body of Christ, it is important for us to remember that Jesus paid the highest price of all for the Church, that He loves His people, and that He still remains in the *midst* of them.

A Light in Darkness

Change

You have the power of the Holy Spirit at your disposal to uproot and remove spiritual weeds from your life — *if* you really want them removed!

You Can Get Over It

It gives God the *deepest gratification* to take us with all our quirks, blemishes, and inconsistencies — the mess we were when we came to Christ — and to unleash His divine power *to effectually and productively bring forth a tangible, noticeable change* in our lives that is *permanent*.

Sparkling Gems From the Greek, Volume 2

God wants to change you so that you can successfully live in the midst of imperfect people. If you'll open your heart to receive what God has for you, He will fill you with His dynamic, supernatural power and help you overcome your own weaknesses so you'll be able to handle all the problem people you have to deal with — and to do it with *joy, peace,* and *victory*! Instead of constantly asking God to remove all the problem people from your life, why don't you ask God to release His power to change *you* so you can walk in peace and victory even when people fail or disappoint you.

Sparkling Gems From the Greek, Volume 1

If the Holy Spirit shows you an area in which you need to make a change, don't moan and groan about mistakes of the past that you can't do anything about. Simply ask for forgiveness and repent, then commit yourself to the process of self-correcting in this area of your life.

Last-Days Survival Guide

Character

We *all* have glitches and flaws in our character. Not one of us is perfect. Fortunately, small flaws are correctable as long as we have receptive and teachable hearts. But if a person refuses to see his need for change and is closed-hearted to suggestions made by those who love him, this is evidence of *the most serious* character flaw — an unteachable heart. From the outside, this person may look like he's just what we're looking for, but we must not forget to consider the *deeper issues* of the heart.

Sparkling Gems From the Greek, Volume 1

You need to know that God has plenty of time, and He is not in a hurry, nor is He focused on the clock, as we usually are. He is more concerned about character, integrity, faithfulness, and purity of heart than about the calendar.

Sparkling Gems From the Greek, Volume 2

If you are mightily anointed by God, it is simply a fact that your schedule will get busier, your demands will increase, and your challenges will grow. But as long as you allow God to develop your character along the way, you will find that you're able to successfully manage anything He puts on your plate!

Sparkling Gems From the Greek, Volume 1

Get quiet in God's presence and humbly ask, "Lord, what do You see in my character, my abilities, and my heart that has caused You to include me in Your purposes? And what do You see in me that needs to change or be perfected so that I can serve You with excellence and longevity?"

Christmas — The Rest of the Story

Children

Everyone sparkles a little differently in life, but everyone *does* sparkle, given the chance. It is God's design. So find your child's gifts and strengths and practice magnifying those things. It's all right if your child is different from you. He or she can have your same heart and same basic beliefs, but God fashioned and destined that child for a future that will be different from yours. Hence, He has gifted your child uniquely to be able to fulfill that divine call.

Unlikely

It is difficult — to say the least — to watch a grown child, grandchild, or sibling go through hard times in their own families — and it is especially difficult when you know that you could help them. But if the door is not open for you to speak into their lives, you must remain silent on the sidelines because your counsel is not welcomed. In such cases, it is vital to accept your silent role as a prayer partner to undergird them before the throne of God, and as you stand in faith for your family members, God will move on their behalf and will eventually open a door for you to become the help you desire to be.

Last-Days Survival Guide

Never think your children or grandchildren are too young to understand spiritual things. If you nurture their hearts, children can easily understand basic spiritual truths. I have seen many parents make the mistake of thinking their children will get around to inquiring about spiritual things on their own when they get older. But often, when they are older, it can be too late because they are already distracted, disinterested, or spiritually hardened. It's better to start talking to children about spiritual things when they are young so they will come to Christ at an earlier age when their hearts are tender.

Unlikely

Children need affirmation of who they are from the outset of their young lives; they do *not* need to be questioning their sexual identity. Instead, parents need to tell them, "You are a wonderful young boy, and you will grow up to be a great man," or, "You are an amazing young girl, and you will grow up to be a great woman."

*How To Keep Your Head on Straight
in a World Gone Crazy*

So often, young children struggle silently because they are not mature enough to understand what they are feeling, or because they do not know how to express it. This is why parents and grandparents need to pray for spiritual sensitivity to discern what is happening below the surface in the lives of children under their care.

__Unlikely__

While our children are still living with us, we must instruct them in how to guard their hearts and minds from the treachery of the world we're living in. It's our job to shield them from harm — spirit, soul, and body — and to teach them how to protect themselves and how to walk accurately on the right path in the midst of the crooked and perverse world that surrounds them. We must make every effort to steer clear of the world's attitudes and teach our children and grandchildren how to do the same.

__Last-Days Survival Guide__

Chosen

One thing is certain — people are not chosen by *accident.* Names are not scribbled on paper, thrown into a big bag, shaken up, and pulled out of the pile. If God chooses one of us for a special assignment, He does so because He sees something *inside us* that qualifies us to be a part of His team.

__Christmas — The Rest of the Story__

Even though you may not have any genius residing in your genes nor any nobility running in your blood, that isn't a strike against you! You can't lay claim to these factors as excuses for not being used by God! God isn't looking for people who are geniuses or well-born, high-class blue bloods. He's looking for *anyone* who will say *yes* to His call!

Sparkling Gems From the Greek, Volume 1

You and I have been chosen by God to live in this crucial hour — and as part of His Church, we have a spiritual inheritance to lay hold of that will empower us to live as overcomers in the midst of the storm. As we listen to what the Holy Spirit is saying and prepare ourselves by standing on the promises of God's Word, we can expect to experience the empowering strength of the Spirit upholding us and seeing us through to victory in every situation.

Last-Days Survival Guide

If your flesh ever tries to rant and rave that you're not worthy enough to be used or that you're just an accident, you need to take authority over your flesh and tell it to shut its stupid mouth! Then you need to declare, "God chose me, and He planned a great future for me. He wants to use me. I'm not going to listen anymore to this foul garbage from my lying flesh and unrenewed emotions. I have an awesome destiny! In fact, I'm a significant part of God's plan!"

Sparkling Gems From the Greek, Volume 1

Before God ever spoke the earth into existence — before His booming voice ever called out for the first layers of the earth's crust to be put into place — He had already spoken our names! He selected and elected us *before* the very first layers of the earth were created. And He had a plan for us right from the start!

Unlikely

Church(es)

Like a miner who goes deep into the earth to extract rock that contains gold, Jesus stepped into the darkness of sin in the human race to extract the Church from this lost world. The Gospel was preached, the lost were convicted of sin, and the Word of God, like rushing water, poured over the souls of the redeemed to remove rubble, wreckage, and waste from their lives. For 2,000 years, Jesus, our Great Refiner, has been washing the Body of Christ with His Word and overseeing the purifying and refining of His precious Church!

Sparkling Gems From the Greek, Volume 2

Since the outpouring of the Holy Spirit on the day of Pentecost, God has been progressively constructing a new Temple where His Spirit can dwell and work mightily. And in this new Temple, each born-again believer is singularly *a living stone* that God is using to place side-by-side with other living stones to progressively construct the Temple He has always longed to indwell.

Apostles and Prophets

The church is God's assembly in every town and city — composed of people who have been saved and called out to make eternal decisions that will affect the very atmosphere of their local region. It means God never intended for the local church to be simply a quiet, hidden body of believers, but He intended for each church to be His voice and ruling power in its community — a special assembly comprised of people who have been called out to make decisions that will impact the atmosphere of their local environment for God.

Sparkling Gems From the Greek, Volume 2

In a committed church, believers walk away *confronted*, knowing what God is requiring of them. When God speaks to these congregations, His voice echoes loudly like the voice of a commander! In these churches, sickness is healed, bondages are removed, sin is dealt with, slothfulness is shunned, and weak, wimpy, "don't-make-it-too-hard" thinking is non-existent.

Life in the Combat Zone

God designed the local church to be a place of victory where faith is built up, the soul is encouraged, and wisdom and strength are imparted. It's to be a community where faith lives and triumphs through love and concern for one another. There is nothing like living in an atmosphere of faith and love where you're surrounded by believers who really believe the Word of God and practice it!

Dream Thieves

The Church of Jesus Christ is the container of the Holy Spirit on planet Earth! Even though we may be fragile and seem inferior or imperfect, the fact remains that God has deposited His Spirit inside the Church, and *we contain an endless supply of the oil of the Holy Spirit!*

Sparkling Gems From the Greek, Volume 2

It's never been more crucial for the Church to humbly seek God's face for wisdom, understanding, and insight concerning His path and His plan for us in this hour. Rather than succumb to fear, we must press into Christ and into the power of the Holy Spirit so that we can make a mark for eternity in as many lives as possible before the age ends.

How To Keep Your Head on Straight
in a World Gone Crazy

You may sometimes feel disheartened by what you see or know about the Church. You may even be tempted to think that the modern Church is in such an irreversibly sad condition that it will never turn around for the better. But whenever your mind is bombarded by such thoughts, it is vital to remember that Jesus loves His Church, that He bought it with His own blood, and that the Holy Spirit is still actively working to purify it.

A Light in Darkness

The most exciting days of the Church are not behind us — they are *ahead* of us — and our Commander-in-Chief is urging us to move forward and take our place on the front lines of battle!

Life in the Combat Zone

Cloud of Witnesses

When you have become illuminated with direction for your life, business, family, or ministry, you need to know that the contest has just begun. You are on the field, all eyes are on you, and the fight of faith is on! If you'll look up into the bleachers of Heaven for just a moment, you'll see that they are stacked all the way to the "clouds" with people just like you!

Sparkling Gems From the Greek, Volume 1

The bleachers of Heaven are *filled* with people who have already faced the enemy and won their fight. They *faced the impossible*, they *accomplished the unthinkable*, and they stand as *proof* that you can make it too — and they're all cheering you on to victory! Just listen with the ears of faith, and you'll hear them saying, *"Go for it! You can do it! Your faith will carry you through!"*

Sparkling Gems From the Greek, Volume 1

Comfort

There has never been a generation in history with more material possessions and comfort than this present generation, but in spite of our abundance of goods and ongoing pursuit of pleasure, the worldwide happiness index is at the lowest point on record at the time of this writing — especially in industrialized nations where wealth abounds.

Last-Days Survival Guide

Many Christians back away from God's call and plan for their lives after considering all the possible challenges they may face. Forging into unknown territory where they've never gone before requires a greater cost than many are willing to pay. They may be bored with their present job, but at least they have job security! They may know in their hearts they were born to achieve more than they're currently achieving — but at least they're comfortable!

Dream Thieves

Does your daily lifestyle reveal that you love entertainment, pleasure, comfort, and happiness the most? Are you consumed with yourself and your own needs and offer no service to anyone else if it requires you to sacrifice your time, energy, or comfort? Or can you honestly say that you are living your life primarily for Jesus, fulfilling His plan for you in these last days? *If God were to comment on your lifestyle, would He say that it is dedicated to Him and to fulfilling His plan? Would your priorities match those of a selfish or unselfish lifestyle?*

Sparkling Gems From the Greek, Volume 2

Commitment

Today — *right now* — God needs a special brand of believers to boldly challenge the kingdom of darkness in the authority and dominion of Jesus Christ and to *storm* the gates of hell! He is looking for those special believers who will hear His voice, surrender to His call, and willingly enter the combat zone to do battle for the cause of His Kingdom.

Life in the Combat Zone

The Bible is full of people, no different than you or me, who heard a word from God, responded in faith, came into divine alignment with what God said, and ultimately saw His word to them fulfilled in their lives. And because of these people's commitment to believe and to possess what God had promised, they changed history!

Dream Thieves

Very few will be required to make a commitment that requires their death, but regardless, that is the level of the actual commitment that Jesus Christ is asking each one of us to make. If we make the commitment to be faithful to the end — regardless of the price that must be paid — being defeated will simply not be an option.

Sparkling Gems From the Greek, Volume 2

Had the believers of early centuries taken a lackadaisical approach to their walk with God, the Church of Jesus Christ wouldn't have gotten very far! *Those early believers were more committed to their task than their oppressors were to theirs.* Early Christians knew what their mission was in the world. They defied Satan as well as the Roman emperors who persecuted them mercilessly — *and they outlasted them all.*

Life in the Combat Zone

Satan will do everything within his power to coax you to move off your position of faith. He'll use family members, friends, associates, and even circumstances to thwart the plan of God for your life. The devil will use people you know and love to say things that simply shock you! This is his attempt to get you to back off the promise you have received. But if you are certain you are doing what God told you to do, don't budge an inch, no matter how much verbal opposition you encounter!

Sparkling Gems From the Greek, Volume 1

Most moments of defeat are produced, not by a demonic attack, but by a *lack of commitment* to stay in the fight. But when we dig in our heels, refuse to surrender, and use our authority in Jesus Christ to resist the devil, he *flees in terror* from us!

Life in the Combat Zone

Common Sense

It is time for us to use our heads and apply both spiritual and common sense to our lives. We need to responsibly build walls of protection around ourselves, our families, and our friends, for such spiritual walls can shield us and those we love from evil forces that are already prevalent in the world around us.

Last-Days Survival Guide

It is unfortunate, but many believers assist the devil in his efforts to attack them by being irresponsible or negligent in key areas of their lives. Many people have money problems because they have spent too much money or used their credit cards way beyond the limit of what they could afford; others get sick in the wintertime because they go outside without proper clothing; marriages get into trouble because the spouses never spend time together or do anything to nurture their relationships. Christians like to blame the devil for everything that happens, but the truth is, people usually help the devil out a little along the way!

Sparkling Gems From the Greek, Volume 1

When questionable spiritual food is being put on your plate, God expects you to respect yourself — and the work He is doing in your life — enough to refrain from eating it and go elsewhere. It's your God-given responsibility to guard your spiritual well-being and to always consider the long-term ramifications of what you are consuming.

How To Keep Your Head on Straight
in a World Gone Crazy

Comparison

God intentionally made you different from others, and you are actually a result of His divine design. Your mannerisms, insights, and style that are different from others may be the very qualities that make you uniquely positioned to fulfill a specific need. If you will quit comparing yourself to others — if you will stop disparaging the very qualities that cause you to stand out from those around you — you'll open the door to freedom from a spirit of inferiority so your unique gifts can begin to shine brightly as God intended.

Sparkling Gems From the Greek, Volume 2

If you feel *inferior* to others, remember that God regularly calls unskilled and uneducated people. Just think of the majority of the apostles whom Jesus hand-picked to serve at His side and to lay the foundation of the Church. The apostles were fishermen, tax collectors, common people — *not* theologians.

Sparkling Gems From the Greek, Volume 1

Perhaps you have felt that you fall short in comparison to others whose gifts and talents shine especially bright. But if you've kept your gifts and talents under wraps, you may be shocked to discover how gifted and talented you really are and how much potential influence is inside you just waiting to be tapped. *You just have to give yourself the opportunity to shine!*

Sparkling Gems From the Greek, Volume 1

Compassion

Never forget that divine compassion is a mighty force that reaches even into the flames of judgment to snatch people out of destruction!

How To Keep Your Head on Straight
in a World Gone Crazy

Becoming critical of those caught in deception will not help set them free, and it will negatively affect you. So address the error if needed, pray for them, and let the compassion of Jesus Christ flow from your heart toward them to help open their eyes and bring them back to where they need to be.

How To Keep Your Head on Straight
in a World Gone Crazy

Even though a sinning believer may have gotten himself into trouble because of his own actions, we must not shut off the flow of God's compassion that resides within us. Believers who have become spiritually deceived need a touch of God's power more than they ever did before! Therefore, we cannot let the enemy sow hardheartedness into our hearts toward people who have become spiritually ill or backslidden. Their plight is very serious, and they need our help and prayers of intercession!

Sparkling Gems From the Greek, Volume 1

Complaining

There is too much at stake for you to make the mistake of sitting around and feeling sorry for yourself. You'll only begin to experience true significance when you accept the fact that God has chosen you and you decide to live up to the glorious calling He has placed on your life. No matter how large or small the task, no matter how big or tiny the assignment, joy and satisfaction will be yours when you start accomplishing what God brought you into this world to do!

Sparkling Gems From the Greek, Volume 1

If you and I take our God-given assignment lightly — approaching it with a casual, easygoing, take-it-easy, relaxed attitude — we'll never go far in the fulfillment of our calling or dream. It takes diligence and hard work to achieve anything worthwhile, and complaining about how hard it is won't make the process any easier.

Sparkling Gems From the Greek, Volume 2

We don't always get what we want or live in the lifestyle we prefer. But if we're not getting exactly what we want and we can't do anything to change the situation, we have a choice: 1) We can constantly complain and make it worse on ourselves and everyone else; or 2) we can make a mental adjustment and decide that we're tough enough to handle the situation until things change. The second choice is the one God wants us to make, for this is the one that demonstrates the attitude of Jesus Christ!

Sparkling Gems From the Greek, Volume 1

When you stop murmuring, moaning and groaning and disputing with God — and you stop muttering in a low-toned voice against what He is asking you to do — you will be on your way to experiencing the power of God to assist you in whatever change you need to make.

Sparkling Gems From the Greek, Volume 2

Condemnation

Don't buy into the devil's lies and badger yourself with thoughts that you have nothing to offer! God's Spirit lives in you — and if you'll dare to let Him do it — He will burn so brightly in your life that you will become an illuminating force to people all around you. But if you refuse to bring your gifts and talents out from under wraps, no one will ever know what God has put inside you. And if you neglect those God-given endowments too long, eventually they will begin to diminish, just like a fire that ultimately goes out for lack of oxygen.

Sparkling Gems From the Greek, Volume 2

There are moments when we all question whether our lives have been worthwhile, and often the devil torments us and tempts us to believe the lie that we have lived in vain. Many people combat hopeless thoughts that they haven't made a difference in anyone else's life. If that describes you, don't move too fast and judge yourself wrongly. If you'll wait, in time you'll see fruit that you are unaware of right now. You have touched more people than you realize. You may not be able to see it right now, but the fruit is out there nonetheless.

Unlikely

Confession

If you believe in your heart that Jesus purchased your healing and you put your *heartfelt faith* together with the *confession of your mouth*, you can literally bring that healing into manifestation in your physical body.

You Can Get Over It

You need to open your mouth and start acknowledging who you are in Jesus Christ! By acknowledging the basic truths of what you have been given in Jesus, you will release so much divine energy that it will radically transform your life. The recognition of these spiritual treasures that reside within you will pick you up, lift you high, and carry you right over into the realm of victory you desire!

Sparkling Gems From the Greek, Volume 1

Creative power is released when the heart and mouth get in agreement! That's why you must be careful about what you believe in your heart and say with your mouth, because when your heart and mouth get "in sync," it makes things happen!

You Can Get Over It

Commit yourself with all your heart and strength to stand in faith on the Word of God, no matter how crazy it may sound to your natural mind. Then meditate on the scriptures the Holy Spirit quickens to your spirit. Ask Him to make the Word more real and rock solid to you than the natural things that surround you. This is the way you come to a stance of faith in which you truly understand and confess from your heart what God is saying to you.

Dream Thieves

Confession of Sin

Don't let your heart become hard by allowing unconfessed sin to build in your soul. *Quickly* confess sin and submit it to the cleansing power of Jesus' blood, and as you do, you'll immediately receive forgiveness and mercy as the blood of Jesus cleanses you from any act or thought that has grieved the Spirit of God.

Last-Days Survival Guide

First John 1:9 tells us that if we confess our sin, God will forgive us! The word "confess" is a Greek word that means *to say the same thing as God says*. This means, rather than debate with God about where you have failed, *it's time for you to get into agreement with God about your shortcomings.* And when your confession is heartfelt, the Bible says that God is faithful and just to forgive you. The word "forgive" is a Greek word that means *to release, to let go*, or *to totally dismiss*. In other words, if you've made a real heartfelt confession about where you have blown it, God promises that He won't hold it against you. In fact, He'll release you from it and send that failure as far away as the east is from the west (*see* Psalm 103:12).

Sparkling Gems From the Greek, Volume 2

By quickly confessing sin and submitting to the cleansing power of Jesus' blood, it keeps us free of self-condemnation and attacks and keeps our hearts pliable.

Last-Days Survival Guide

Confirmation

The Lord partnered with early believers by confirming the Word they preached through "signs following" (*see* Mark 16:20). What if there had been no "signs following"? The message would have been true, but the supernatural confirmation gave strength to the message that was preached. In this way, Christ *partnered* with the early ministers of the Gospel through the ministry of the Holy Spirit. When the gifts of the Holy Spirit operated in conjunction with the preaching of the Gospel, they provided a tangible demonstration of this supernatural *partnership* of Jesus Christ with the Early Church.

Why We Need the Gifts of the Holy Spirit

If God is going to speak something significant to you about His will for your life, it is likely that He will tell you personally about it first. For instance, He may speak to you during prayer or reveal to you as you study the Bible that a change is coming. Or perhaps you and your spouse are praying together and suddenly you both begin to sense an upcoming change, or you may receive that same word of direction while sitting in church and listening to your pastor preach. Later the Lord may even bring someone to you who says to you, "I sense a change is coming to your life." That kind of confirming word — affirming what you already know — is *powerful*.

The Will of God — The Key to Your Success

If you need a confirming word concerning the will of God for your life, the Holy Spirit will be faithful to orchestrate it. And the bigger and more "out of the ordinary" your assignment seems to be — the more dramatic the confirmation will likely be. Whatever the case regarding the call God has ordained you to fulfill, He knows exactly what you need to hear to be fully assured that you are on track and running the race He has set before you!

The Will of God — The Key to Your Success

Conflict

We are called to speak the truth *in love* — *not* to "bludgeon" each other in the way we communicate what's on our minds. We must ask God to teach us how to present the truth in a manner that makes it easier to receive.

Sparkling Gems From the Greek, Volume 2

Don't allow yourself to become a judge of another person's inward motivation. God is the only One who sees the heart. You may think another person's actions reveal a heart that isn't right with the Lord. But you really don't know what is in that person's heart, so leave it alone. *Don't get into the judgment business.* Let the Lord deal with the deeper matters of someone else's heart that you can't see nor correct.

You Can Get Over It

When you think about the way people have wronged you in the past, does it affect your desire to love them? What have these conflicts revealed about *you*? Is your love for those unkind people consistent, unwavering, unshaken, and unaffected? Or have the conflicts revealed that you have a fickle love, which you quickly turn off when people don't respond to you the way you wished they would?

Paid in Full

Give others the benefit of the doubt. *People often act in a way that is misperceived by others.* Maybe they don't realize how their actions are being perceived and therefore project attitudes or actions that are contrary to what they actually intend. Have you ever been misunderstood, or has anyone ever called your motives into question? Did it shock you to hear what others misperceived about you, especially when you knew your intentions were right? This happens to everyone from time to time, and just as you want others to believe the best about you, it's important for you to reverse that grace and believe the best about others.

You Can Get Over It

Confrontation

When you are required to confront someone and speak the truth, remember the principle of doing unto others as you would have them do unto you. In other words, be mindful to speak the truth in love to that other person as you would want to have truth spoken in love to *you*. Ask yourself this question: *How would I want the truth spoken to me?*

Sparkling Gems From the Greek, Volume 2

Don't confront anyone until you've first made it a matter of prayer.

You Can Get Over It

You may dread the moment you have to sit down with a person on your team to discuss what is wrong in his attitude. But the other team members will also be thankful that you took your leadership role seriously and refused to let a bad attitude negatively affect everyone else on the team. In the end, you'll bolster your own leadership position in the eyes of others because you did the right thing. Your willingness to confront a problem will cause your team to respect you more, and hopefully you will have helped that person whose attitude needed to be corrected.

Sparkling Gems From the Greek, Volume 1

Confusion

Fear always produces confusion.

Paid in Full

Lying threats and false accusations are the enemy's attempts to beat a hole through your mind and emotions so you can't think rationally. He comes to pave a road of fear into your mind and to fill your mind so full of fear and confusion that you eventually lose the courage you need to step out in faith and obey God's call on your life.

Dressed To Kill

I am convinced that the failure to be quiet is one reason people get confused in life. They get so busy that they no longer are in touch with themselves — what they believe, what they need, and what they feel. Instead, they just keep moving through life like robots. You need times of deep contemplation in order to stay in touch with your own heart.

Sparkling Gems From the Greek, Volume 2

We must seek the face of God to know how to respond to confusion and help people find peace, healing, and restoration. Those who are wayward, confused, and bound in sin are not to be rejected because of their deception. They need the forgiveness, deliverance, and freedom offered through the Cross of Calvary.

How To Keep Your Head on Straight
in a World Gone Crazy

Consistency

Be consistent and constant in your commitment. Refuse to relent! Stay stubborn and unbending even in the face of opposition until your objective is achieved. Your consistency and determination will push the powers of hell aside and obtain the victory you desire!

Sparkling Gems From the Greek, Volume 1

Fickle, flighty, erratic behavior will never produce the fulfillment of God's will in your life. It takes consistency and determination to push aside the powers of hell and obtain the victory you desire.

Sparkling Gems From the Greek, Volume 2

Regardless of how heavy the pressure seems to be or how much trouble mounts against you, it is imperative that you refuse to move or to surrender. *Stick* to your position, *abide by* what you believe, and *stay put* no matter what tries to come upon you.

A Light in Darkness

Consumerism

If you have fallen into the trap of self-consumption — if you are never satisfied and always wanting *more* — you must heed the Holy Spirit's voice as He tries to wake you up. He wants you to realize that the enemy is trying to drag you into a financial cesspool that has the potential to ruin you financially and put undue stress on your family and relationships.

Last-Days Survival Guide

Jesus likened pigs to people who don't appreciate the holy things that are freely given to them from the depths of another person's life. It's sad to say, but many believers live and act just like pigs because they are careless, mindless consumers of other people's time and energy. They never think about how a person obtained his wisdom, what it cost for him to obtain it, or how many years it took for him to come to his present place of growth in God. These people who act like pigs just take and take. And after they have drained that person of all his strength, they don't even take the time to say thank you for what they have consumed!

Sparkling Gems From the Greek, Volume 1

A pernicious and pervasive fiscal lack of control will emerge in the very last of the last days, and as a self-entitled society throws off all restraints, people will be hurled into excessive living, exorbitant spending, and mindless consumerism.

Last-Days Survival Guide

Conviction

How can you make a dead man see? You can't, for he is dead. How can you cause a dead man to feel? How can you convince a spiritually dead man that he needs to change? It is impossible for a dead man to respond, but thanks to the Holy Spirit, we were supernaturally awakened to our sinfulness, brought to a place of undeniable conviction, recognized we were sinners, and at that divine moment, our souls heard Him say, in effect, "Awake thou that sleepest, and arise from the dead, and Christ shall give thee light" (Ephesians 5:14).

The Holy Spirit and You

There is a supernatural, anesthetizing effect of the Holy Spirit when He speaks difficult truths to His people's hearts. His correction does not discourage, condemn, or leave hearers in a downtrodden condition, but instead, He speaks truth in a way that protects and soothes as it corrects so that the end result is comfort, encouragement, hope, and strength — and one who speaks for God can depend upon the anesthetizing effects of the Holy Spirit to help listeners receive the correction without feeling like they are being "bludgeoned" by truth.

Apostles and Prophets

Unsaved people and backslidden Christians should be *deeply disturbed* when they hear God's message. The message should even deliver such an intense *stab* to their hearts that it *penetrates* their conscience, *slices open* their souls, *punctures* them in their inmost being, and *cuts* them so deeply on the inside that they cry out for help. The message must be delivered in such anointing and power that it stings their hearts and minds as they become aware of their sin, to the point that their souls feel an *ache*. We must know that they need truth to change them, and not a painkiller to make them feel good while failing to remedy their very serious problem. The root of the problem must be lovingly identified so it can be dealt with and eliminated.

Repentance — What It Is,
What It Isn't, and How To Do It

Correction

You are a living document — and God is reading the pages of your life to observe how you live, how you speak, how you treat others, and so on. He is doing investigative research to determine if you are ready for a promotion or a greater anointing. Don't be too surprised if God finds a few errors that need correction, for none of us is perfect. If there are issues that need correcting — and I'm *certain* there are — you must allow the Holy Spirit to put you through a process to correct those flaws *before* you get the big break you have been dreaming of or before God promotes you to a higher level of responsibility.

Sparkling Gems From the Greek, Volume 2

When the "wheat" of the Word is injected in large doses into an otherwise dangerous situation, those life-giving words of truth have the power to nullify the poisonous spiritual influences that are present and turn the situation around (*see* 2 Kings 4:41). The Word of God can correct and reverse any ill effect of spiritual poison, whether intentionally or unintentionally introduced, that has negatively impacted God's people.

Apostles and Prophets

Christ always prefers repentance to judgment, but if repentance does not occur, He moves in the direction of the offender to bring correction and judgment where it is needed — yet He moves *slowly* with the hope that repentance will occur before He has to apply his bronze feet of judgment (*see* Revelation 1:15). Lifting one foot at a time, Jesus moves slowly to give each person an opportunity to avoid judgment by repenting before suffering the consequences of continued error or sin.

Sparkling Gems From the Greek, Volume 2

No matter how slowly or carefully Jesus proceeds in correcting people or His Church, the effects of correction are always painful to some degree. Correction is inherently a painful process and often bitter to the taste, but Christ in His infinite mercy attempts to minimize pain. The purpose of divine correction and judgment is not to wound, but rather to cleanse, heal, and restore.

No Room for Compromise

Never forget that bringing people higher is one of the primary goals of a leader. So if you are entrusted with the care of others in any arena of life, do everything you can to lead them to a higher level of excellence — even if it means correcting them in love!

Sparkling Gems From the Greek, Volume 1

Courage

The New Testament urges believers to prepare themselves for a fight with courage and a commitment to win, regardless of the difficulties that might lie ahead — and this is not a suggestion — *it is a command.*

Christmas — The Rest of the Story

Every person has faced something fearful at some point in his or her life. If you are feeling this way, I want to encourage you to stay faithful to the very end, because victory lies at the end of the battle you are facing right now.

Sparkling Gems From the Greek, Volume 2

As representatives of Almighty God, we have a responsibility to raise the standard of His truth in every situation — being willing to stand at odds with every law that is opposed to Scripture, to dig our heels into scriptural truth, and to *refuse* to bend with the times — no matter what everyone else around us is doing.

How To Keep Your Head on Straight
in a World Gone Crazy

This is a time for you to step forward and use the authority Jesus Christ gave you to bring deliverance, freedom, and peace to each place that the devil has tried to bring chaos, harm, and hurt. The situation that exists in the world today is your opportunity to let the power and glory of God shine through you!

Signs You'll See Just Before Jesus Comes

We are called to pick up our cross and follow Jesus, regardless of the price we are required to pay. Scripture never teaches that we are to draw back from our faith when hardships approach. Rather, Jesus asks for our commitment and faithfulness, even unto the point of death, if that's what is required as a part of our journey in Him.

Sparkling Gems From the Greek, Volume 2

Critics

Jesus didn't change His behavior or His message to fit the doubters in the crowds of people He taught. In fact, knowing that they were present, Jesus poured it on even more strongly — and as a result, they eventually left Him and, for that time at least, bothered Him no more. Just like Jesus, we are not to change the way we present ourselves or our message simply because of who is in the audience or because of whom we're talking to at the moment. We have no need to apologize for what we believe or for the power of God that works through us. If we shrink in fear, observers will perceive it as weakness, but if we stand forth boldly and pour out what we really believe with the convicting power of the Holy Spirit, it will silence our critics.

Sparkling Gems From the Greek, Volume 2

There is a negativism in human nature that often causes people to sit back and watch someone take a step of faith while speculating about that person's potential failure. They may verbally express support to that person, but inwardly they often harbor unspoken reservations. People like to hang back and watch for your next move. If your step of faith fails, or if you don't follow through on your commitment, they may conclude that you can't really hear the voice of God or that your vision was bigger than your faith. But if they actually see you follow through on your words and accomplish something truly noteworthy that bears great fruit for God's Kingdom, you'll win their hearts, and the next time you announce you're going to do something that sounds outrageous and wild to the natural mind, people will be much more inclined to believe you!

The Point of No Return

The Cross

Through His death on the Cross and His resurrection from the dead, Christ crushed Satan's whole empire, stripped him of his authority, and forever destroyed his tyranny over humankind. Because of what Jesus did, the devil's head was and is crushed, and he is forever a defeated foe.

Fallen Angels, Giants, Monsters,
and the World Before the Flood

As Jesus hung on the Cross, blood drenched His torso, poured from His head and brow, and ran like rivers from the deeply torn flesh in His hands and feet. His body swelled up and became horribly discolored, and His eyes were matted with the blood that poured from the wounds in His brow — wounds caused by the crown of thorns that bore down into His skull as the soldiers pushed it hard upon His head. The whole scene was ugly, unsightly, repulsive, sickening, vile, foul, and revolting.

Paid in Full

When I read of what Jesus endured during the long hours before He was sent to be crucified, it nearly overwhelms me. Jesus committed no sin and no crime, nor was any guile ever found in His mouth, yet He was judged more severely than the worst of criminals. Even hardened criminals would not have been put through such grueling treatment. And to think that all this happened *before* He was nailed to a wooden cross — which was the lowest, most painful, debasing manner in which a criminal could be executed in the ancient world!

Paid in Full

The victory is already yours! Your healing, your miracle, your financial blessing — all of these are already yours! Jesus accomplished a total, complete, and perfect work on the Cross of Calvary and in His resurrection from the dead!

Dressed To Kill

Crown

A day is coming when Jesus will step forward, dressed in the regal splendor of the exalted King of kings, and place a crown of life upon the heads of those who have faithfully run their race to the very end. The Savior Himself will be personally involved in the giving of this priceless reward. There could be no greater reward than Jesus Christ Himself personally placing this victor's crown on the brow of Christians who have endured to the end and victoriously finished their race of faith.

A Light in Darkness

First Corinthians 9:25 refers to a *crown of incorruption*, which is a special crown given to believers who practiced *physical self-governance* and therefore ran a successful race in life. Those who practiced self-discipline and refused to let the flesh hinder their race of faith can look forward to receiving this precious reward.

Sparkling Gems From the Greek, Volume 2

First Thessalonians 2:19 refers to the *crown of rejoicing*, which theologians often refer to as the *soul-winner's crown*. It is a crown given to those who brought others to Jesus Christ. Oh, think of the joy those who have brought others to Christ will experience when they receive a *crown of rejoicing* or *a soul-winner's crown*.

Sparkling Gems From the Greek, Volume 2

Second Timothy 4:8 refers to the *crown of righteousness*, which is specially designated for those who longed for Jesus' appearing and lived holy lives in anticipation of His return. This is the crown that Paul referred to when he wrote about his own death and the crown that Jesus would give to him.

Sparkling Gems From the Greek, Volume 2

First Peter 5:4 refers to the *crown of glory,* which is sometimes called the *pastor's crown* because it is a special reward that will be given to shepherds who faithfully pastored and taught God's people.

Sparkling Gems From the Greek, Volume 2

James 1:12 and Revelation 2:10 refer to the *crown of life,* which is a crown often referred to as the *martyr's crown* because it is given to those who suffered for their faith, those who died for Christ, or those who were committed to finishing their race of faith regardless of the difficulties they encountered in this life.

Sparkling Gems From the Greek, Volume 2

If you are running in a fierce race of faith that is requiring every ounce of your spiritual, mental, and physical strength, I encourage you to lift your eyes to Heaven and see Jesus with your crown in His hands. One day your race will be finished, and if you made it all the way to the end, He'll place a crown on your head — a *victor's crown* — because you finished your race of faith!

Sparkling Gems From the Greek, Volume 2

Crucified Life

Just as priests followed a protocol of offering sacrifices each day, Christians are to follow a *daily protocol* of offering ourselves to God, for offering ourselves as a living sacrifice is our lifelong priestly occupation.

Christmas — The Rest of the Story

By living a crucified, sanctified life on a continual basis, we are able to neutralize any attack the enemy would try to wage against our flesh. This is because dead men and women do not have the capacity to respond! You can kick dead people; spit at dead people; curse at dead people; or try to tempt, deceive, and seduce dead people — but no matter what you do, they do not respond!

Dressed To Kill

There was no such thing as a living sacrifice in the ancient world because sacrifices that weren't dead were not considered a sacrifice. If a person walked away from an altar with a living animal, all he did was make a big spectacle. And we can put on a show and say a lot of impressive words about how we want to surrender our lives to God — but until we actually do it, it is nothing more than a spectacle. For us to become a living sacrifice, we must be willing to "crawl onto the altar," surrender ourselves — yielding that which is precious — and be willing to renounce all claims to ourselves as we fully surrender to the purposes of God.

Christmas — The Rest of the Story

The body will not yield itself voluntarily as a living sacrifice, and this act of committal and consecration will never occur by accident. So to present our bodies as a *living sacrifice*, we must decide once and for all to surrender our life to God — and to affirm that commitment daily.

Christmas — The Rest of the Story

Culture

God has anointed *you* to reach the people He has placed on your heart. They may be different than you, they may have a different skin color than yours, they may live in a different part of the world than where you were born, or they may live on a different side of town. But the Holy Spirit knows how to reach people in every culture, and if you will lean on Him and carefully follow what He tells you to do, He will give you the method and the manner to reach a particular group of people, no matter how difficult it may seem to you.

Sparkling Gems From the Greek, Volume 2

When we are reaching out to people who are outside of the faith, God expects us to use our heads in the way we approach them. To reach into a lost culture, we must remember that we are leaving the world of "church" and reaching into spiritual darkness. That's why we must have the help and the wisdom of the Holy Spirit as we seek to reach these people with the message of Christ!

Sparkling Gems From the Greek, Volume 2

There are many people in your own city who don't know God and who didn't grow up in church, and you can't assume that they understand the words and phrases that are familiar to you as part of the Church world where you have lived much of your life. The Christian community uses wonderful, meaningful terminology that the world doesn't know or understand. For example, the words "amen" and "hallelujah" are dear and precious to us, but to a world that is lost in darkness, those words sound strange — and when you use them, it often makes people want to tuck their tails and run!

Sparkling Gems From the Greek, Volume 2

D

Debt

By managing your finances in a fiscally responsible manner, you remain free from the bondage of unnecessary, frivolous debt — you are able to pursue your calling without the hindrance and distraction of crushing financial obligations to creditors slowing you down. However, if you repeatedly succumb to your flesh and use your credit card to purchase items you don't need and can't afford, you will inevitably end up swamped in debt and financially ruined. If you'll listen to the Holy Spirit, He'll help you put together a plan to exercise temperance in your life that will lead you to a place of financial freedom!

Sparkling Gems From the Greek, Volume 2

If every debt and credit-card bill you owed was suddenly paid off, how would you act? Well, Jesus *paid in full* your debt to sin, and I want you to consider the far-reaching implication of that truth. Sickness, torment, grief, and guilt have no right to oppress you or demand anything from you. Jesus paid your bill, cancelled your debt, and left you with a zero balance!

Paid in Full

By listening to the Spirit of God, using common sense, exercising self-control, and planning your purchases in advance, you can live a life that is more debt-free than the way you're living right now. It will take determination to do it, but if you really want to become free of debt — and remain free forever — it is possible to achieve it.

Sparkling Gems From the Greek, Volume 2

Deception

There is an onslaught of deception attacking our culture from every direction and a propensity to rationalize away truth and replace it with politically "progressive" thinking. And unfortunately, like a sickness invades and sickens the human body, this end-times deception, like a spiritual disease, has seeped into every part of society, and now it is in our education system, courts, government, on television — and in virtually all forms of art and media.

Signs You'll See Just Before Jesus Comes

The way to circumvent spiritual deception is by knowing, understanding, and being rooted in the truth of God's Word.

*How To Keep Your Head on Straight
in a World Gone Crazy*

The enemy is using the voices of influential people in entertainment and the media — those who already have been beguiled and seduced to believe a lie — and His goal is to victimize a last-days generation and lead them into ways of thinking and behaviors that damage their minds and steal, kill, and destroy on as many levels as possible.

How To Keep Your Head on Straight
in a World Gone Crazy

According to Jesus, deception will affect every part of society and spread across the globe like a growing cancer. In both First Timothy 4:1 and Second Timothy 4:3 and 4, Paul also alerted us that even the Church would be affected by this spirit of deception and delusion — warning us that we must stick with the clear teaching of Scripture and strengthen ourselves in the Word of God.

Signs You'll See Just Before Jesus Comes

Decisions

Changing behavior requires a decision to do things differently — to speak differently, to think differently, and to act differently. It all starts with a decision.

Sparkling Gems From the Greek, Volume 1

Every choice has a consequence, so are you making the choices today that will produce the results you want tomorrow?

Paid in Full

It is important to *decide beforehand* how you're going to respond to negative situations! Instead of blowing them out of proportion, make the decision before anything happens that you and the Holy Spirit are bigger and stronger than any problem that will ever come your way. The two of you together, armed with the all-powerful name of Jesus, can tackle and overcome anything that ever comes against you!

Sparkling Gems From the Greek, Volume 2

Many times the right choices we make can seem small and insignificant, but the Word of God declares that we should never despise the "small things" (*see* Zechariah 4:10). Those little beginnings — those tiny decisions we make every day to do the right thing — can give birth to the most incredible and awesome miracles of our lives!

Dream Thieves

Deliverance

The Word of God carries creative, restorative power that can *deliver* us from every power of darkness and *infuse* our lives with the music and aroma of Heaven. Literally everything you need is in God's Word — if you will simply unlock it and release what's in it, it will supply answers to every problem you face and provision for every one of your needs.

Last-Days Survival Guide

We can add absolutely nothing to what Jesus did at the Cross of Calvary. It was a total, perfect, and complete work, and in that glorious work of redemption, Jesus purchased our complete and total deliverance from the powers of the evil one!

Dressed To Kill

The word "delivered" comes from a Greek word that depicts *an intervention* or *a rescue operation intended to snatch a person out of physical or spiritual peril.* The use of this word in the New Testament tells us categorically that God's power is available to rescue us, even if it feels we've just been rescued in the nick of time!

Last-Days Survival Guide

Demons

No matter what demonic strategy may come against you this day or how many demons are assembled together for your destruction, you *never* have to go down defeated. Jesus *plundered* the enemy when He rose from the dead! So when you look into the mirror, you need to learn to see yourself as one who *already* has the victory. You *already* possess the authority necessary to keep Satan under your feet where he belongs. Remember, you are no longer a victim — *you are a victor*!

Sparkling Gems From the Greek, Volume 1

James wrote that demons "tremble" at the thought of Jesus. That word "tremble" is from a Greek word that means to *bristle*, as when the hairs stand up on a person's neck when he is suddenly "spooked" or startled by an unexpected noise. This means that when demons find themselves in the presence of a believer who is exercising his authority in the name of Jesus, it sends them into shock, panic, and dismay. Figuratively, it causes the hair to stand up on their necks. It *terrifies* them! Since you have the Holy Spirit living in you and you have the name of Jesus Christ to use at your disposal, it means you are in a position to make demons tremble!

Sparkling Gems From the Greek, Volume 2

Demonic hordes are tasked with bombarding people's minds with the goal of modifying their thinking and leading them, through deception, into destructive behaviors and regretful decisions. Only demon spirits could propagate evil on such a wide scale — which is precisely what the Holy Spirit prophesied in First Timothy 4:1.

How To Keep Your Head on Straight in a World Gone Crazy

If you really know Jesus as your Lord and Savior — if you are in Christ — you can be sure that you have authority over demonic powers in the power of His name. You are empowered by the Holy Spirit, and you have been given the name of Jesus to take authority over and to cast out demons. You are empowered by the Spirit of God and have real God-given authority in the spirit realm!

Sparkling Gems From the Greek, Volume 2

Departing From the Faith

A departure from the faith, which the Holy Spirit prophesied about, does not refer to a blatant, outright rejection of the faith — although it may eventually lead there. It is something much more *subtle* than that. It is a gradual, step-by-step, almost undetectable departure over a period of time.

How To Keep Your Head on Straight in a World Gone Crazy

A drift from the Bible has created a doctrinal vacuum in the Church — a void currently being filled with dynamic business ideas, financial advice, and motivational messages instead of the Word of God that the Holy Spirit is bound to honor with signs and wonders. It is certainly true that some of the motivational messages delivered from the pulpit are beneficial in people's lives, but this help is temporary and can often be found in a book by some psychological guru. When everything is said and done, only the Bible has the power to permanently transform.

Sparkling Gems From the Greek, Volume 2

Careful observation reveals the sad truth that some ministers are pandering to the itching ears of a last-days generation. Instead of dealing with issues as Jesus did, these ministers refuse to address any issue of morality or deal with any sinful behaviors.

***How To Keep Your Head on Straight
in a World Gone Crazy***

Many traditional denominational churches were born in revival and in the power of the Spirit and were pioneered by men and women who believed the Bible and gave their lives for the preaching of the Gospel. But not all traditional churches have stayed loyal to their original, God-given message and mission. Although their doctrinal tenets and creeds remain largely unchanged, the actual practice of their faith represents a shocking departure from those foundational truths of the Bible.

Last-Days Survival Guide

Desire

I would rather work with a less talented person who has desire than with a talented person who has no desire. What good are a person's gifts and talents if he doesn't have the inward drive to get up and use those gifts for God's glory? It's better to train someone who doesn't have a lot of experience and is less qualified than others but who has *desire*, is willing to pay the price, is motivated to put in the time and effort, and is ready to make sacrifices to become all that he or she can be.

Promotion

Even though every person has a dream for success, that doesn't mean every person will attain it. It takes great effort and hard work to achieve success in any realm of life. Many people who dream of success will never experience it because they don't desire it enough and aren't willing to put forth the effort to make it happen.

Promotion

No one but God knows what lies in your path, but when you face unexpected problems that seem impossible to overcome, remember any obstacle can be overcome, any challenge can be conquered, any mountain can be successfully climbed — *IF* you have the inward desire and motivation to achieve your goal. God is not unprepared, and He will help you!

Unlikely

Destiny

Think of it — God's marvelous plan for your life is living and breathing deep inside you right now. Even if your mind hasn't realized or comprehended it all yet, it's there, waiting to be tapped into. And when you finally realize it, embrace it, and begin to pursue it, that divine plan will unleash supernatural power to carry you forward toward its fulfillment.

The Will of God — The Key to Your Success

To do the impossible, you must be willing to stretch — and that means being willing to go to places that are totally unknown to you and to people to whom you are not naturally drawn. It may sound scary, but God's grace will empower you to do it *if* you're willing to say *yes* and obey!

The Will of God — The Key to Your Success

My friend, you are no mistake. Before God ever formed this universe, He had already planned the course for your life. If you haven't yet discovered your divine purpose, the day will come when you will wake up to God's plan — whether it's the day you receive Jesus as your Lord and Savior or years after you are born again. That divine plan will seem new and glorious to you — but, in reality, God's purpose for your life has been in existence for eons and eons of time!

Dream Thieves

Whatever you're facing right now, this is *not* the time for you to give up. On the contrary — it's time to jump back in the race and run with all your might to fulfill your God-given purpose and destiny!

Last-Days Survival Guide

It might be that the place to which you are called is outside your comfort zone, and you wish you could escape to somewhere else far away. But if you know that God has spoken a word over your life, don't second-guess Him — *trust* Him — and trust that He is working to fully develop the gifts He has placed within you so you can fulfill your divine mandate. *He knows exactly what you need!*

The Will of God — The Key to Your Success

If you know it's time to step out in faith, you must take your eyes off the raging, turbulent waters before you and fix your eyes on Jesus Himself. He is the Author and Finisher of your faith, and you can be sure that what He starts, He will always finish. He is with you at the beginning of your journey, in the middle of your adventure, and He will empower you to make it all the way to the finish line.

Sparkling Gems From the Greek, Volume 2

Determination

If you want to achieve God's will for your life, you must live your life every day as Paul did — with an attitude of holy boldness and Holy Ghost-imparted determination. This alone will take you through the obstacles and attacks of the enemy, ultimately bringing you to the place God desires for your life.

Dream Thieves

Putting on Christ is a daily mindset — a daily, hour-by-hour determination!

Sparkling Gems From the Greek, Volume 1

God's power works in people who have resolve — those who have decided they will never turn back until the assignment is finished.

Sparkling Gems From the Greek, Volume 1

When God calls us to fulfill *our* assignment, we must be willing to do what He asks and go where He sends us, even if it means we must work in places that are difficult or in cities and nations where it is spiritually hard. Yes, we may encounter challenging situations that make it difficult for us to do our job. But regardless, with God's help, we will be enabled to push through each distraction or problematic situation and refuse to be affected by what we see, hear, or feel.

Sparkling Gems From the Greek, Volume 2

Devotion

Do you see yourself as someone who is running the spiritual Olympic event of his or her life, or are you simply "jogging for Jesus?" If you're serious about fulfilling God's plan for your life, it's time to shift into high gear and start putting all your spiritual, mental, and physical energies into getting the job done. You have to remove all distractions and commit yourself to a life of discipline, balance, and devotion.

Sparkling Gems From the Greek, Volume 1

Commit to the regular intake of the Word of God, for I guarantee you that this decision will immediately begin to increase the level of your faith. Especially in challenging times, you must take your stand on the Word of God, exercise your faith, listen to the Holy Spirit, and obey whatever He tells us to do!

Last-Days Survival Guide

If an individual or a church is not completely devoted to doing whatever is necessary to retain spiritual passion, it is likely that over time, the initial passion will slowly dissipate.

A Light in Darkness

We must care deeply about the matters that mean most to God.

Last-Days Survival Guide

Jesus requires His people to remain *devoted, trustworthy, dependable, dedicated, constant,* and *unwavering,* even in the face of the worst circumstances imaginable. Breaking their commitment to Him under the weight of external pressures, no matter how extreme, is not an acceptable option.

A Light in Darkness

Difficulties

The only thing more frustrating and painful than making a mistake or going through a difficult time is watching someone you care about go through difficulty — particularly when it's a situation of his or her own design. There are times when people need someone to step in and help them get their lives in order again.

Paid in Full

Often when problems erupt in our lives, we yearn to escape the difficulties that surround us and dream about running away to some new location. However, in most cases, there *is* no escape. It is a fantasy to think we can run and hide from the issues that face us. Jesus firmly encouraged the disciples to face their challenges head on, no matter how difficult the situation became. This should come as no surprise, considering Jesus faced incredible persecution throughout His ministry — enduring even the Cross and the grave.

No Room for Compromise

Life will occasionally take you through difficult places — such as those times when you discover that people are disappointed with your performance. When you find yourself in such a situation, go hide yourself away for a few minutes and call out to the Lord. He understands, and He will help you know how you must respond.

Paid in Full

Satan doesn't hide in the closet and pop out at night to personally attack us while we're sleeping! Because he is the "god of this world," he uses the world to do battle with us. In other words, he uses people, events, situations, circumstances, and difficult dilemmas to obstruct us from reaching our goals.

Sparkling Gems From the Greek, Volume 1

Jesus is the Chief Example, Teacher, Master — the One we are called to copy — so learn from the life of the Master, and walk through your situation in the same manner Jesus walked through His most difficult challenges.

Paid in Full

Diligence

If you and I want to see our dreams fulfilled, we must give our *full attention* to what God has called us to do. It must have our full consideration, our undivided attention, and our full mental and spiritual concentration. Ceaseless, around-the-clock, nonstop devotion is essential in order to be *diligent*. To remain diligent, we must be engrossed, totally absorbed, and fully engaged. We must immerse ourselves in faith, prayer, and meditation regarding God's call on our lives. All of this takes a hundred percent of our focus and effort if we are going to accomplish what God has placed in our hearts.

Unlikely

If you and I take our God-given assignment lightly — approaching it with a casual, easygoing, take-it-easy, relaxed attitude — we'll never go far in the fulfillment of our calling or dream. It takes diligence and hard work to achieve anything worthwhile, and complaining about how hard it is won't make the process any easier.

Sparkling Gems From the Greek, Volume 2

Evil is always lurking in the shadows, waiting for us to drop our guard and fall asleep on the job. In those vulnerable moments of lethargy, the enemy is positioned to seize his opportunity and attack, often with devastating consequences. Therefore, it is essential that we are always on guard — diligent, wide-awake, and doing our part to protect ourselves from the evil that is in the world.

No Room for Compromise

Disappointment

In moments when we experience the unpleasantness of someone's dishonorable behavior, remember that even Jesus had an insincere person — Judas Iscariot — on His team. So don't let it surprise you if you occasionally experience a disappointing personal encounter with a fellow Christian.

Sparkling Gems From the Greek, Volume 2

Relational hurts can be so painful that people often end up entirely focusing on their hurts and disappointments and forget about all the wonderful people who have been and remain a blessing to them. Satan uses hurt, pain, and personal let-downs to get people so side-tracked by what one person or a small group of people did that they forget about all the good and kind things that others have done for them.

Sparkling Gems From the Greek, Volume 2

Unrealistic expectations — whether placed on leaders by followers or on followers by leaders — always lead to disappointment.

Promotion

Make the decision not to permit yourself to be disturbed or disappointed because the attendance at a meeting is smaller than you anticipated. Even if the numbers are small, it may be that you have reached the heart of someone who will one day have great influence and power — and that would make your results very successful indeed!

Sparkling Gems From the Greek, Volume 2

Discernment

It is important for us to learn how to think right, use our sound minds, stay sensitive to the Lord in our hearts, and keep our heads on straight in this world that is going crazy as we approach the end of this age.

How To Keep Your Head on Straight
in a World Gone Crazy

You need to be careful concerning what you see and what you hear, and you need to be careful about who *interprets* what you see and hear! *Those who influence your thinking have great power over your future.* So be very careful of what you see, what you hear, and who you let interpret things for you.

The Point of No Return

If you find it difficult to discern what direction the Holy Spirit is leading you, it may be that you're too busy, or there may be so much mental noise and clutter that you can't easily hear what God is saying. Perhaps the influence of the people around you is hindering you from stepping out in a certain direction or from developing certain gifts, or maybe you're too comfortable where you are and your own complacency is keeping you from taking a step that requires stretching your faith and totally depending on God. But don't be afraid to obey the Lord, because He's not going to hurt you or mislead you!

Sparkling Gems From the Greek, Volume 2

We must be careful not to indulge ourselves in every spiritual manifestation that is presented without exercising discernment — and this means both spiritual leaders and followers must assume responsibility to ensure that the wine being offered to us to drink is in reality the work of the Holy Spirit.

How To Keep Your Head on Straight
in a World Gone Crazy

One surefire way to test whether a new revelation or experience is from God is to examine the fruit it bears in your life and in the lives of the people around you.

Testing the Supernatural —
How To Biblically Test Dreams, Visions,
Revelations, and Spiritual Manifestations

Take as much time as you possibly can in any new venture for Jesus — and be sure of the actions you take. Before you act on any opportunity publicly, first "learn the landscape" of your new environment. Take time to really understand the opportunities and possible problems around you. Make sure you are completely informed of all the pertinent facts about your new environment — facts that will help you move forward smoothly in fulfilling your new assignment without unnecessary delays or detours. Then pray diligently about the information you gather and seek the Lord's wisdom on how that information applies to your assignment.

Unlikely

Discipleship

We are not called just to win masses to Christ and then leave them behind as spiritual infants. Rather, our God-given task is to help people walk out of immaturity and lead them onward into spiritual maturity.

Sparkling Gems From the Greek, Volume 2

Jesus' disciples both followed and obeyed Jesus. They were committed to explicitly follow His teachings and do His bidding. All of these were requirements for a person to be a disciple. They were not mere followers — these were committed disciples who explicitly followed *whatever* Jesus asked of them.

A Life Ablaze

If you are facing difficult times — if you are being accused of things you didn't do, being blamed for things of which you have no knowledge, being mistreated or discriminated against — this is the moment for you to turn your eyes to God's Word and to study what He did and how He responded in situations similar to yours. It is then your task to copy Him. If you'll take this approach to the challenges you're facing right now that seem so distressing, you'll begin to see those situations as opportunities to become more like Jesus!

Sparkling Gems From the Greek, Volume 2

Peter wrote that we are to follow in the "steps" of Jesus. The word "steps" really means *footprints*. It pictures us putting our feet exactly where Jesus first placed His feet, stepping in His very footprints and following His actions in every circumstance we face. This means we must learn to walk in Jesus' steps, even if it seems His stride — *His standard, His example, His way of living and loving and forgiving* — seems much bigger than the level we're used to walking in right now. With those footprints before you, you can do what He did, you can say what He said, and you can walk how He walked. *What a blessing that you don't have to figure it all out by yourself!* Just look at Jesus' steps and stretch forward by faith to step in His footprints.

Sparkling Gems From the Greek, Volume 2

Discipline

The Church has more authority than the devil and more power than the devil, because we have the Greater One living in us. The Church of Jesus Christ is loaded with heaps and heaps of raw power, but at this time, that power is disconnected and disjointed by a Body that lacks discipline, organization, and commitment! Once we match the discipline, organization, and commitment that the enemy possesses, we will begin to move in the awesome demonstration of God's power!

Dressed To Kill

The discipline of the Lord is just as real today as ever before. If a child of God deliberately ignores God's Word and knowingly goes astray, God will graciously give him an opportunity — and perhaps many opportunities — to come back home of his own free accord. But if that person is really a child of God and refuses to come into compliance with what He has set forth in His Word, then God — out of great love for that person — will take other measures to bring him or her back home. It may not feel like it at the time, but this spiritual discipline is divine love in action!

Sparkling Gems From the Greek, Volume 2

Let's face it — there is nothing more thrilling than to see progress in your life. But to get the kind of progress you desire, you will be required to do something more than you've been doing. You will have to say no to your flesh, denying its appetites and disciplining yourself to do what God says even if your flesh doesn't want to do it. This process often feels long and laborious, but afterward when you can *see* and *appreciate* the results, you'll be so glad you didn't quit!

Sparkling Gems From the Greek, Volume 1

I advise you that in the process of reaching out to seize what you are dreaming for, do not take shortcuts or skip important steps that are essential to keeping you solid along the way. Get established in the basics so God can know you are ready for Him to put His hand on you and move you to a greater assignment. *First things first!*

Unlikely

Discouragement

One of Satan's greatest weapons is discouragement, and he knows exactly when to use it. He waits until you are tired, weak, and susceptible to his lies. Then he hits you hard in your emotions, trying to tell you that you are accomplishing nothing valuable in life. But if you will yield to the Holy Spirit who dwells in you, He will supernaturally revitalize you. He will rejuvenate you. He will refresh you with a brand-new surge of supernatural life. He will fill you with so much resurrection power that you will be ready to get up and go again!

Sparkling Gems From the Greek, Volume 1

The manifestation of your dreams is probably just around the corner, and that is why the devil is working overtime right now to discourage you! He wants you to discard your faith because he knows that if you hang on much longer, you'll see the desire of your heart come to pass. *So hold on and keep believing — because it won't be much longer until you are standing in the middle of the long-awaited manifestation of your dream!*

How To Receive Answers From Heaven

There are a myriad of reasons why people stay away from church when they are discouraged. Perhaps they're embarrassed that their faith isn't working as fast as they think it should, or perhaps they're ashamed that they're still struggling with problems they think should have been conquered long ago. They may not want anyone to know they're still wrestling with the same old problems, so they disappear from sight. If this describes you, don't let embarrassment or discouragement keep you away from other believers. You need their strength! You need their testimony! You need their encouragement! You need to hear them say, *"You can do it! You can make it!"*

Sparkling Gems From the Greek, Volume 1

Disobedience

It is simply a fact that if a person is living a blatant life of sin or disobedience to the Word of God and the Christian community knows about it, that behavior will disqualify him from leadership in the Church. Or if an individual's actions don't correspond with the Bible's requirements for spiritual leadership and he does nothing to self-correct, the Bible makes it perfectly clear that he shouldn't be considered for a leadership position.

Sparkling Gems From the Greek, Volume 2

Sometimes the plan of God for our lives is delayed — not because of the devil, but because of us!

Dream Thieves

Through Adam's disobedience, sin entered the world and death was passed on to all men. But just as sin entered the world through Adam, the gift of God came into the world through the obedience of Jesus Christ. Now the grace of God and the free gift of righteousness abounds to all who have called upon Jesus Christ to be the Lord of their lives!

Paid in Full

A day is coming — and in large part, is already here — when children will no longer submit to or follow the leadership of their parents. They will deny their parents' right to lead them, often disrespectfully, and will even assert their own right to make decisions for themselves without parental influence or intervention — including decisions that in many cases will be life-altering or detrimental to their long-term well-being.

Last-Days Survival Guide

Disrespect

You may disagree with an authority figure on some matter, but that does not give you the right to be disrespectful toward that person in authority over you — even when you're not in that person's presence.

Last-Days Survival Guide

When people behave disrespectfully toward their boss, their department director, their pastor, or their parents, they are demonstrating that they are not smart and certainly not mature. When you see this, it should send up a red flag before you to let you know the maturity level you are dealing with in the lives of these individuals. Even if they are called to the ministry; even if they have been to Bible school; even if they have been members of your church for a long time — the fact that they would act disrespectfully toward authority reveals that these people are still young in terms of maturity.

Sparkling Gems From the Greek, Volume 1

Those who refuse to cooperate with the authority figures they are subject to will never advance well in life unless they choose to change — and if they choose to stay discordant and continue to refuse to submit to authority, it is likely they will be uninvited from participating in the future.

Last-Days Survival Guide

Because rebellion is running rampant against every established form of authority, there is disrespect and dishonor for the authority of government, parents, police, and pastors — truly against nearly every form of established authority.

A Life Ablaze

The Bible clearly teaches that as the prophetic clock ticks toward the final countdown, widespread disrespect for authority will grow to become even more out of control and serve as a sign that we are reaching the cusp of this end-time age.

Last-Days Survival Guide

Distractions

One of the fastest ways Satan can knock you out of your race and keep you from finishing victoriously is to get you distracted by surrounding circumstances. Remember that a runner who takes his eyes off the finish line to look at all the commotion around him will *never* finish first. While he's looking around, others who are more focused will pass him by and leave him in the dust. He'll end up far behind everyone else, feeling like he can never catch up or finish his own spiritual race. So if God has put a dream or vision in your heart, don't allow any distraction to stop you from reaching your goal!

The Will of God — The Key to Your Success

The temptation to get distracted by thoughts that pull you off track usually comes when you're on the brink of an incredible breakthrough. God is getting things in alignment in your life, and hell's forces are being driven back. But then the pressure becomes so intense that you give in to fear and decide to slip away to try your "luck" elsewhere.

Life in the Combat Zone

God is watching us to see our actions and reactions — to see how we treat people, how we respond to pressure, and whether or not we have the tenacity to stay on track when distractions try to thwart our obedience. Before He taps us on the shoulder to give us a new assignment, He carefully observes to see how well we have done with the last assignment. Did we do it as He expected? Did we finish it completely, or did we leave parts of the assignment incomplete? Did we do it in a way that glorified the name of

Jesus? God wants to know if we are faithful, trustworthy, reliable, dependable, true, and unfailing. Rather than take a shot in the dark and simply hope for the best, God bases His decision on *discovery.*

Sparkling Gems From the Greek, Volume 2

Just like Jesus, you must keep your eyes permanently fixed on the desire God planted in your heart that pertains to your part in His plan. If your vision wavers, you'll begin to lose your firm grasp on your commitment. But this is *not* the time to loosen your grip — it's the time to redouble your efforts to *hold on tight!* You must steadfastly look *forward* toward the goal God has set before you. Refuse to get distracted by any circumstance that surrounds you or any negative emotion or thought that would try to derail you!

Life in the Combat Zone

Diversity

The exclusion of Gentiles from the church at Jerusalem had the negative consequence of eliminating diversity from their congregation. Only one nationality was represented within the church, and this was not a true picture of the new man God was creating. It was not — *and will never be* — His will for the makeup of any congregation to be restricted to one particular race, nationality, or ethnicity.

The Will of God — The Key to Your Success

We must remember that diversity *adds variety and spice to the Church!* As members of the Body of Christ, we each have unique and important roles to play, and we must learn to appreciate and respect the views and opinions of others in the Church. Learning to deal successfully with other believers — to cope with their differences and learn to appreciate them — is one of the greatest achievements we can reach in life. We don't have to agree with every believer on every issue in order to be good Christians.

Sparkling Gems From the Greek, Volume 2

In the church at Antioch, blacks, whites, Jews, Gentiles, bond, and free all mingled together in leadership and worship, and this was something that had never existed before. Remarkably, God used a plethora of nationalities and cultures that represented a broad perspective of the Gospel and its mission to paint a powerful picture of what the Church should look like — a colorful tapestry of people from all walks of life.

Apostles and Prophets

What would life be like if everyone was exactly like you? There would be gaping holes and terrible deficiencies all around us. Rather than allow differences in personalities to rub us the wrong way, we need to let the Holy Spirit teach us to see the benefit that each person we meet has to offer!

Sparkling Gems From the Greek, Volume 2

Divine Guidance

Like a master craftsman teaching an apprentice a new skill, the Holy Spirit will direct and guide you. He'll show you what's needed, He'll open your eyes, impress your mind with supernatural direction, and lift you up when you've stumbled. He will develop you, foster your growth, cultivate your gifts, and teach you about the things of God and about life.

The Holy Spirit and You

Without the Holy Spirit's guidance, we are left to find our way on our own. This no doubt means we will waste valuable time, energy, and money, not to mention shed a lot of unnecessary tears along the way! The Holy Spirit sees what we can't see; knows what we don't know; and understands the best routes, the most efficient shortcuts, and the safest paths to take. Since this is the kind of Leader the Holy Spirit is, we would be wise to let Him lead us!

Sparkling Gems From the Greek, Volume 1

If you are going to move beyond your fear of the unknown and experience real, supernatural Christian living, you must come to a place of surrender to the Holy Spirit. In this act of surrender, you give Him permission to be your Heavenly Coach.

The Holy Spirit and You

The Holy Spirit wants to show us how to take the safest route, He knows exactly how to get us safely to our future point of destination, He knows the future, and He wants to enlighten us with all the information we will need in every situation. *This is part of His ministry to you!*

Last-Days Survival Guide

You can be sure that when the Holy Spirit puts a thought in your mind to do something, it is a right thought, or when He plants an idea in your heart, it is a right idea, or if He nudges you in your spirit to do this or that, He always has a reason for it. He sees and knows something you don't know and is trying to guide and direct you according to wisdom. He is always the Spirit of Truth, and as the Spirit of Truth, you can bank on the fact that He will never mislead you.

The Holy Spirit and You

Divorce

Because of the rampant self-centeredness in society today, many view marriage merely as a vehicle of self-gratification through romance and intimacy. In this psychological approach to married life, one's primary obligation is not to one's family but to one's self, and marital success is defined not by successfully meeting obligations to one's spouse and children, but by a strong sense of subjective happiness in marriage.

Last-Days Survival Guide

The Holy Spirit prophesied that a season would emerge at the end of the age in which individuals in covenant relationship will drift apart until they reach a point of *irreconcilable differences* between themselves, and they will reason that a less complicated solution is to walk away from the relationship — hence, *breaking their truce* or *breaking their covenant*.

Last-Days Survival Guide

A disregard for covenant relationships will eventually infiltrate all facets of society — resulting in *en masse* divorce, contractual breaches of all kinds, and every other form of covenant bond being fractured or destroyed. Because this pattern will be so rampant, it stands to reason that it will also try to infiltrate the Church.

Last-Days Survival Guide

Doctrine of Balaam

There are those today who assert that since Jesus already dealt with sin on the Cross, the outward actions of Christians have no effect on their relationship with God. This is the same dangerous and false teaching that Balaam used against the men of Israel. Jesus' triumph over sin does not alter the fact that He demands *holiness* and complete *separation* from the world for His people.

No Room for Compromise

God saw to it that every person who had cooperated with Balaam's doctrine against Israel was judged — both the Moabite and Midianite women who initiated it and the men of Israel who compromised their conviction and followed the bait right into the trap. In addition, what Balaam *sowed*, he eventually *reaped*. When Moses and his troops began to slay the Moabites and Midianites who had participated in this trap, they discovered that Balaam was among them. So along with everyone else who was killed, Moses' troops executed Balaam with the sword as well (*see* Numbers 31:8). Thus, we see that the law of sowing and reaping held true in the life of Balaam — which stands as an eternal warning to anyone who falsely believes they can ensnare God's people without suffering consequences for their actions.

No Room for Compromise

Doctrines of Demons

It was prophesied long ago that seducing spirits with doctrines of demons would lead masses into deception in the last of the last days. That is the time frame we find ourselves in, and in fact, we are observing society throwing off the voice of Scripture to create a new world with a new moral code that is both messy and chaotic.

How To Keep Your Head on Straight
in a World Gone Crazy

Seducing spirits with doctrines of demons have gradually lured believers away from a rock-solid position on Scripture so that they will accommodate the moral mess in the world rather than be motivated to change it.

Last-Days Survival Guide

As God's people, we must be alert to the fact that Satan is loosing hordes of seducing spirits with doctrines of demons in these last days to lead an entire generation into delusion. Satan has launched a covert operation to seize minds — *especially young minds* — to lead them off track.

How To Keep Your Head on Straight
in a World Gone Crazy

Double-Minded

Think of what a monstrosity it would be to see a person with two heads. One head directs the man to do or say one thing, while the other head directs him to do or to say the opposite. This indeed would be monstrous on more than one level. But James used this very example of a person who is "double-minded" to alert us to the fact that people who are tossed to and fro spiritually are often like a man with two heads. Because they are not established in the Word of God, they are tossed here and there, and they are spiritually "unstable" — or constantly going "back and forth" like that man with two heads.

Apostles and Prophets

When a person is spiritually unstable, he is spiritually restless, spiritually unsteady, and spiritually up and down in his spiritual life. If a person's habitual spiritual instability does not stop, it will begin to seep into and affect *every road* or *path of life* on which he walks.

Apostles and Prophets

Double-Tongued

Have you ever known a person who agreed with whomever he was talking to at the moment? When he was with you, he agreed with you, but when he was with someone else who had a different opinion, he agreed with that person as well. Did that person's opinion fluctuate so quickly that it nearly shocked you? It is very difficult to build trust with a person like this because you never know if he is really with you, or if he's just agreeing with you to your face until he can turn around and disagree with you behind your back. This often reflects a person's lack of integrity, and it is difficult to build a significant relationship with a person who is double-tongued.

Sparkling Gems From the Greek, Volume 1

The Greek word for "double-tongued" presents the picture of someone who says one thing to one person about a situation, but then says something altogether different about it to someone else. This individual is either *inconsistent* in what he tells people, or he is just simply *dishonest*. Sometimes this characteristic of being "double-tongued" indicates that a person is a people-pleaser. He wants everyone to like him, so he agrees with whomever he is with at the moment. This person may be concerned that if he takes an opinion contrary to his immediate audience, he will lose favor or influence with them. So instead of speaking his true convictions, he finds himself violating his conscience. Beyond just remaining silent if he doesn't agree with something that others say, he actually verbalizes *agreement* with those in his presence, knowing that what he says is not really what he believes. This trait of being double-tongued is a serious character flaw.

Sparkling Gems From the Greek, Volume 2

Dream Thieves

When we finally discover a portion of God's will for us, His plan begins to awaken in our hearts — we come to understand what job to take, what business to start, what ministry God has called us to fulfill, and so forth. But if we don't hold fast to our God-given vision, tightly embracing what He has shown us, the "dream thieves" will see to it that we slowly let our dream slip away from us. We must seize that dream — wrap our arms of faith around it, hold it down, grasp it tightly, and place all our weight on top of it. If we don't, the dream thieves of life will come to steal the wonderful plan God has for our lives. If they succeed in doing so, they will steal our uniqueness and our individual purpose in the magnificent plan of God — and nothing would be more tragic than this.

Dream Thieves

You can be sure that if you take a stand of faith in response to a word you received from God, every possible negative thought will come against your mind. Not only will the devil try to use people and circumstances to thwart the plan, he will try to affect your own mind with all kinds of negative thoughts and accusations! He'll do everything he can to talk you out of doing what God has called you to do. *Don't be surprised by this!*

Sparkling Gems From the Greek, Volume 1

Dreams

The greatest tragedy you could ever experience would be to let go of your God-given dream and allow the fire in your heart to go out. To do that is the equivalent of letting go of your special individuality, your divine call, and your God-given giftings.

Dream Thieves

Once you really know what God wants you to do, you must set your heart on the assignment God has given you — without budging, hesitating, flinching, or doubting. Once you truly know God's will for you, you must follow through by obeying what He's told you to do — no matter what your friends, your family, or your surrounding circumstances have to say about it!

Dream Thieves

Dreams are powerful. They usually seem impossible at first, but those who dare to do the impossible are the ones who eventually see the impossible come to pass in their lives. Everything great starts as a dream. Consider the example of Thomas Edison, who worked so long and furiously to realize his dream of the light bulb. Although Edison failed literally thousands of times in the earliest pursuits of his dream, he learned from every failure and pushed forward. Finally, his dream came to pass, and it changed the course of human history. What if this brilliant man had given up and given in to discouragement? Someone else along the way would have invented the light bulb, but Edison wouldn't have had the great honor of being a part of it!

Sparkling Gems From the Greek, Volume 1

Before the foundation of the world, God had a plan for your life. As He knit you together in your mother's womb, your Heavenly Father breathed dreams into your spirit aligned with that plan. Those God-given dreams reflect your special individuality, calling, and divine giftings. You are called to be conformed to the image of Jesus Christ, not to the image or opinions of your family and friends.

Dream Thieves

E

Early Believers

Early believers lived in a world full of conflict, violence, and upheaval — so as the Early Church leaders developed, analyzed, and taught sound doctrine inside the Church at large, they also needed to equip the saints to deal with the hostile surroundings outside the Church.

Dressed To Kill

Jesus' physical absence didn't stop early believers from performing miracles, raising the dead, casting out demons, healing the sick, or bringing multitudes to a saving knowledge of Jesus Christ. Because the Holy Spirit was with them, this meant the ministry of Jesus continued uninterrupted in their midst.

Paid in Full

Early believers relied completely on the Holy Spirit — and in doing so, they experienced demonstrations of God's power, miracles, healings, mass evangelism, the full operation of the fivefold ministry gifts, and the gifts of the Spirit in amazing abundance.

The Holy Spirit and You

What Jesus did, what Jesus said, and how Jesus operated was the model for everything the early believers did as the Christian era began. Jesus demonstrated His need for the partnership of the Holy Spirit, and He allowed the Spirit's miraculous power to be released through His ministry.

A Life Ablaze

Early Church

In the Early Church, believers faced unremitting persecution and were confronted by a host of hostile powers that were arrayed in opposition against them. The immoral culture, pagan religions, the government, unsaved family and friends — all of these external forces put constant pressure on the early believers to forfeit their faith and return to their old ways — but they firmly believed that if they had endurance, they would survive and outlast all the opposition. They believed that if endurance was operational in their lives, the question was no longer *if* they would overcome their battle — only *when* they would overcome.

A Light in Darkness

When you examine the history of the Early Church, you find that the majority of early Christians were not nobility. They were just regular people who were unspoiled by the luxuries of life, content with little, inured to fatigue, and accustomed to hard work — perfect soldiers in the army of the Lord!

Life in the Combat Zone

It took a while for the Early Church to *put to shame* all the evil forces that had come against it. But in the end, that's what happened! The Church eventually emerged in power and changed the face of history. The common, regular, run-of-the-mill people God had chosen were so mighty and powerful in the Lord that they "conquered the world" for Christ during their day.

Unlikely

Equipped with "the whole armor of God" (Ephesians 6:10-18), early believers lived victoriously for the Lord in the midst of the worst predicaments — predicaments much worse than you have ever known. Although Satan buffeted the Early Church with unimaginable torture and outward persecution, he could not destroy her!

Dressed To Kill

The Early Church was comprised of people who had been pagans, and they knew very little about the work of Christ and the things of the Spirit. Nevertheless, their ignorance didn't hinder them, and they quickly became spiritual powerhouses in that dark period of human history.

The Holy Spirit and You

The similarities between the Church at the end of the First Century and the Church that exists today are remarkable. Back then the Church struggled with tolerance of sin, false doctrine, a falling away from one's first love, passionless spiritual routines, and spiritual cold-heartedness. These are the same issues the Church struggles with today.

A Light in Darkness

Ears to Hear

When Christ speaks, all other voices are silent, all arguments cease, and no one else is able to utter a sound. Christ — and Christ alone — is heard when He speaks as the King of kings and the Head of the Church. This voice is so majestic and commanding that no force or power on earth can resist it. When *this* voice speaks, *everyone* listens.

A Light in Darkness

We must learn to continually keep our spiritual ear tuned to the Holy Spirit's counsel and follow Him implicitly, taking each of our cues from Him.

The Holy Spirit and You

Jesus doesn't want His Church to be taken off-guard or by surprise. Regardless of what lies in the future, He has already seen all that will transpire on this earth. Jesus' love for us is so great that He will warn us in advance of impending difficulties — *if* our hearts are open to hear and heed what He has to say. Christ's love compels Him to forewarn His people about coming danger to *forearm* them for challenging times that await them.

A Light in Darkness

History bears witness that the Spirit of God always warns His people in advance when difficult times are coming. There are abundant historical records spanning the centuries that relate accounts of believers and missionaries in hostile nations throughout the world who were forewarned by the Holy Spirit of future hardships. Such divine warnings are intended to prepare believers to face the impending challenges, *if* they will hear and heed the voice of the Spirit.

Sparkling Gems From the Greek, Volume 2

Jesus has already provided answers to every issue His people will ever face. If we will open our ears to hear what the Spirit is saying to the Church, we will know how to respond to every challenge that confronts us in these perilous times God ordained us to live in. He purposed for us to live in this generation and to fulfill His purposes for this moment.

No Room for Compromise

If we will listen to the Holy Spirit, we can know when we are to remain in the battle or when it is wiser for us to withdraw, break camp, and relocate to new territory where greater victories will be won. The Holy Spirit will lead us — *if* we will quiet our hearts and listen for His voice.

Sparkling Gems From the Greek, Volume 2

Eating

Society may throw off control and restraint when it comes to food consumption — a decision that can often prove fatal — but we must resist this destructive tendency in our own lives.

Last-Days Survival Guide

The word "lasciviousness" is translated from a Greek word that describes *excess*, but it primarily refers to the *excessive consumption of food* or *wild, undisciplined living that is especially marked by unbridled sex.* It is listed in Second Peter 2:6 as the principal sin of the cities of Sodom and Gomorrah and the reason that God overthrew them. But notice the word "lasciviousness" also refers to *the excessive consumption of food.* This means that in God's mind, it is just as perverted to overindulge in food as it is to engage in sinful sexual activities! *So how does this make you feel about overeating?*

Sparkling Gems From the Greek, Volume 1

God has a good plan for your life and a long race for you to run, but for you to finish your race, you have to take action to get yourself in shape. If you don't, you could jeopardize your ability to finish your race well. As you eat every meal, remember the wisdom found in First Corinthians 10:31: "Whether therefore ye eat, or drink, or whatsoever ye do, do all to the glory of God." Before you eat, always ask yourself: *Can I eat this kind of food and this portion of food to the glory of God?*

Last-Days Survival Guide

Eating Meat

Paul emphatically urged believers not to eat meat that had been sacrificed to idols — not because meat itself was evil or "possessed" by demons, but because they had to trespass into dark and spiritually dangerous territory in order to purchase it. It was for this reason as well that Christ vehemently opposed those who advocated eating meat offered to idols.

No Room for Compromise

No matter what argument for compromise someone might propose, the fact remained that eating meat offered to idols or roaming about a pagan temple were spiritually poisonous activities that could ultimately bring ruin and destruction into the lives of careless believers.

No Room for Compromise

Edifying

The word "edifying" in Greek carries the ideas of *stewardship, management,* and *positive upbuilding.* It is closely related to an architectural term meaning to *enlarge* or *amplify* a house, and it depicts the careful following of an architectural plan to *enlarge, increase,* or *amplify* as well as the act of *leaving something in an improved condition.*

Testing the Supernatural

Have you ever known a person who always had something good to say about someone else? Doesn't that person leave a sweet taste in your mouth? You feel good about the time you spend with such a positive, sweet-speaking individual. In fact, you feel challenged to rise higher and be better every time you leave that person's presence! The Holy Spirit urges us in Ephesians 4:29 to become a wellspring of good words when we talk to and about others — so we must determine that our words will build others up and leave them in a much-improved state of being!

Sparkling Gems From the Greek, Volume 2

The God-ordained *architectural plan* we have been given to follow is the inspired Word of God. It has been provided to help us *steward, administrate,* and *positively upbuild* our lives. If we will operate according to the plan of Scripture and not question it, change it, or veer from it, it will *edify* us and *leave us in an improved condition.* In other words, it will *enlarge, increase,* and *amplify* our lives.

Testing the Supernatural

Education

You need to treat education like it is important, but you also need to understand that having an education is *not* the equivalent of having wisdom. Education gives you information and facts; but wisdom gives you principles, solutions, and answers. It gives you special insight that helps you know what to do, and it contains principles that will lead you out of that baffling situation and into a place where things begin to work again!

Sparkling Gems From the Greek, Volume 1

I believe people should get as much education as possible. But school-issued pieces of paper are not the criteria that impress God and get His attention. There have been many educated people whom God could not use. Although they were brilliant according to the flesh, they were not worthy of being chosen because their hearts weren't right.

Unlikely

Although *tolerance* and *free thinking* should be encouraged in universities, most professors are actually *in*tolerant and disdain those who stick with more traditional ways of thinking. It seems tolerance is primarily extended to those who embrace the new morality and excepts those who adhere to biblical morality and traditional Christian beliefs.

Last-Days Survival Guide

The education system is public for the most part and, as such, is federally funded. Educators are mandated to indoctrinate teachers in training and to write curricula for the classroom that undermine biblical authority (and *all* godly authority), as well as respect for God. This humanistic curriculum blurs the lines of truth, incites confusion, obliterates common sense, and punishes independent thinking. Any thinking that is outside the box of the "kinder, gentler" world of progressive humanism is not only frowned on, but is often met with violent, punitive resistance.

How To Keep Your Head on Straight in a World Gone Crazy

Effort

Even though a person has a dream for success, that doesn't mean he will attain it, for it takes great effort and hard work to achieve success in any realm of life. Many people who dream of success will never experience it, because they aren't willing to put forth the effort to make it happen.

Sparkling Gems From the Greek, Volume 1

We live in a world that loves to take it easy. We want instant results — and we want them *right now*. Technology has made almost everything instantly accessible. Our entire

Western lifestyle is centered around making things as easy, fast, effortless, and painless as possible. A newer generation is so accustomed to getting everything they want that they don't understand there is a price to pay for true success. But whether they like it or not, the fact remains: True greatness, great achievements, and real success won't float to them on clouds that suddenly materialize above their heads. If anyone wants to achieve something great and significant, he or she will have to put a lot of hard work and effort into making it happen. To achieve the greatness God desires, we will have to be determined, committed, and willing to do anything necessary to accomplish what He has for us.

Sparkling Gems From the Greek, Volume 1

Emotions

When your emotions are not under the lordship of Jesus, they can become a weapon that quickly leads you in the wrong direction, making you say and do things you later regret — but emotions under the control of the Holy Spirit can be a *mighty instrument* in the hands of God.

Christmas — The Rest of the Story

God gave you emotions to help you feel passionate, alive, and joyful. He even gave you emotions to alert you when something is wrong, but your emotions don't need to control you. If your emotions rule you, they will manipulate you like a puppet, and you'll end up as a slave to your emotional whims — up one day and down the next.

Last-Days Survival Guide

Because the devil loves to make a playground out of your mind and emotions, you must deal with him like a real enemy. Rather than fall victim to the devil's attacks, you must make a mental decision to seize every thought he tries to use to penetrate your mind and emotions. Rather than let those thoughts take you captive, you have to reach up and grab them and *force* them into submission! You must take *every* thought captive to the obedience of Christ!

Sparkling Gems From the Greek, Volume 1

When Jesus was surrounded by liars who unjustly accused Him and called for His death, He didn't wither and collapse emotionally, nor did He beg or negotiate His way out of the situation. He knew who He was and what He had come to do, and He held fast to His trust in the Father. Jesus knew that His life was in God's hands, not man's.

Paid in Full

Emotions are expensive, you must wisely choose how you are going to spend them!

Sparkling Gems From the Greek, Volume 2

In your walk with the Lord, you *will* experience times when the devil pushes buttons in your emotions to keep you all bound up and depressed. Other times the enemy will disguise his voice to make you think God is talking to you in order to get you off track or cause you to cast off your deepest dreams as pure imagination. But whenever these attacks occur, just tell the devil to shut up and stop dropping those dimwitted thoughts of nonsense into your head. Tell him to hit the road! Let him know you're not going to bite that bait any longer, so he might as well go fishing somewhere else. You're not a sucker anymore! You know how he works now, and you've determined that he isn't going to steal, kill, or destroy one more good thing in your life!

Sparkling Gems From the Greek, Volume 1

Empowerment

We must always remember that when God calls us, He also equips, provides, sustains, and empowers us to do more than we think or even imagine we can do.

The Point of No Return

We *all* have opportunities and temptations to bail out — sometimes on a daily basis — but God's supernatural strength will empower us to *stay* in the fight, to *keep running* the race, and to *hold on* to the call He first gave us.

Life in the Combat Zone

When something happens that seems to prohibit you from doing the will of God, remember that you are not the first to encounter such difficulties. Others have been in the same quandary. In time, however, the devil's attack ceased and the way for them to move ahead became clear. In the same way, you can be sure that God is going to empower you and give you the wisdom you need to get where you need to go!

Sparkling Gems From the Greek, Volume 1

Encouragement

Encouragement is one of the most profound gifts you can bring to the life of another person. Your words can lift someone from the depths of despair to the heights of hope.

Dream Thieves

You are surrounded every day by people who are struggling in their personal lives, in their minds and emotions, and in their relationships. They may not open up to you about it, but many people are deeply struggling — and they need your encouragement!

Last-Days Survival Guide

Every believer needs to be lovingly provoked at times, irrespective of his or her position in the Body of Christ — and the greatest men and women of God are no exception. Even the most anointed servants of the Lord are still subject to the wiles of the devil and the lies of the flesh, just like anyone else. Everyone needs a loving push in the right direction now and then!

Dream Thieves

Have you noticed that when Christians need encouragement the most, it's often the time they start running from church? They decide to skip church, stay home, and do something else instead. *They isolate themselves when they're in their greatest need of encouragement!*

Sparkling Gems From the Greek, Volume 2

Let's not forget that there are others around us who need encouragement just as much as we do. We shouldn't be led by our eyes only — not everyone who smiles is happy!

Sparkling Gems From the Greek, Volume 1

Rather than fixate only on *your* need to be encouraged, try taking your eyes off yourself to see those around you who are also in need of strength. Think of someone you know whom you can strengthen by coming alongside him to speak words of comfort, consolation, or bravery. Maybe you can take that person to lunch; call him on the telephone; drop him a note; or go out of your way to see how he is doing. Remember, you're not the only one who needs encouragement!

Sparkling Gems From the Greek, Volume 1

Endurance

If the pressures of life have been closing in on you — making you think about giving up — *don't do it!* Ask the Holy Spirit to give you the endurance you need to finish the race you're running. He wants to give you *staying* power so you can make it all the way to the end of your race of faith!

The Will of God — The Key to Your Success

When you are waging war against the forces of hell, *endurance* is the name of the game. If you can endure, you'll win the battle. Satan's tolerance for losing in every showdown with you will inevitably wear out. He'll recognize that you have endurance, and he'll know that he can't beat you. His only option will be to bow out and leave the fight.

Life in the Combat Zone

Anytime you resolve to maintain a position of faith, your choice to stand firm and resist the enemy's strategy causes God to supernaturally join you in that situation. In that space, He begins "kneading" supernatural patience and endurance into your heart and soul — and He doesn't stop until you are completely *filled* and *saturated* with endurance from top to bottom!

The Will of God — The Key to Your Success

The Bible is piled high with stories of people — *people just like you* — who stood in faith and endured difficulties to accomplish what God instructed them to do. You are surrounded on every side with these powerful examples — those who were challenged in their faith, yet who held on to the Word of God and didn't deviate from God's plan, and as a result, they saw God's promises come to pass in their lives!

The Will of God — The Key to Your Success

If you are going through a difficult time, you may be tempted to obsess over questions like, *How did this happen? What did I do wrong? Why did God allow this to take place? How did I let Satan get in and do this to me?* But your questions won't change your situation. What's important is that you deal with the devil's attack bravely, endure hardness if you must, and come out of that combat zone a winner!

Life in the Combat Zone

Make the decision once and for all that quitting is *not* an option and say, "I will not back down from my firm position of faith!"

The Will of God — The Key to Your Success

Entitlement

When a person feels entitled to everything, he loses his thankfulness for nearly everything. Why should a person be thankful when he feels he is entitled to anything he is ever given? This sense of entitlement is destructive to individuals, and it leads society as a whole into a state of *unthankfulness*.

Last-Days Survival Guide

Today society is filled with people who are ruled by a sense of entitlement. When a person — or society itself — embraces a sense of entitlement, it produces a *"Me! Me! Me!"* attitude.

Last-Days Survival Guide

When people live with an unrealistic sense of entitlement, they rarely *feel* grateful for what they receive because they think it's rightfully theirs anyway. No matter how much they receive, they expect more and they believe they are entitled to more simply "because" — regardless of their performance or having done anything to merit it.

Last-Days Survival Guide

An entitlement mentality is a blight on any society that can eventually undermine a nation's economic stability, because it focuses on *taking*, not *giving*. Not only can this mindset erode a country's economic system, but it also hinders men and women from reaping the benefit of God's higher system of *effort and reward*.

Last-Days Survival Guide

Entry Points

We need to be serious about our lives because the devil is always looking for a door, a window, or a crack — *an entry point* — through which he can access us. We must circumspectly look at our lives to see if there is any area we have left open or unguarded that has allowed the devil to find a way to attack us.

Sparkling Gems From the Greek, Volume 2

Living a life of obedience shuts every door and makes it very difficult for the devil to find entry into our lives. On the other hand, we must acknowledge that if we are living in disobedience in any area of our lives, those areas may become the very entry points by which the devil gains access to try to disturb our peace and stop our forward momentum.

Sparkling Gems From the Greek, Volume 2

Many attacks we experience can be attributed to the devil acting in accordance with his own evil nature, but the truth is, often *we* have left a door open that allows the enemy to find his way into our lives and launch his fiery darts from an inside position. It's up to us to do all we can to shut every door and to make sure they *stay* shut. And during those times we are under attack, it would behoove us to ask: *"Holy Spirit, is there any area in my life where I've left a door open and allowed this intruder to find his way in?"* Before we take authority over the devil in the name of Jesus, let's *find the access point and STOP him at the door!*

Sparkling Gems From the Greek, Volume 2

Environment

God will use your environment — the people, places, and opportunities around you — to shape and sharpen your gifts. And while He is in the process of developing your gifts, He will simultaneously use you to sharpen the gifts in others.

The Will of God — The Key to Your Success

Your biggest potential enemy (besides your own wrong thinking and the devil himself) is the environment in which you live. If you constantly live in an atmosphere of doubt and unbelief, you'll have a lot more difficult time maintaining a walk of strong faith. You need to know that a doubt-filled environment will eventually negatively rub off on you!

The Will of God — The Key to Your Success

It is possible that you might be too comfortable where you are in this particular phase of your life, and your comfort zone may be hindering you from having to stretch and totally depend on God. If so, you might begin to sense a "divine discomfort" as the Lord prepares you to say *yes* to His call to "step out of the boat" and follow Him into a new place of challenge and purpose.

The Will of God — The Key to Your Success

Your friends and your job are not so important that you should let them destroy your spiritual life. If you cannot successfully handle the environment you're in, get out of there! The Lord will provide a better job and better friends than you've ever had in your life!

Sparkling Gems From the Greek, Volume 1

There is no record in the book of Acts of preachers, apostles, or believers attending pagan temples to meet people, advertise their messages, help them identify with local populations, or become more "seeker-friendly" to the unchurched. When the message of Jesus Christ came to a community in darkness, God's power meshed with Christ's call for people to repent — and God called people *out of* those dark environments into His holy community. There was never an option to remain in both worlds. To enable believers to make this break with the world around them, the Holy Spirit empowered them to walk free.

No Room for Compromise

It's just a fact that your environment tends to affect you and the way you think. For example, if you used to smoke or if you used to have a drinking problem, it's obviously not a smart idea for you to hang around smokers or drinkers — *unless*, that is, you want to be influenced to return to your old habits. Hanging around people who still do these things may lure you to pick up a cigarette and take a smoke or to allow yourself one more small drink. Those little allowances may possibly be the very hook that the devil uses to drag you back into the bondage from which Jesus Christ already delivered you, and that's why it's vital for you to understand that the environment surrounding you is very important!

Sparkling Gems From the Greek, Volume 1

Error

When society sets God aside, *error* is released, and this eventually leads to *ruin* on multiple levels. It is like an inevitable "chemical reaction" that will always occur if the right elements are mixed together.

How To Keep Your Head on Straight
in a World Gone Crazy

Dealing with error is not pleasant, but there is a time when it must be done bravely, lovingly, and in the power of the Holy Spirit.

How To Keep Your Head on Straight
in a World Gone Crazy

If correction doesn't come to an errant leader's life, his words and teachings have the potential to become food that makes others sick. Because his influence is strong, it is likely that those who are close to him will pick up whatever has contaminated him and become infected with the same spiritual problems. And it doesn't take very many erring individuals to transmit sickness to an entire church body when they hold positions of influence.

Last-Days Survival Guide

It might be difficult to imagine that a congregation with loyalty to Christ would simultaneously be infected with an internal spiritual disease. However, Satan has learned that if he can't destroy a church with external pressure, he has to attack it from within. Often believers are so focused on combating external opposition that they overlook the greater enemy that has risen up in their midst.

Sparkling Gems From the Greek, Volume 2

Small amounts of error can be tolerated without lasting harm if the believer soon returns to a steady diet of healthy spiritual fare, but if spiritual food containing even small amounts of error is consistently ingested over a long period of time, that error will begin to sicken believers and can eventually prove to be spiritually "fatal" — leading to the shipwreck of their faith (*see* 1 Timothy 1:19).

How To Keep Your Head on Straight
in a World Gone Crazy

Those who promote spiritual error will soon discover that Jesus will act in mercy and compassion to attack spiritual disease and cleanse it from His Church. Christ loves the Church so much that, *if* necessary, He will even remove those who resist Him to eradicate the false doctrine and worldly compromise so His Church can be strong and healthy.

No Room for Compromise

I urge you to remove any plate tainted with error from your table and learn to identify and receive only good spiritual food that will make you strong in faith and godly character.

How To Keep Your Head on Straight
in a World Gone Crazy

Those who advocate compromise often wrongly mistake Christ's *longsuffering* for His *tolerance* of compromise. It is true that Jesus loves everyone, even those who are in error, but if error begins to pollute a church, a time will inevitably come when Christ's patience will cease and His sword will swing into action. He will lift His righteous blade and swiftly excise the spiritual disease before it fatally spreads to the rest of the church.

No Room for Compromise

Eternity

God is a Keeper of records and there is a book in Heaven called "The Book of Life" which holds the names of everyone who has put his or her faith in Jesus Christ.

Build Your Foundation

As you live, be intentionally cognizant of the reality that eternity is in front of you. If you do this, it will affect what you think, what you say, what you do, how you use your time, and how you spend your money. It will make you want to live your life with a view toward eternity.

Last-Days Survival Guide

Too often we devote the bulk of our time to our homes, gardens, cars, businesses, or other worldly affairs. Although we must give attention to the basic things that are necessary to life, we make a huge mistake if we focus on these temporal matters while neglecting the eternal spiritual issues that will pass from this life into the next. Only what is done for the Lord will last. Everything else will be left behind in a world that will one day be consumed with a fervent heat. Since everything will be dissolved, doesn't it make sense that we invest in our spiritual futures as well as in our present lives?

Sparkling Gems From the Greek, Volume 1

Countless numbers of good people have died and gone to hell because they didn't die in Christ. It is not about works; it's about the spiritual state people are in when they die. The Scriptures guarantee that if a person dies *in* Christ, he will be *in* Christ for all of eternity, but if a person dies in a lost spiritual state, he or she will spend eternity in hell, apart from God and in an irrecoverable and lost state forever.

Build Your Foundation

The stakes are not only *high* — they are *eternal*.

How To Keep Your Head on Straight in a World Gone Crazy

Evil

In the midst of a current worldwide shift toward lawlessness, we are witnessing evil spiritual forces setting an entire spectrum of destructive fires, which are designed to consume as many lives as possible. This highlights with even greater force how crucial it is that we stick with the Bible and hold to the authority of Scripture in this late hour.

How To Keep Your Head on Straight in a World Gone Crazy

Because of Jesus' death on the Cross and His resurrection from the dead, the forces of hell are *already* defeated.

However, even though they have been legally stripped of their authority and power, they continue to roam around this earth, carrying out evil deeds like criminals, bandits, hooligans, and thugs. And just like criminals who refuse to submit to the law, these evil spirits will continue to operate in this world until some believer uses his God-given authority to enforce their defeat!

Sparkling Gems From the Greek, Volume 1

If not restrained, evil in any generation will become more and more bold, brazen, and aggressive.

How To Keep Your Head on Straight in a World Gone Crazy

Very often, evil finds access into your mind and imagination through your eyes, so make a covenant with your eyes as part of your deliberate plan to build a wall of protection around your life. Psalm 101:3 says, "I will set no wicked thing before mine eyes...."

Last-Days Survival Guide

When God's power arrives on the scene, evil spirits swiftly go out — and when they depart, the physical and mental afflictions caused by those spirits leave with them. Evil spirits are literally *ejected* or *evicted*, just as an unwanted person would be ejected or evicted from a house.

A Light in Darkness

The floodgates of evil are swinging open wide as society races toward a cataclysmic collision with crises of a magnitude never before seen, and societal attitudes and moral standards have shifted and plummeted to depths that are almost unimaginable.

Last-Days Survival Guide

Evil is always lurking in the shadows, waiting for us to drop our guard and fall asleep on the job. In those vulnerable moments of lethargy, the enemy is positioned to seize his opportunity and attack, often with devastating consequences. Therefore, it is essential that we are always on guard — diligent, wide-awake, and doing our part to protect ourselves from the evil that is in the world.

No Room for Compromise

You cannot avoid the fact that you will sometimes face unpleasant situations in which you feel mistreated, abused, or discriminated against. As long as you live in a world where the devil operates and unsaved people have their way, evil and injustice will touch your life from time to time.

Paid in Full

Even the strongest believer can be worn down by the constant onslaught of evil surroundings.

Last-Days Survival Guide

Evolution

When the fundamental belief that man is made in God's image is replaced with the notion that man is merely a part of the evolutionary process, the dignity God gave man by creating him in His own image is seriously undermined, and human beings begin to be viewed as mere objects in an evolutionary process who can be altered scientifically or medically without moral considerations or consequence.

How To Keep Your Head on Straight
in a World Gone Crazy

It is an inevitable outcome that when society rejects biblical knowledge, people will begin to embrace the belief that humans are nothing more than objects of the evolutionary process. As more and more reject the premise that man is made in God's image, a growing number find it easier to promote surgical altering of the gender identity God has given to each person born on the earth.

How To Keep Your Head on Straight
in a World Gone Crazy

Examination

"Due diligence" is always smart to do before anyone finalizes a deal and signs his name on a contract that legally binds him. In the same way, God does "due diligence" before He decides whom He will and will not use. If it is logical to do research before signing a contract involving a large sum of money, think how much more logical it is for God to *validate, confirm,* and *certify* that we are ready for a big task before He promotes us into a visible position where we will represent Him before many people.

Sparkling Gems From the Greek, Volume 2

You need to know that God has plenty of time, and He is not in a hurry, nor is He focused on the clock, as we usually are. He is more concerned about character, integrity, faithfulness, and purity of heart than about the calendar.

Sparkling Gems From the Greek, Volume 2

You are a living document — and God is reading the pages of your life to observe how you live, how you speak, how you treat others, and so on. He is doing investigative research to determine if you are ready for a promotion or a greater anointing. Don't be too surprised if God finds a few errors that need correction, for none of us is perfect. If there are issues that need correcting — and I'm *certain* there are — you must allow the Holy Spirit to put you through a process to correct those flaws *before* you get the big break you've been dreaming of or before God promotes you to a higher level of responsibility.

Sparkling Gems From the Greek, Volume 2

Exercise (Physical)

Your body is an instrument given to you by God — but to keep it working in good shape, you have to *use* it and *move* it.

Last-Days Survival Guide

Inactivity — a lack of regular, physical movement — is a great contributor to weight gain, obesity, life-crippling immobility, and health problems that would generally disappear if people would simply become more mobile.

Last-Days Survival Guide

If you continue going the way you are going right now, is your physical body going to be a fine-tuned instrument that God can use, or is it going to be the very tool the devil uses to bring you into discredit and shame? Who is running your life today — you or your flesh? Don't join the ranks of those who were once used by the Lord but are now set aside and ruined because they refused to bring their bodies into subjection!

Sparkling Gems From the Greek, Volume 1

When it's time for you to head to the gym or get on your home exercise equipment, expect your flesh to put up a fight and look for an escape. Determine beforehand that you're going to steadfastly *subdue* and *conquer* that fleshly "pull" to give up on your commitment. You have to let the flesh know that it is *your* servant — and *you* are the boss!

Sparkling Gems From the Greek, Volume 2

Experience

God has a way of using the experiences of our early days — even our very bad experiences — and redeeming them as only He can. He forges them into a glorious purpose for our lives and uses our seasons of obscurity, loneliness, brokenness, clumsiness, and even *failure* to weave together a plan so *unlikely* that only He could bring it to pass. Our future doesn't lie in our own impressive resume or grandiose list of accomplishments, but in our faithfulness and consistency day to day as we walk with God and build a "resume" of accomplishments, exploits — *and even godly character* — with Him.

Unlikely

When God calls you, He will equip and prepare you to effectively complete your assignment on time. He will use every aspect of who you are — your background, your level of education, your past occupations, your life experiences — to bring about His will in your life.

Sparkling Gems From the Greek, Volume 2

While Jesus grew up, He spent time in the nearby city of Sepphoris where his father Joseph worked and where His grandparents on Mary's side of the family lived. Jesus' exposure to the enormous wealth of the city, as well as the banking industry, the theater, and the lush surrounding farmlands later provided Him with many life experiences and analogies that He could not have known had he never ventured from Nazareth. This explains why Jesus was able to speak with knowledge and authority on a wide range of subjects and to many different kinds of people. He would not have been able to do that had he never ventured outside the bounds of His small hometown.

Christmas — The Rest of the Story

Pearls are not easily found. To obtain the richest and most beautiful pearls, a diver must dive again and again. Then after lifting shells from the sea floor, he must force open the mouth of each shell and dig through the tough meat of the muscle, poking and searching for the tiny white pearl that was formed over a long period of time. These pearls are precious, rare, valuable, and hard to obtain. This is how you should view the things God has done in your life. You can't put a price on what you have learned through your life experiences. Like precious pearls, those life lessons are inestimable in their value because they cost you something. *You had to go deep into God to obtain those spiritual treasures.*

Sparkling Gems From the Greek, Volume 1

F

Failure

Failure doesn't have to be final, and every setback you experience doesn't mean it's the end of the road for you or your future!

The Will of God — The Key to Your Success

If you're like a majority of people, you have probably spent a lot of time putting yourself down and badgering yourself about your failures — and you've likely been tempted to largely forget about the great work God has done in your life. But it's time for you to put an end to that downward spiral. Stop berating yourself over your missteps and start thanking God for the progress you've already made!

Sparkling Gems From the Greek, Volume 2

A closed door does not mean failure!

Dressed To Kill

If you allow it, the devil will hound you relentlessly with thoughts of failure, and little by little, you'll find yourself becoming trapped in the memories of past disappointments. *Don't let that happen!* It's time for you to *speak out loud* and remind the devil that those failures and negative memories are in the *past*. They are under the blood of Jesus and therefore no longer applicable! Resist those thoughts of failure just like you would resist the devil. *Command them to get behind you and to stay away forever in Jesus' name!*

Sparkling Gems From the Greek, Volume 2

Faith

Faith is the spark that ignites the impossible and causes it to become possible — and when a person's faith is activated, it sets supernatural power in motion that enables that person to do what he normally would never be able to do! Once faith has been activated and remains activated, a person becomes enabled and empowered so that he is capable and competent to do whatever it is God has told him to do. *Such a person can even do the impossible!*

Sparkling Gems From the Greek, Volume 2

When the power of God and faith are operative in your life, you are like a huge army tank with the ability to move your position forward without taking any losses!

Dressed To Kill

Commit yourself with all your heart and strength to stand in faith on the Word of God, no matter how crazy it may sound to your natural mind. Then meditate on the scriptures the Holy Spirit quickens to your spirit. Ask Him to make the Word more real and rock solid to you than the natural things that surround you. This is the way you come to a stance of faith in which you truly understand and confess from your heart what God is saying to you.

Dream Thieves

Pick up your feet and take that first step into the unknown! That's where your faith will explode and the adventure will take off. You'll never know the joy of truly serving God in a life of faith by sitting at home, watching television, avoiding new challenges in life, or ignoring what you know that the Holy Spirit is asking you to do!

The Point of No Return

When faith finally finds what it needs or wants, it does not move until it GETS what it seeks. Or you could say that faith is like a bulldog that has finally found the bone of its wildest dreams. Once the bulldog wraps its jowls around that bone, no one is going to pull the bone out of its mouth! Someone may tug, pull, and try to jerk that bone out of the bulldog's mouth, but it will not let go. The bulldog is going to "stand by" that bone and never relinquish it.

Dream Thieves

The fact is, in God *all* things are possible. Therefore, *it's up to you and me* to get our thinking in line with God's Word. And as you build up your faith to the level it needs to be for the new challenge, you will experience an explosion of supernatural power that literally carries you over into the realm where impossible things become possible!

Sparkling Gems From the Greek, Volume 2

If you're sitting on the banks of your life — fully aware that God is calling you to cross the river and enter a new realm of faith and power — don't look back to Egypt and all of its creature comforts. Look across the river to the land of promise where the milk and honey flows! *Keep your eyes on the milk and honey!*

The Point of No Return

Faithfulness

God is your Divine Protector! He is your *Hiding Place*, your *Strong Tower*, your *Shield*, and the *Mountain* that surrounds your life! He promises to be with you at all times and to *never* abandon you. All He asks is that you "stay put" in the center of His will where He has called you — *refusing* to move or give up and rejecting every scare tactic of the enemy to abdicate your post.

The Will of God — The Key to Your Success

When we put our hand to the plow that God has placed in front of us, and we do it with all our might, He always gives increase, making us fruitful in our endeavors and entrusting us with more.

Unlikely

It can be difficult to focus on the future when present circumstances seem to descend like a fog that obscures your spiritual view — but whatever you are facing today didn't take God by surprise! If you'll stay faithful to do what God tells you to do and refuse to let go of His hand, He will lead you on a path that will take you straight out of the crisis and into His plan for your life. The fog *will* eventually lift and you'll bask in the glorious light of day, right in the middle of God's perfect will!

The Will of God — The Key to Your Success

It isn't always how well we fight that really counts in life but that we keep on fighting. A "never-give-up" kind of attitude will eventually produce victory every time!

Dressed To Kill

I encourage you not to lament whatever "small thing" you may be doing right now as being too tiny or unimportant. Believe me when I tell you that nothing is being wasted in what you are doing right now. God is *committed* to training you now so you can be a success in the future!

Unlikely

False Doctrine

From the beginning of time, wherever there was something true, Satan tried to twist and pervert it to present something false in its place.

Testing the Supernatural

Defective doctrine — if allowed into a church or into a believer's life — in due course will produce a stinking mess, for deceptive doctrine is nasty, and it has such long-term, detrimental effects that it should be treated like stinking excrement to be urgently removed from the house.

How To Keep Your Head on Straight in a World Gone Crazy

It is difficult to understand how early believers who sat under the teachings of the apostles could have been led astray by Gnostic teaching, but it happened. And since it could happen then, it can certainly happen now. Many Gnostic-like doctrines are reemerging and being perpetuated today — just as the Holy Spirit forecasted in First Timothy 4:1.

Testing the Supernatural

Today some skillfully allege that the concept of God's wrath is antiquated and outdated and that God's wrath was poured out on Christ, so consequently (they say) there is no more divine wrath to be released in a future judgment. But anyone educated in theology understands the outright fallacy of this assertion.

How To Keep Your Head on Straight
in a World Gone Crazy

The enemy's strategy is to "breach the walls" and bring in heretical error that will produce a powerless, weakened version of Christianity where sin is tolerated, separation and holiness are ignored, and the need for ongoing repentance is disregarded.

How To Keep Your Head on Straight
in a World Gone Crazy

False Ministers

In early New Testament times, false ministers were trying to get believers to "bite" their bait and get hooked! And think about it — a hook of deception in one's jaw would make it difficult for that person to break free and get away from that false apostle with his deceptive teaching. These people with false motives wanted control and leverage in the lives of churches and believers with the hope that it would result in notoriety and financial gain.

Testing the Supernatural

The Bible prophesies a particular group of spiritual leaders will arise at the end of the age and present a counterfeit version of truth, claiming to be on the "cutting edge" of progressive thinking and even of new theological concepts and ideas. But in reality, this particular category of leaders will be out of sync with authentic apostolic preaching and teaching contained in the pages of the New Testament.

How To Keep Your Head on Straight
in a World Gone Crazy

It is damaging to true ministry gifts when false ministers gain a public foothold and stain or ruin the reputation of the ministry.

Testing the Supernatural

The Ephesian congregation refused to tolerate or endure false ministers, and their desire to protect the integrity of God's Word and to uphold the honor of public ministry was one of the characteristics about this local church that made it commendable to Jesus.

Testing the Supernatural

The Holy Spirit prophesied that a host of false teachers will arise and large numbers of people will be attracted to these leaders who offer modified versions of truth. He also said that these *ear ticklers* will proliferate rapidly in these last days as this erring generation "heaps" such teachers unto themselves (*see* 2 Timothy 4:3).

How To Keep Your Head on Straight
in a World Gone Crazy

False Prophets

If a prophetic message — or *any* message given in *any* form, for that matter — is given that is contradictory to the Word of God, those who are in spiritual leadership have a God-given responsibility to correct it.

Apostles and Prophets

God's concern about false prophets was not aimed at prophets who prophesied the long-range plan of God. It was for those who predicted immediate events — perhaps even setting dates to accompany them — that did not happen as forecasted, for the impact of this is disheartening to the people of God and "discrediting" of true prophets. Remember, God said if anything doesn't occur that a so-called prophet foretold *would* occur within a short time frame, it is right to be untrusting of that prophet and to keep a distance from him.

Apostles and Prophets

People counterfeit all kinds of things. For example, fake currency is regularly being produced and circulated from place to place. But just because there are counterfeit bills in circulation, does it mean you refuse to use money? Of course not, because you need money to live. Rejecting money because of a few counterfeit bills would be a wrong response. In the same way, to reject all prophets and all prophetic ministry simply because you've had a bad experience with them is a wrong response. Since God gives nothing needlessly and He has given prophets to the Church, we *need* them. Therefore, you need to learn how to recognize the legitimate ones, as well as the telltale signs of those who are illegitimate prophets.

Apostles and Prophets

There are some ministers who were false from the start, but there were others who started out pure and then, through the lure or advantage of profit, veered off course and prostituted themselves. Rather than being pure vessels who spoke on behalf of God by the Holy Spirit, they began using their spiritual giftings for self-gain or self-promotion to work money out of sincere people's pockets into their own pockets, and due to their hidden agendas and ulterior motives, nearly everything in their so-called prophetic operation had become "false."

Apostles and Prophets

Family

Armed with knowledge, we can protect ourselves, our families, and our loved ones from the destructive trends that will be associated with the closing days — and we can resolve to stand strong and do the will of God, shining as lights in the darkness that will certainly increase just before Jesus returns.

Last-Days Survival Guide

If your family has fallen victim to perilous times — if your home is out of order or if your children no longer respectfully listen to what you say — you need a break-through and a drastic change. I can assure you from the Word of God that to reassume your position as the leader in your home and regain your children's obedience and respect *is* possible. You can turn things around in your home and family!

Last-Days Survival Guide

God has always been in the habit of calling entire families, and He wants to call *your* family and give them a special purpose too!

Christmas — The Rest of the Story

If we pay heed to the Holy Spirit and build our homes according to God's Word, we can have strong families even in the last of the last days. But because we are living in this end-time hour, it is vital that a hedge is built around our marriages and families.

Last-Days Survival Guide

If we've lost precious opportunities in any area — includ-ing time lost with our families — we can *reverse* that condition. Through our recommitment to ourselves and to the Lord, we can buy back time that has been lost, wasted, or forfeited — and with the Holy Spirit's help, we can accomplish in *a short time* what we thought was forever lost. We really can *redeem time* and get back on course!

Last-Days Survival Guide

Favor

The longer you walk with God, the more you learn that He foots the bills when you are where He has asked you to be, doing what He has asked you to do. That doesn't mean you won't ever face financial challenges, but when you are doing what God has asked, your obedience opens the door to greater favor and provision.

The Will of God — The Key to Your Success

It's a spiritual law that deliberate and diligent obedience ultimately brings divine favor and blessings.

The Will of God — The Key to Your Success

In the New Testament, the word "grace" is occasionally translated *favor* because a person who receives it has been *supernaturally enabled* as a result of receiving a manifestation of *favor* from God. The word "grace" refers to God graciously imparting a special touch that *enables, empowers*, and *strengthens* a recipient of it. *It is a divine touch that transforms an individual and gives him the ability to do what he could not do before.*

Why We Need the Gifts of the Holy Spirit

Fear

Fear is a powerful force — and if fear gets a grip on your mind, it will produce cowardice in you. If you let it go unchecked, eventually you'll become afraid of everything and everyone. If you allow it to do so, fear will eventually control your life!

Life in the Combat Zone

Some people are so controlled by fear that they pray *fretful* prayers instead of *faith-filled* prayers. I must admit that I've had moments in my own life when I've prayed more out of fretfulness than out of faith, but praying fretful prayers doesn't get you anything. It is non-productive praying because God does not respond to fretfulness. He responds to *faith*!

Sparkling Gems From the Greek, Volume 1

If fear tries to assault us, we have to let peace stand in front of our hearts and minds as a guard — and with our mouths, we must declare: *"ACCESS DENIED!"*

Signs You'll See Just Before Jesus Comes

There may be moments when you're tempted to be afraid and to flee from where you know God has assigned you for this season. But if you will quiet yourself and listen carefully, the Lord will give you a reassuring word of encouragement. When fear or pressure is affecting you, it's likely the enemy is pressuring you to abandon your God-given assignment.

The Will of God — The Key to Your Success

Instead of yielding to fear, we must command it to *stand down* and leave us in Jesus' name — acknowledging that fear itself is evil and that it has been *defeated* by Jesus Christ.

Last-Days Survival Guide

Whoever or whatever controls a person's mind ultimately has the power to dictate the affairs and outcome of that person's life. Thus, if a person allows his mind to be doused with panic or fear, he is putting fear in charge of his life. Because God wants us to remain in peace regardless of the tumultuous events that transpired around us, Scripture urges us not to allow fear-filled thoughts to penetrate our minds, will, and emotions.

Sparkling Gems From the Greek, Volume 1

If not dealt with, fear and paranoia can cause people to act in illogical and unreasonable ways.

Christmas — The Rest of the Story

If you've been tempted to fear or to feel hopeless about the changes happening in this age, it's time for you to tell fear to *leave* in Jesus' name! Then ask God to help you allow His delivering power to work through you to bring freedom to people who are confused or gripped with fear. The world is looking for hope — and you have a great hope to give them!

The Will of God — The Key to Your Success

Fear of God

The need to *fear the Lord* is so important that the Scriptures command us to do it more than 300 times in various ways throughout the Old and New Testaments.

A Life Ablaze

When the fear of God holds a healthy place in our lives, it *protects us* from sin, it *keeps us* from wrong behaviors, and it *saves us* from the effects of bad choices. When we have a healthy fear of the Lord, it *liberates us* from the fear of many things in life that would steal our peace.

A Life Ablaze

Let me use electricity to describe the fear of the Lord. God's Word and His awesome power are amazing! Both of them bring life, light, illumination, healing, and deliverance. Both quicken the dead to come alive again and improve our lives in ways that are indescribable. Yet if God's Word and His power are mishandled — that is, if they are treated casually, disrespectfully, or irreverently — the consequences can be very negative. Just as we have no need to fear electricity if it is handled correctly, we never need to be afraid of God *if* we are living in obedience to His Word and responding properly to His mighty power. We need to be afraid only of the consequences we will reap if we are deliberately living in disobedience to the principles of His Word or if we mishandle His power.

A Life Ablaze

As you grow in your understanding of the fear of the Lord, there is no question that it will release the power of God like a surging flood that brings the miraculous into every sphere of your life!

A Life Ablaze

Fellowship

Have you noticed that when Christians need encouragement the most, it's often the time they start running from church? They decide to skip church, stay home, and do something else instead. *They isolate themselves when they're in their greatest need of encouragement!*

Sparkling Gems From the Greek, Volume 2

Satan knows that if he can get you to fall out of fellowship with other believers — *at the very moment when you need fellowship and encouragement the most* — then he can probably keep you down and defeated. It's true that you can read the Bible at home by yourself, and you need to do this — but fellowship with other believers is essential for everyone, and that includes you. That is why church is the last place the devil wants you to go when you're feeling low! He knows if you go to church, you will be touched by the Presence of the Lord, you will get encouraged by other believers, and in the end, and you'll crawl out of that hole the enemy has put you in and rise up to a place of heavenly victory!

Sparkling Gems From the Greek, Volume 1

From the beginning of the Church Age to the last of these last days, God's people have been getting together to strengthen their relationships, to share the love of Christ, and to enjoy one another in "private houses" — outside of a church setting. If you've never opened your own home for such an event, maybe this is the year for you to step out by faith and invite a small *or large* group of people over for an evening of fellowship.

Sparkling Gems From the Greek, Volume 2

Fight

Why would we ever try to fight our battles alone when the Greatest Warrior in the universe — the One who possesses ultimate power — is willing to fight for us?

Paid in Full

God is calling upon you to stand up and *fight* — giving your concentrated efforts to stand *firm* for what you believe. Fight in a manner that is noble, admirable, and worthy of the reward that awaits you. *And remember — the greater reward usually requires a greater fight.*

Sparkling Gems From the Greek, Volume 2

We have the name of Jesus, the blood of Jesus, and the mighty sword of God's Word, and through the power of prayer by the Spirit of God, we are called to diligently keep watch and faithfully do our part to *thwart* Satan's ability to carry out his evil strategies!

How To Keep Your Head on Straight in a World Gone Crazy

God is looking for a special brand of believers who want to enter the combat zone and live there according to His will and His ways. He needs resolute, committed Christians who know their place of victory in Christ and will challenge the devil, storm the gates of hell, and remain faithful until the job is accomplished. God is seeking spiritual warriors who will step forward to be enlisted ahead of the rest of the ranks, ready to fearlessly look the enemy in the eye and do battle!

Life in the Combat Zone

Regardless of how well or how badly believers are doing in the midst of their fight, at least they are fighting! While others have given up, they have not, and these are the very kind of people whom you should view as comrades in the faith!

Dressed To Kill

Fivefold Ministry

I feel the need to categorically state that everyone is *not* called into fivefold ministry — and that the gifts of *apostle*, *prophet*, *evangelist*, *pastor*, and *teacher* are much rarer than the large conglomeration of people who today call themselves by these names or who are called these names by those who misuse the terms to describe them. The overuse of fivefold ministry names has given the incorrect impression that these Christ-given gifts can be found in large doses and that people can be self-titled and self-called. The result is the awe, respect, and weightiness that Christ intends for these authentic gifts to possess among us — so they can perform their building, equipping, and unifying function — is degraded.

Apostles and Prophets

Christ uses fivefold ministry gifts to assist in bringing *correction* where it is needed, to *fix* what is broken, and *to equip* and *to prepare* the Body of Christ for works of ministry so that it is not hindered by issues that have not been dealt with along the way, and to help each member of the Body become *connected* and *assembled* into right places, which will result in the Body of Christ becoming *fully operational* and *fully functional.*

Apostles and Prophets

Satan knows the important, strategic place in the Church held by the fivefold ministry, so he never stops working his diabolical plan to destroy every apostle, prophet, evangelist, pastor, and teacher he can reach. He knows that if he can hit a leader and knock him or her out of the battle, he can wound a significant part of the Body of Christ with one blow!

Life in the Combat Zone

There may be times when those who stand in the ministry must work at other jobs until they can work full time in the ministry, but Ephesians 4:12 strongly implies God's best is that they do these ministries in the Church as *a full-time line of work.* Fulfilling their role as Christ-given ministry gifts requires concentration and hard work, and for them to do what Christ has called them to do, it is the responsibility of the Church to financially support those called into these positions so they can do it with no financial stress and provide the full benefit of their ministries to the Body of Christ.

Apostles and Prophets

Flesh

A life dominated by the flesh is a hard life. It is filled with excess, imbalance, extremity, laziness, self-abuse, hatred, strife, bitterness, irresponsibility, and neglect. The way of the flesh is the hardest route for any individual to take; yet the flesh cries out to be in charge, screaming to have its own way, demanding to be the boss. Unless you take your flesh to the Cross and mortify it by the power of God, it will keep screaming until you finally surrender to it and allow it to produce its ruinous effects in your life.

Sparkling Gems From the Greek, Volume 1

Fleshly nature does not want to be laid on the altar. It desperately desires to be in full control and actively resists God's pleading for surrender.

Apostles and Prophets

Don't let your flesh tell you that you can keep covering up your problems with temporary solutions, because those temporary solutions will eventually wear off or run out — and when they do, the same issue you faced before will resurface again.

Last-Days Survival Guide

The truth is that the devil's attacks against our lives wouldn't work if our flesh didn't cooperate. If we were truly mortifying the flesh on a daily basis and living lives that are "dead to sin" as we are commanded to do in Scripture, we would not respond to demonic suggestions and to fleshly temptation. Dead men are incapable of responding to anything. Thus, we see the power of a crucified life!

Dressed To Kill

If you really want to live a supernatural, Spirit-led life, you have to deal with your flesh, which wants to control you. You must mortify, or defeat, the flesh, and allow the Holy Spirit to have His way. The struggle may seem great, but it's the route to live a fruitful Christian life.

Sparkling Gems From the Greek, Volume 2

Flexibility

I have met very few people who enjoy change. Most people like to be where they feel comfortable, and flesh naturally gravitates to what is easy. It seems so effortless to take the path of least resistance. We are drawn to what is familiar and will usually shy away from anything that will "rock our boat."

The Will of God — The Key to Your Success

God may call you to a people or place that you would not naturally choose. He may call you to a church filled with people of a different race and color or an unfamiliar situation you would normally avoid. He may call you to a different city or a different part of the country or to another part of the world. Regardless, you can rest assured that *wherever God calls you is the best place for you to be!*

The Will of God — The Key to Your Success

Although God expects us to use our brains, we cannot always follow what *seems* right to us. We must diligently follow exactly what God has instructed us to do, otherwise, we will experience negative consequences, which can include strife, stress, fear, dread, broken relationships, delayed blessings, unfulfilled dreams, and an endless list of other pains and problems. The bottom line is when God speaks to us, we must do *what* He says *the way* He says to do it!

The Will of God — The Key to Your Success

We need to obey *everything* God tells us to do, even if we don't understand. We must not have the attitude, "Lord, I'll obey You when I understand all the facts." If we wait till we understand everything, we will never obey God.

The Will of God — The Key to Your Success

Forbidden Practices

God is very clear that He does not approve of those who try to peer or probe into the spirit realm by their own initiative. When people try to do this on their own, demons are more than happy to accommodate them with an experience.

Testing the Supernatural

The Bible makes it clear that it is not our business to attempt to pry through spiritual doors that God has not opened.

Testing the Supernatural

God demands His people's absolute obedience when it comes to not prying, peering, or attempting to penetrate the spirit realm by their own initiative. This does not mean we shouldn't pray or seek God and be open to His initiating such an experience. Praying and seeking God opens our hearts so He can speak to us. But we see over and over again in Scripture that God Himself is the initiator of real God-sent experiences.

Testing the Supernatural

Most occultic practices require those involved in it to initiate experiences as they try to peer or probe into the spiritual realm by themselves. This is an evil, scripturally forbidden practice.

Testing the Supernatural

Forgiveness

Once your sin is placed under the blood of Jesus, *it is under the blood of Jesus forever.* God will not deal with you about it in eternity, because that sin has become nonexistent in the mind of God.

Build Your Foundation

God has put your sins behind His back forever, never to look at them again. He has chosen to release you from those sins completely — *as if you never did them.* God doesn't have a poor memory. He could remember if He chose to, but He has *chosen* to never remember them again. *He has thrown them into the depths of the sea, where He will never retrieve them to bring them up to you again!*

Sparkling Gems From the Greek, Volume 2

Millions of Christians are held captive by bitterness, resentment, and unforgiveness because they will *not* determine to do what is necessary to live free of offense As a result, they have no joy, no peace, no victory in their lives, and they're miserable because they haven't made the choice to jump through the escape hatch God has provided for them and leave all that negative garbage behind.

You Can Get Over It

Your future depends on how well you are able to connect and work with other people, so rather than allow the pain from past experiences to paralyze you, it's time for you to put the past away, decide to quit focusing on how others have failed you, and begin to search for a new group of people or friends so you can start over again. If you don't do this, the devil will have the victory over you — paralyzing and immobilizing you, effectively preventing you and your gifts from ever being fully realized. *Don't give the devil the pleasure of that victory!*

Sparkling Gems From the Greek, Volume 1

I may have a *reason* to be upset with someone, but I have *no excuse* to stay upset, especially when I remember how much mercy has been shown to me in the past for stupid mistakes and foolish statements I've unintentionally made. *How can anyone who has been shown as much mercy as I have judge others who have made similar mistakes?*

You Can Get Over It

Hasn't the Lord forgiven you many times for sins you have committed against Him? How often has He forgiven you for doing the same thing again and again? If you've *received* this kind of mercy, isn't it right that you should *give* the same mercy to others?

You Can Get Over It

We must make a decision that if we're ever blindsided by something hurtful that others do or say, we will forgive and allow the Holy Spirit to begin working in our hearts. That way we can be healed and restored as soon as possible so we can return to the front lines of battle where we're called to fight!

Life in the Combat Zone

Because Jesus was willing to offer His own blood for the full payment of our sinful debt, we are forgiven, utterly debt-free, and "PAID IN FULL" was stamped on our lives!

Paid in Full

Exercising true forgiveness means that you can no longer hold the grievance against that person — and just as God removed your sin as far as the east is from the west, you must decide that this person is *freed* in regard to a past offense. Once you forgive your offender, you can't drag up the offense again and again, because you have released him completely and now he is freed, released, and liberated from that sin. *You forfeit your right or privilege to ever pull out that offense later and use it against him. It is GONE!*

You Can Get Over It

When the devil — or any person, for that matter — tries to throw a stone of judgment against us by mentally tormenting us about past actions we've already been forgiven for, we may boldly answer: *"Christ has reviewed all the evidence and already cast His vote. He has found me innocent!"*

No Room for Compromise

Foundation

A building can be glorious, but the foundation is the most important part. It holds the greatest part of the weight and is the most expensive part of the building, yet it is the most inconspicuous part.

Build Your Foundation

Having a strong foundation of fundamental spiritual truths provides a platform on which we can build everything else in our lives. It informs our Christian experience and affects the way we perceive what is right and what is wrong. It tells us what we are to believe and what we need to reject. It gives us tools and instruments by which to make decisions and helps us come to correct conclusions.

Build Your Foundation

The Church is filled with people who ought to be spiritual adults by now, but they are still spiritual infants because they have not been exercised by the Word of God. Consequently, there is a great number of modern-day Christians who are confused about what is morally right and wrong. They remain silent on issues like homosexuality, gender confusion, adultery, fornication, and so forth, that destroy people's minds, emotions, families, and *lives*. And they do it primarily out of confusion or out of fear of being viewed as judgmental. Without the foundation of the Word of

God, they are left "blowing in the wind" on many subjects (*see* Ephesians 4:14).

Build Your Foundation

The only foundation strong enough to hold you steady in times of trouble is the Word of God.

A Life Ablaze

Fragrance

The Word of God holds within it *the fragrance* of Heaven, so if you are tired of the "stink" in your life — in your home, your relationships, or any other area — it can all be changed. As you receive, embrace, and act on the Scriptures, your obedience will literally unleash the fragrance and aroma of Heaven in every area of your life.

Last-Days Survival Guide

Nothing will change the "odors" of wrong words and attitudes and of stale, carnal living in your home more quickly than opening the Word of God and acting on it. That Word — once received, embraced, and acted upon — releases heavenly fragrances to replace the foul smell of strife, frustration, and carnality that have lingered too long in your environment.

Last-Days Survival Guide

When we leave a person and a conversation, we must make it our endeavor to leave the fragrance of Christ's love in our wake.

Sparkling Gems From the Greek, Volume 2

Fruit

If you're wondering how long it's going to take for *your* fruit-producing season to finally arrive, don't be discouraged. The bigger a tree is, the longer it takes to send its roots down deep enough into the earth to draw nourishment and give itself a firm footing against wind, weather, and pestilence.

The Point of No Return

God's desire for all of His children — including you — is to "be planted in the house of the Lord" and "flourish in the courts of our God" (Psalm 92:13). To be "planted" and "flourishing" is one of the greatest blessings of submitting to the spiritual authority under which God places you.

A Life Ablaze

When I analyze my life and my ministry, I always look to see if what I have done was something that "started with a bang and ended with a fizzle," or if it was something that has endured the tests of life and time. All fruit is good, but according to Jesus, having *"fruit that remains"* is what is most important.

Unlikely

We must be very careful to look at the fruit of people's lives when considering them for key positions in our churches, ministries, businesses, or organizations. You can make quite a discovery about people if you'll just take the time to carefully observe their lives! If you want to know what is inside a person, just observe his attitudes and how he relates to other people. His *fruit* will tell you the truth about who he really is. Good fruit belongs to good trees, and bad fruit belongs to bad trees. It's that simple. The fruit *never* lies.

Sparkling Gems From the Greek, Volume 1

Future Judgment

Judgment is a reality that every one of us will face. Believers will stand before the Judgment Seat of Christ, and unbelievers will stand before the Great White Throne Judgment.

Last-Days Survival Guide

It's crucial that we understand there is a future judgment of the unsaved. The revelation of this truth will ignite our hearts to obey God more fully regarding our responsibility to share the saving news of Jesus Christ and to ask the Holy Spirit to open the eyes of the spiritually blind so they can come to Christ and avoid this final judgment.

Build Your Foundation

Those who do not believe in God's justice should remember that His justice is so steadfast that when the world of Noah's day persisted in their egregious, sinful behavior and refused to repent, God judged that entire ancient civilization. In fact, He judged it so entirely that He wiped it out — leaving only a handful of Noah's family surviving.

How To Keep Your Head on Straight
in a World Gone Crazy

What happened to Sodom and Gomorrah was *an event so catastrophic* that when the event was finished, there was absolutely nothing left of these areas but smoke. The Bible teaches this is a prototype of a coming future judgment that will be released at the end of all ages upon a society that is "ungodly."

**How To Keep Your Head on Straight
in a World Gone Crazy**

G

Gender Dysphoria

Many thought they would never see the day when society would be so confused that it would question whether a man is a man or a woman is a woman, yet people are bombarded from every direction with the notion that changing one's sex, or gender, is perfectly normal.

How To Keep Your Head on Straight
in a World Gone Crazy

When people don't know if they are male or female, or when they actually embrace the belief that there are *dozens* of genders from which to choose — this is indicative of a deeply delusional state. *Only seducing spirits and doctrines of demons could convince intelligent people to embrace such absurdity.*

How To Keep Your Head on Straight
in a World Gone Crazy

We need to establish it in our own minds that it is absolutely right for us to hold to the belief that the attempt to surgically change a man into a woman or a woman into a man *is* a perverted and twisted business.

How To Keep Your Head on Straight
in a World Gone Crazy

Issues about gender fly in the face of God's original intent concerning creation, marriage, procreation, life, creativity, and fruitfulness according to His will, plan, and design. This deviance from what Scripture clearly teaches is a demonic attempt to overthrow these God-given institutions and the model of His crowning creation.

How To Keep Your Head on Straight
in a World Gone Crazy

Those who struggle with the serious issue of gender confusion need a mental healing — not a surgery to try to make their physical makeup match their mental confusion. We need to help them with the *right* tools, which is not a surgeon's scalpel.

How To Keep Your Head on Straight
in a World Gone Crazy

We are watching moral confusion rage among the civilized nations of the world as never before in our lifetimes, and this confusion is no clearer anywhere than in the debate over gender identity — a manifestation of confusion so severe that it stuns most thinking minds.

How To Keep Your Head on Straight
in a World Gone Crazy

Generosity

When you go out of your way to meet the needs of the Gospel, God will go out of His way to make sure *your* needs are met. In other words, when you meet the needs of God's Kingdom, He will see to it that your needs are met — *but* when God meets *your* needs, He will do it *lavishly, abundantly, excessively,* and *richly!*

Sparkling Gems From the Greek, Volume 2

As Christians, most of us understand at varying levels that it is our job to combat the forces of darkness in this world — through prayer, our walk of humility and obedience before God, and the proclamation of His Word — but we must also make the effort to combat these dark forces through more natural means. I'm talking about something as simple as opening our wallets and sharing our resources with those in need!

Signs You'll See Just Before Jesus Comes

The generosity of the Early Church ignited a dynamic cycle of blessing and power as a synergistic "snowball effect" began to take place in the Spirit. God moved, the people gave, and then God generously distributed demonstrations of His power to confirm the truth of Christ's resurrection through great signs and wonders.

A Life Ablaze

If we give Jesus our time, our finances, our possessions, our businesses, and our talents, He will multiply our gifts both for our good and for the good of the multitudes.

Dream Thieves

I realize we live in an age when insurance pays death benefits and the government often assists women who have lost spouses. Many widows today are not suffering financially as they did years ago. But there are still many widowed women who suffer great financial and social needs when their spouse dies, and God commands us to do whatever we can to be a blessing to them in their times of suffering.

Unlikely

When hearts come alive with the fire of God, one manifestation of that divine fire is the desire to open wallets and purses and allow an outflow of His generous heart to pour through us. Stingy hearts are closed hearts; open hearts are generous.

A Life Ablaze

Gentleness

The word "gentle" is a translation of a Greek word that depicts one who is *mild, kind, temperate, calm,* or *gentle.* It denotes one whose character comforts, calms, softens, or even brings healing.

Testing the Supernatural

Gifts of the Holy Spirit

The gifts of the Spirit lift Jesus right off the pages of history and bring Him into the midst of the Church today. They remove Jesus from a purely historical, fairy-tale category and bring Him right before our eyes so we come to know Him and His power experientially!

Why We Need the Gifts of the Holy Spirit

If there is no operation of the Holy Spirit's gifts in your life or in the church you attend, there is an entire supernatural dimension of Jesus Christ that is missing from your life and church. Your mind may be filled with accurate information, and that is always a good thing. But God never intended for your salvation to exist only on an intellectual level. He gave the Holy Spirit to the Church to bring the overflowing, abundant life of Jesus Christ right into the midst of His people!

Why We Need the Gifts of the Holy Spirit

The gifts of the Holy Spirit confirm the Person and work of Jesus Christ, and they give testimony to the fact that Jesus is still alive, still healing, and still working miracles today.

The Holy Spirit and You

The gifts of the Holy Spirit operated so powerfully in Corinth that sin, wrong attitudes, and carnality were supernaturally brought to the surface. Through these demonstrations of the Spirit, whatever needed to be addressed was exposed and dealt with *God's* way. The sin that might stay hidden below the surface in other churches could not remain hidden in Corinth, because the abundant flow of the revelatory gifts of the Spirit at that church ensured that it *would* become exposed. It was the gifts of the Holy Spirit that *brought these sinful issues to light* so God could *purge* the sin from their midst.

Why We Need the Gifts of the Holy Spirit

Everything the Holy Spirit did for Jesus — and everything He did for the disciples and the Early Church — He still desires to do today. Two thousand years later, His name, His character, His behavior, His work, and His ministry have not changed.

The Holy Spirit and You

We must embrace the gifts of the Spirit, knowing that God gave them to the Body of Christ because we *need* them. He never intended for the gifts of the Holy Spirit to be a cause for embarrassment. In fact, He gave them to make us smarter and sharper! God wants the gifts of His Spirit to impart supernatural wisdom and revelation to us, and He designed them to take us higher and to enable us to demonstrate His love and His power on the earth!

Why We Need the Gifts of the Holy Spirit

Today many churches have backed away from the operation of the gifts of the Spirit. The unspoken implication is that it's not popular or culturally acceptable to be known as people who speak in tongues or to associate with people who operate in those spiritual gifts. They say they're concerned that the gifts of the Spirit will scare people away. But I can tell you the gifts of the Holy Spirit did *not* scare me — and if you've had an encounter with the power of the Holy Spirit, they probably didn't scare *you* when you were first exposed to them.

Unlikely

Those educated in Church history would never argue about whether or not these supernatural manifestations have been in operation throughout more than 2,000 years of the Church's existence. There are abundant historical records to affirm that these gifts have *never* ceased. The attempt to rationalize away the gifts of the Holy Spirit by saying they ceased with the death of the apostles is intellectually dishonest and historically inaccurate.

Why We Need the Gifts of the Holy Spirit

The magnificent gifts of the Holy Spirit are grace-given, so there is no room for boasting or self-glory in our possession of them. They are not natural talents developed by our own ability, but they are supernatural graces that are divinely imparted by the Spirit of God.

Why We Need the Gifts of the Holy Spirit

Giving

God finds it pleasurable when a believer gives sacrificially. When it happens, He throws open the door to embrace the *giver* and the *gift*!

Apostles and Prophets

It is vital for us to determine that, first and foremost, we will dedicate our resources to God and stay ready to give into His work as He leads — for each of us is responsible to take part in advancing the preaching of the Gospel around the world, funding missionaries and organizations that are focused on taking the Good News to their neighbors and to the ends of the earth!

Last-Days Survival Guide

Be unmoved in your commitment to support the work of God, regardless of what is happening in the economy.

Every time you write a check for the furtherance of God's Kingdom, *God is watching.* He sees each time you cut back on something else but refuse to skimp on your tithes and offerings. *God sees it all, and He takes note of your unwavering commitment to support His work.* And as a result, God will provide for you in ways that your natural resources could never provide. *God will multiply your seed back to you in ways you could never expect or anticipate.*

Sparkling Gems From the Greek, Volume 2

When our giving is done gladly and truly costs us something, God's heart is deeply touched and He responds magnificently. Scripture bears out that the greater the sacrifice, the greater the response from God.

A Life Ablaze

There is no greater *benefactor* or *philanthropist* than a person who is filled with the Spirit and who is producing the fruit of the Spirit in his or her life!

Sparkling Gems From the Greek, Volume 1

Goodness

God is not the God of a clinched fist, but the God of an open hand!

How To Receive Answers From Heaven

The word "goodness" in Greek was used to portray *a person who is generous, big-hearted, liberal, and charitable with his finances* — in other words, *a giver.* Thus, the fruit of the Spirit called "goodness" is that supernatural urge in a person to reach beyond himself to meet the natural needs of those around him. When a believer is walking in the Spirit, his eyes are supernaturally opened to see the needs of humanity and his heart is moved to meet those needs.

Sparkling Gems From the Greek, Volume 1

Does the memory of the power of God working in your life still leave you with a sense of awe, or has time dimmed your fervor and affection for God and dulled your appreciation for His goodness?

Paid in Full

Gospel

We must never forget that the *Gospel* is the *power of God* that leads to salvation, and there is never a reason for us to be ashamed of the Gospel or to apologize for the requirements God has set forth for all who would come to Him.

Sparkling Gems From the Greek, Volume 2

There's power in the proclamation of the Gospel to snatch a person right out of a lifetime of bondage and plant his feet firmly on the right path. On that path is everything that person could ever need: light for his feet, freedom for his mind, strength and resolve for his will, and vision for a bright future. *That's* what God's Word can do! It is therefore no wonder that Satan tries to stop the preaching, teaching, and ministry of the Word! Mental, emotional, and spiritual strongholds are *demolished* when the Word of God is proclaimed!

Sparkling Gems From the Greek, Volume 2

The Gospel not only comes *from* Christ — *it is firmly in His possession.* Jesus is the *Originator,* the *Giver,* and the ultimate *Supervisor* of the faith; and it is for this reason that we must always cherish and correctly teach the faith.

No Room for Compromise

The Good News of Jesus Christ *was* and *is* the best news anyone has ever heard!

Christmas — The Rest of the Story

We are the recipients of the truth of the Gospel and its amazing benefits, but Christ is the One who paid for it with His blood to make it available. *What One bleeds for, another lives for* — and Christ shed His own blood for the truth of which we freely partake.

Sparkling Gems From the Greek, Volume 2

Gossip

Gossip is evil and is almost never based in truth. When one person hears a rumor, he passes it along to another person, who then repeats it to someone else — and so it goes from one person to the next, growing more and more ridiculous with each telling. Finally, an entire story is being told that has no truth in it whatsoever.

Paid in Full

Evil speaking with the intent to cause harm, raise suspicion, or slander is defined by Jesus as being in league with darkness and is a practice that He hates.

A Light in Darkness

Talking badly about others behind their backs is a type of nasty conversation that should not be tolerated in the Church. As far as God is concerned, this type of communication *reeks*, and those who consume this type of talk find it to be so putrid that it sickens them, just as spoiled meat would do. Just as a rotten apple must be removed from a bucket of apples or it will eventually spread and ruin the entire batch of good apples, this is how ruinous corrupt communication can be to those who listen to it, as far as God is concerned. Everything about corrupt communication has a *putrefying effect* on others.

Sparkling Gems From the Greek, Volume 2

Instead of poking around in matters that have nothing to do with us, we are to keep our mouths shut, keep our eyes from wandering, and focus on our own personal affairs. We have no right to delve into the private matters of other people for whom we have no responsibility. *Period.*

Sparkling Gems From the Greek, Volume 2

Grace

Grace is God's divine empowerment to do what we could never do on our own. It is His ability to live beyond our ability and carry out His will for our lives.

The Will of God — The Key to Your Success

Regardless of where you live and what you are facing — regardless of how bad the situation looks to your natural eyes — the grace of God is flowing *downstream*. He is lavishly pouring it forth in *abundant* measure! In fact, it is impossible to imagine, measure, or even dream of the amount of divine grace God is sending in our direction. No banks can hold the flood of grace He is sending our way! The *flood* of grace will always far surpass the flood of sin and darkness!

Sparkling Gems From the Greek, Volume 1

Grace first produces *inward change*, but it also always comes with *outward evidence*. It is never silent; it is never invisible — it always manifests in a visible way!

Why We Need the Gifts of the Holy Spirit

When you've given your best and you don't feel like you have another ounce of energy left to give, or when it looks like your resources are drained and you're unable to take one more step, that is *exactly* the moment when Jesus Christ becomes your personal Benefactor. He will step forward to donate a *massive, overwhelming, generous* contribution of the Holy Spirit's grace and power for your cause!

The Holy Spirit and You

Sin may have once existed in abundance in your life, but the grace of God has far exceeded anything that the devil or any past sin ever attempted to bring to pass in your life. The grace of God working *in you* is higher, preeminent, unsurpassed, and unrivaled by any past rule of sin in your life. There you are — a former temple of sin — and now you have become a place where God with all His miracle-working power is at work. It should leave you *speechless* to consider what God has done and is doing in you!

Unlikely

Gratitude

We live in an end-time season when people are so *self-*focused, *self-*consumed, and covetous that they are rarely grateful for anything — and if they *are* grateful, that attitude is often short-lived and soon forgotten.

Last-Days Survival Guide

Let's be honest! Perhaps things could be better than they are in your life right now. However, you probably will admit that they are not as bad as they could be! The truth is, you have *a lot* to be grateful for! Gratitude is a choice. You and I must turn our eyes *toward* the good in our lives and *away* from the foul things that try to hold our focus — and *choose* to be grateful. It's not that we're hiding our heads in the sand concerning those bad things — we're simply focusing on what is good and choosing to display an attitude of thankfulness!

Sparkling Gems From the Greek, Volume 2

The word *thankful* is concerned with a person's attitude toward his good fortune rather than his feelings toward anyone responsible for it, and it suggests that someone is relieved or pleased about a situation or a turn of events. But someone who is *grateful* realizes that someone else has helped him or treated him kindly, and he has warm feelings toward that person. Thus, the word *grateful* suggests more of an impulse to thank someone than *thankful* does.

Last-Days Survival Guide

Great Commission

Jesus doesn't intend for us to "reach just a few people" in every country or to send missionaries to "just a few places" in every country. The intention of Jesus was that we, His Church, would rise up so strong in the Spirit and so militant in our faith that we could literally reach the entire world and give *every member* of *every nation* the opportunity to be a disciple of the Lord Jesus Christ.

Life in the Combat Zone

Any study of Church history shows God's power goes hand in hand with the Spirit-led efforts of any person, church, or organization committed to proclaiming the Gospel to the lost. But when God's people withdraw from Christ's command to reach the lost, His divine power begins to slowly wane in the Church.

Unlikely

In the Early Church, believers had a militaristic mentality and were absolutely committed to the faith. They were going to turn the world upside down and take it for Jesus Christ. And to see this vision realized, they gave their lives for their cause. Some early Christians were thrown in jail, and some were killed, yet they continued to defy Satan and outlast numerous Roman emperors. *They did, in fact, change the world forever!*

Life in the Combat Zone

Souls are *precious* to God — so precious, that He sent His only Son to the earth to redeem people with His blood.

Since people are that precious to God, they must be precious to us as well. Let's use the God-given opportunities we have to warn people that a life lived apart from Jesus will result in *serious* eternal consequences. We must do all we can to bring them into the safe harbor we have found in Jesus Christ!

Sparkling Gems From the Greek, Volume 2

Like a diligent farmer who works his field — plowing through hardened soil and sweltering heat during the hottest time of the year — we cannot neglect our responsibility to sow. Even if the task is difficult, we must never forget that our place is to be in the field.

Life in the Combat Zone

Great High Priest

Christ's feet carry the golden hue of frankincense because He lives in the atmosphere of prayer, where He intercedes as the Great High Priest for every person He has ever washed in His blood.

Sparkling Gems From the Greek, Volume 2

As the Great High Priest, Jesus *is, has been,* and *always will be* interceding for the Church.

A Light in Darkness

When God the Father sent His Son into the world, Jesus left His heavenly home and took upon Himself human flesh. And because of this great exchange, He has stood in our place, He has felt what we feel, He is touched with the feelings of our infirmities, and He intercedes for us with great compassion as our Great High Priest.

Sparkling Gems From the Greek, Volume 2

When Jesus hung on the Cross, He was both Lamb and High Priest. In that holy moment, Jesus — our Great High Priest — offered His own blood for the permanent removal of sin. After that, God never again required the blood of lambs for forgiveness.

Paid in Full

Greek

Paul knew he was called as an apostle to the Gentiles and, therefore, his primary audience was Greek-speaking believers who were pagans before they came to Christ. So in his teachings, he used words and examples that native Greek-speakers could easily relate to and understand.

Apostles and Prophets

Consider how English is read and spoken around the world today, and it will help you understand the role that the Greek language played in the First Century. It was spoken almost everywhere in the Roman Empire, irrespective of the native dialects that might be used in the privacy of one's home. Even highly educated Jewish scholars of Alexandria, men who were very advanced in Hebrew studies, spoke Greek in their daily lives.

No Room for Compromise

When it was time for Paul to pen his timeless epistles, the Holy Spirit reached deep into the apostle's vast repertoire of language, literature, and history and used his knowledge to convey incredible spiritual truths. Because there was no precedent for Christian vocabulary at the time, it had to be established, and since Greek was the foremost language of the First Century, the extensive Greek vocabulary was the perfect source from which to draw.

Apostles and Prophets

The fact is that *if* the New Testament had been written in Hebrew, its message would have never penetrated the worldwide audience Jesus came to redeem. The use of Hebrew would have limited the availability of the message, whereas Greek opened doors for the message of Christ to spread to the far reaches of the Roman Empire. Furthermore, if the imagery used in the New Testament was solely borrowed from the Old Testament, pagans would have missed the significance of most of the illustrations since they were unfamiliar with Hebrew culture. Therefore, God in His wisdom chose to use the imagery, symbolism, and figures of speech that the pagan world would understand. It's true that the New Testament does use images and concepts that were drawn directly from the Old Testament, but the overwhelming majority of words and images in the New Testament are borrowed from the Greek world.

No Room for Compromise

Grieving the Holy Spirit

When we act like the world, talk like the world, behave like the world, and respond the same way the world does, we cause the Spirit of God to feel shock, hurt, and grief. When we deliberately do what is wrong, we drag Him right into the mire of sin with us, because He lives in us and goes wherever we go!

Sparkling Gems From the Greek, Volume 1

Sin not only affects us, but it also grieves the Holy Spirit in us! Having material possessions, social status, and so forth, in your hand is one thing — but having these things in your *heart* is another. When the things of the world get in your heart and you become preoccupied with them, you have crossed a serious line!

The Holy Spirit and You

You would never think of throwing mud and garbage all over a beautiful cathedral. Your conscience probably couldn't bear the guilt of knowing you had personally desecrated a finely decorated church building. Yet *you* are of far more worth than a cathedral, and the Holy Spirit doesn't live in buildings — He lives in *you*. In spite of this, we throw mud and garbage into our lives all the time, not thinking of how it must grieve the Spirit of holiness who lives inside us.

The Holy Spirit and You

When a Christian uses corrupt language — which could include anything that doesn't minister life to someone else — or any language that is rotten and worthless, it grieves the Holy Spirit and brings dishonor to the name of Jesus. Thus, we must avoid being gossipy or using language that is not worthy of Jesus' name or the Holy Spirit's indwelling presence in our lives!

Sparkling Gems From the Greek, Volume 2

The Holy Spirit is here for *us*. That is why He was sent — so when we ignore Him, turn a deaf ear to Him, or consistently disobey what He nudges us to do, it grieves Him.

The Holy Spirit and You

Growth

The Gospel is so powerful that when it is properly declared, one can expect all types of growth to be forthcoming.

Apostles and Prophets

We can till the ground, plant the seeds, pull the weeds, and lavishly water what has been planted, but *only* God can provide the blessing, sunshine, and environment to make it all grow.

Sparkling Gems From the Greek, Volume 2

It takes every one of us doing his or her different job — with God's blessing on it — for doors to open and harvests to be reaped. Divine connections are essential for completing a divine assignment, and respect for every person for the role he or she plays — including God and His role — is important. We must realize that even if we all did our respective parts to make supernatural things come to pass, nothing of value would ever grow if God didn't provide His continuous blessing. So *all* the glory goes to God for what is produced in our lives.

Sparkling Gems From the Greek, Volume 2

There are seasons in which a pause in growth for a time is needed. No farmer lives in continuous harvest. When one season of harvest concludes, it is time for rest and then sowing seed again, watering it for the next period of growth, and harvesting once again.

Apostles and Prophets

God is not interested in sacrificing quality for quantity — He desires *both* for the Church.

Apostles and Prophets

In Colossians 1:6, Paul wrote that the correct preaching of the Gospel naturally produces fruit. As a Christian leader, I find this truth to be so vital, because a lack of growth is a "neon sign" that something has gone awry. Certainly there can be different stages of growth, but if there is a continual lack of growth, it should be taken as a divine indicator that it is time to seek wisdom from above about what needs to change.

Apostles and Prophets

Guilt

Guilt is a prison that will keep you perpetually bound and *unchanged*.

Repentance

A person who confesses his sin with no intention of changing is doing nothing more than admitting his guilt. He is *not* exhibiting genuine repentance, for true repentance is always accompanied by the fruit of corresponding actions.

Sparkling Gems From the Greek, Volume 2

Remorse expresses the *guilt* a person feels because he knows that he *has done wrong*, that he *will continue to do wrong*, and that he *has no plans to change* his course of action. He feels shameful about what he is doing but continues to do it anyway, which results in a state of ongoing guilt. This guilt produces *no change* in a person's life or behavior, but genuine repentance would fix this feeling of guilt and remove it completely.

Repentance

Happiness

Seeking pleasure and happiness is not God's greatest will for you. His greatest will for your life is that you truly love Him and are *obedient*. If you are whole-heartedly doing God's will, you will find joy that is longer lasting than fleeting happiness.

Last-Days Survival Guide

We must not let the errant doctrine that we are entitled to be "happy" drive our lives. Pleasing God and obeying His Word must be our driving motion and the cry of our heart!

Last-Days Survival Guide

Happiness is based on circumstantial pleasure, merriment, hilarity, exuberance, excitement, or something that causes one to feel hopeful or to be in high spirits. These fleeting emotions of happiness, although very pleasurable in the moment, usually go just as quickly as they came. All it takes is one piece of bad news, a sour look from a fellow employee, a harsh word from a spouse, or an electric bill that is larger than what was anticipated — and that emotion of happiness can disappear right before a person's eyes!

Sparkling Gems From the Greek, Volume 1

The *only* way we can be truly happy is by doing what God has asked us to do. Every other form of happiness is temporary and an unreliable measuring stick in determining how pleasing we are to God or how well we are walking in obedience to Him.

Last-Days Survival Guide

Hard Times

Hard times are inescapable, but God's power unfailingly sustains those who are determined to be faithful to Him. Even if the fires of adversity rage until it seems they will never cease, trials are *always* temporary. Satan uses fires to test, but God allows those same fires to purify. Church history has proven that the persecuted Church always emerges purer than gold and mightier in Spirit, not weaker. *Always.*

A Light in Darkness

It is an inescapable fact — verified in Scripture and throughout historical records — that hardships, and often persecutions, come to believers. However, if those believers will stand true to the testimony of the Lord, *there is a special working of God's power available to them.*

Life in the Combat Zone

At times there is nothing you can do to change a situation, and all you can do is walk through it. In those moments, you must remind yourself that your Heavenly Father is greater than everything you are facing and that He has a plan for you and intends to give you a hope and a future.

Paid in Full

A trick of the devil is to get you so self-focused that you are swallowed up in your own needs and fail to see the needs of those around you. But God wants you to shift your focus to others so you can enter the territory that the devil has gained in people's lives, set them free, and help them take back what he has stolen!

Last-Days Survival Guide

Hard Work

If a farmer wants to reap the benefits of a crop, he has to plow and plant, regardless of the difficulties he must face to get the job done. The difficulty of the task doesn't change the necessity of the task.

Life in the Combat Zone

Sowing seed in a field is typically accomplished by one individual. Even though it is very time-consuming for one person to do all the work of sowing the seed, it is still the farmer's responsibility to sow and no one else's. Later when harvest time comes, many workers can come into the field to help reap the harvest. However, the planting of seed — because it is such a crucial job — is the task of the farmer himself.

Life in the Combat Zone

If you and I take our life assignment lightly — approaching it with a casual, easygoing, take-it-easy attitude — we'll never go far in the fulfillment of our calling or dream. It takes diligence and hard work to achieve anything worthwhile, and complaining about how hard it is won't make the process any easier.

Sparkling Gems From the Greek, Volume 2

Harvest

Harvests don't happen accidentally! You have to break up the hard, fallow ground you're standing on; turn and prepare the soil; and plant some seeds. Once the soil is prepared and the seeds are planted, you must water and watch over your seeds in order for them to grow and be healthy. You must regularly search for the smallest hint of insects, pests, and weeds, and get down on your hands and knees to pull out the weeds one by one. After many days of careful watching and hard work, your precious seeds will finally begin to grow and pierce the topsoil, reaching upward to the sun. When the plants reach maturity and it's time for harvest, you have to go into the field to reap your crops while they're still ripe and ready. If you let the crops sit too long, bugs will eat them, or they'll mildew and rot! Absolutely nothing about harvests is accidental!

The Point of No Return

Like it or not, every farmer occasionally experiences a crop failure, but a farmer doesn't stop farming just because of one bad year! He has too much invested in his farm to give up that easily. He has put years of work into that farm, invested lots of money into his machinery, and has given his life to his profession — and he knows that just because one crop failed, it doesn't mean the next one will! Likewise, you have too much invested in your church, ministry, business, or dream to give up now. You may have put years of work into it and planted all your finances in it — but you have invested in too much "spiritual machinery" to stop planting now. Just because one crop failed *doesn't* mean you're finished, so when God speaks to your heart and you know it's time to start planting again, go for it!

Life in the Combat Zone

Spiritual harvests often come more quickly than natural harvests. It may take four months for wheat to be ready to be reaped. However, don't think that it will always take a long time before you see people respond to the Word you sow into their hearts. The souls of men are often ready to be reaped for the Kingdom of God very quickly after the initial sowing.

Sparkling Gems From the Greek, Volume 1

Perhaps you live in a city where the "temperature" isn't right yet for a large harvest. Perhaps the spiritual climate is still being prepared for a move of God's Spirit. Or it may simply be that your colleagues reached harvest time a little earlier than you did. However, none of these scenarios are proof that you have missed out on anything. All they tell you is that your climate is not ready just yet to yield a harvest. *Nevertheless, harvest time will come.*

Life in the Combat Zone

Your spiritual life is so very important, and what you pour into yourself or allow to be poured into loved ones under your charge will eventually produce a harvest. So ask yourself: *If I keep myself and my family in the spiritual environment we are in at the present time, what kind of harvest will it produce in us in the future?*

Last-Days Survival Guide

Healing

If sickness or disease attempts to latch onto you, remember the stripes Jesus bore to obtain healing and wholeness for you. If pain grips your body or if a report of disease threatens to rob your peace of mind, crowd you with fear, or shorten your life, remember that Jesus was wounded for *your* transgressions, bruised for *your* iniquities, the chastisement needed to obtain *your* peace of mind was laid on Him, and by His stripes *you* are healed!

Paid in Full

All healings do *not* occur instantly; some of them take place over a period of time. But Jesus promised that if we will lay our hands on the sick, God's power will be released into the body of the afflicted. If we are releasing our faith and believing for healing power to flow from us to the recipient, healing virtue will be deposited into the sick person's body. Just as medicine slowly works to reverse a medical condition, the power of God that was deposited with the laying on of our hands will begin to attack the work of the devil and progressively bring that sick person back into a state of health and well-being.

Sparkling Gems From the Greek, Volume 1

It is God's will to heal the sick through various means — including, but not limited to, the laying on of hands, the prayer of faith, anointing with oil, and the operation of the gifts of the Holy Spirit — and the Bible teaches that healing is provided in the redemptive work of Christ and is available to every believer everywhere.

How To Keep Your Head on Straight
in a World Gone Crazy

People often ask, "How do I know if God wants to heal the sick today?" Look to Jesus for your answer, because He is the perfect imprint of the Father's nature and will. When Jesus healed someone, it was a demonstration of the Father's will to heal. He never would have acted on His own or out of character with the will of the Father.

The Holy Spirit and You

This is our moment to rise up with authority to pray for the sick with confidence, backed up by healing promises from the Bible, for Jesus clearly prophesied that at the end of the age, the world would be battered by demonic powers that long to ravage, ruin, and *devastate* people's health and lives, but because we have the promises of the Word of God and the power of the Spirit, we are equipped to answer His call to bring healing to the sick at the end of this age.

Signs You'll See Just Before Jesus Comes

In Luke 4:18, Jesus declared that He came to "heal" the brokenhearted. The word "heal" in that verse means to *set free* or *to loosen* from the detrimental effects of a shattered life. The Greek speaks of a *release* from the destructive effects of brokenness. In other words, although there is every reason to experience and feel brokenness, the anointing on Jesus is more than enough to release you from the adverse effects of a broken past. If you have been through the experience of failed relationships, shattered friendships, and broken families, the anointing of Jesus is sufficient to release you from the pain of that experience.

Sparkling Gems From the Greek, Volume 2

Heart

We *all* have glitches and flaws in our character. Not one of us is perfect. Fortunately, small flaws are correctable as long we have receptive and teachable hearts. But if a person refuses to see his need for change and is closed-hearted to suggestions made by those who love him, this is evidence of *the most serious* character flaw — an unteachable heart. From the outside, this person may look like he's just what we're looking for, but we must not forget to consider the *deeper issues* of the heart.

Sparkling Gems From the Greek, Volume 1

The natural heart pumps blood into every part of the body and thereby influences a person's ability to live and function. Similarly, whatever is produced in the human spirit determines the ultimate outcome of a person. If a person's spirit is filled with darkness, it will pump darkness into every part of that person's life. On the other hand, if a person's spirit is filled with the life of God, it will pump life into every part of that person's being. *Whatever is in the spirit is exactly what will be reproduced in a person's life and conduct.*

Sparkling Gems From the Greek, Volume 1

Heaven

God's promise to you is that *anything* you do for Him is *never* a waste! So when your flesh or the devil whispers to you and tempts you to think that no one notices or appreciates your efforts, that your job is insignificant, or that you are wasting your time — *that* is the moment *you* need to remind yourself and the devil that nothing done for the Lord is ever a waste. Every effort, every deed — *everything* you have ever done in obedience to His instructions — will be accredited to your heavenly record!

Sparkling Gems From the Greek, Volume 2

You can be the deciding factor between Heaven and hell for some people. By your witness of the truth and your stance of faith, you can make the difference for eternity for those who are watching you. If for no other reason, we must remain faithful for the sake of the Gospel and for those who need to hear the truth and be rescued from an eternity without God!

Life in the Combat Zone

Heaven will be full of surprises — who is there and who is not there. The thought is not pleasant, but it's important for us to never forget that Heaven and hell are real places. What we *do* or *do not do* with Christ in this life determines everything in eternity.

Unlikely

If you have a friend who doesn't know Jesus, don't you think it's time for you to introduce him to Jesus Christ? One day in the future, that friend will bow before Him anyway, but the question is, from which place will he bow before Jesus — from Heaven, from earth, or from hell?

Paid in Full

When a person comes to Christ, he is snatched from a lost eternity and is immediately infused with a new God-given nature that makes him a member of God's eternal family. In a split second, *eternal life* is imparted into that person that assures him a destiny in Heaven instead of an eternity in an unspeakably terrible place called hell.

A Life Ablaze

One day in the future, Heaven, earth, and hell will resound with the voices of all who have ever lived as they thunderously shout out and acknowledge: *"JESUS IS LORD!"*

Christmas — The Rest of the Story

Hedge of Protection

It is time for us to use our heads, apply both spiritual and common sense to our lives, and responsibly build walls of protection around ourselves, our families, and our friends, for such spiritual walls can shield us and those we love from evil forces that are already prevalent in the world around us.

Last-Days Survival Guide

Faithful believers who submit to the authority of the Scriptures and are willing to do whatever is necessary to build a hedge of protection around their homes do *not* have to fall victim to this destructive end-time attack on families.

Last-Days Survival Guide

It's easier to keep the enemy out than it is to try to get him out once access has been granted through an open door. Although the door to deception has swung wide open in Western society, the Church must "rise and shine" and do its part to remove the thief from the house!

How To Keep Your Head on Straight
in a World Gone Crazy

Hell

We must never forget that hell is real, and people really do go there.

Build Your Foundation

One very real problem is that many Christians today don't really believe in hell. Oh, sure, if you ask most Christians if they believe in hell, they will invariably answer, "Yes, of course, I believe in hell. The Bible teaches it." But if you examine their actions, it will lead you to the conclusion that they don't *truly* believe that their unsaved family members, friends, and acquaintances who haven't been born again are going to hell. If they did, wouldn't it affect them so deeply that they would at least do everything within their power to try to stop them from going there?

A Life Ablaze

God knows what hell is, and He doesn't want *anyone* to go there!

Signs You'll See Just Before Jesus Comes

The mere thought of a friend, relative, co-worker, or acquaintance going to hell should motivate us to do something to prevent that person from his or her eternal fate. That's why it's so imperative that the doctrine of hell be taught and preached from the pulpit. A revelation of hell puts a fire in believers' hearts to pray for the salvation of the unsaved and to ask God for opportunities to share the Gospel with them. Jesus was so convinced of the need to convey hell's reality to people that He spoke about it in the four gospels *three times more* than He spoke about Heaven!

Unlikely

If a person dies without faith in Christ, the Bible is *absolutely* clear — his or her future is eventually a lake of fire — and there is no negotiating about this truth.

Build Your Foundation

One who physically dies in his sins without accepting Christ is eternally lost in the lake of fire and therefore has no further opportunity of hearing the Gospel or of repenting. The lake of fire is literal, and the terms "eternal" and "everlasting" used in describing the duration of the punishment of the damned in the lake of fire, carry the same thought and meaning of endless existence as used in denoting the duration of joy and ecstasy of saints in the presence of God.

How To Keep Your Head on Straight
in a World Gone Crazy

I understand that many people are uncomfortable discussing or even thinking about the topic of hell, but hell is a reality whether we like it or not. People we know will go there if they don't receive the message of Christ that can save them from it.

A Life Ablaze

Today I hear many church leaders talk about the need to reach the "unchurched." That phrase is accurate if they are trying only to reach Christians who are not in a local church. But unsaved people are not unchurched — they are "unsaved." They are in eternal jeopardy.

A Life Ablaze

A day is coming when those in Heaven, earth, and hell will bow their knees in honor of, respect for, humility toward, and in the worship of Jesus Christ. It is not a question of *if* people will bow their knees to Jesus; it is only a question of *when, how* and *where* they will do it. Will they freely do it while still living on this earth? Or will they do it from the vantage point of hell? *Everyone* will bow his or her knee — including those who have already died and gone to Heaven, those who are still alive when Jesus comes, and even those who have died and are eternally separated from God — in acknowledgment of Jesus Christ's lordship!

Christmas — The Rest of the Story

Helmet of Salvation

If your salvation — like a helmet — is not worn tightly around your mind, the enemy will come to chop the multiple benefits and blessings of your salvation right out of your belief system. He will whack away at your spiritual foundation, trying to tell you that healing, deliverance, preservation of mind, and soundness are not really a part of Jesus' redemptive work on the Cross. In fact, by the time he is finished attacking your mind, the only thing he will leave you with is Heaven!

Dressed To Kill

Our intellectual understanding and comprehension of salvation and all that it encompasses must be ingrained in our minds. When our minds are convinced of these realities — when our minds are trained and taught to think correctly in terms of our salvation — that knowledge becomes a protective helmet in our lives!

Dressed To Kill

Once the knowledge of our salvation and all that it is becomes a part of us, it won't matter how hard the devil tries to hit and whack away at us. We will know — beyond a shadow of a doubt — what Jesus' death and resurrection purchased for us. At that point, the enemy will no longer be able to attack our minds as he did in the past, because he won't be able to get past our impenetrable helmet of salvation.

Dressed To Kill

Help

When you are convinced of what God has promised you, you will have a certainty when you pray that God hears you and will do as you have asked. You don't need to feel sheepish or embarrassed — you can come *boldly* to seek help in your time of need.

Sparkling Gems From the Greek, Volume 2

If the Holy Spirit's divine assistance in our lives is going to be effective, He requires our ears, our hearts, our trust, and our obedience. Anything short of this will produce inferior results far short of the supernatural life we really desire. He is there to help us, but we must *let* Him help us.

The Holy Spirit and You

Don't be ashamed to ask God for help. Simply turn to Him with your whole heart and declare, "I am Yours — save me!" Then allow God's power to strengthen you in the midst of the situation you are facing right now.

Paid in Full

God is *always* present to help those who call and wait upon Him in time of need!

Last-Days Survival Guide

Empowered by the ever-present help of the Holy Spirit, God's Word contains all that is needed to *thoroughly* furnish us. With that supernatural equipment, we can launch out into the deep of God's call on our lives and successfully complete our journey in Him.

Last-Days Survival Guide

Heresy

A heretical teaching is any belief or doctrine that is divergent from the core beliefs presented in the Scriptures. By contrast, beliefs that are aligned with Scripture — sometimes called *orthodox* doctrines — are referred to as "sound doctrine" in the New Testament because they agree with the time-tested truths presented in Scripture.

How To Keep Your Head on Straight in a World Gone Crazy

The word "heresy" in Greek carries the idea of *a person or group of people who are sectarian*, and the word "sectarian" refers to *a group of people who adhere to the same doctrine or who ardently follow the same leader*. The adherents of such a sect were usually limited in their scope and closed to outsiders, staying primarily to themselves and often operating in secret. In New Testament times, these groups were considered to be *unauthorized* because they were not submitted to the authority of the church leadership, and because this type of group was viewed to be so disruptive to the Early Church — and because it didn't fall under the spiritual covering of church leadership — it was considered *heretical*, which in this sense meant *divisive*.

Sparkling Gems From the Greek, Volume 1

Hesitation

Think of how many people you know who were given a remarkable opportunity to do something tremendous but failed to take advantage of the moment. Because of laziness, hesitation, fear, or a "take it easy" mentality, the opportunity given to those people slipped away and was lost. *Don't let this describe you!* If God has given you a moment when you can work to achieve something tremendous — or if an exceptional prospect stands before you that will enable you to make a difference in someone else's life — you must give yourself *enthusiastically* and *passionately* to the task that lies before you.

Sparkling Gems From the Greek, Volume 2

Many people have had great ideas, but because they pondered the idea for too long without acting on it, someone else finally came up with the same idea — and then went out and did something about it! The person who originally came up with the idea eventually sees someone else prospering with the idea he had first. How do you think that makes him feel? He knows it could have been him experiencing that prosperity and success, *but now it's too late.* His hesitation to act or his laziness prevented him from getting up and putting that idea into action; as a result, the opportunity passed on to someone who was willing to *do* something with the idea.

Sparkling Gems From the Greek, Volume 1

Holiness

The walk of daily, practical holiness does not happen automatically just because God has chosen you, cleansed you by Jesus' blood, placed His Spirit inside you, and separated you from the rest of the world. To walk in the reality of holiness in your everyday life is going to take a moment-by-moment yielding to God and a dedicated effort to flee all forms of behaviors that are contrary to what He desires for your life.

A Life Ablaze

We must walk in love toward those around us, but we must also walk in holiness. To walk in power, we must walk by a higher standard — and that standard is given to us in the Word of God.

How To Keep Your Head on Straight
in a World Gone Crazy

God justified us and made us to be righteous by faith — and in that act, we moved over into a new category of human beings! We might look like regular people, but in actual fact, there is *nothing* regular about us.

A Life Ablaze

When the blood of Jesus cleansed us and the Holy Spirit moved into our hearts, that divine presence *set us apart* and made us so *different* that God now sees us in a special, holy light that is different from unsaved people.

A Life Ablaze

God called His people *out of* darkness *into* His marvelous light. He knows that skirting around the edges of darkness is *not* the way for His children to flourish in His light.

No Room for Compromise

God has lavished His mercy and grace upon us in Christ Jesus. He willingly came to earth to lay down His life to make us righteous and to move us out of our former state into a new category that He calls *holy*. When God looks at us, He does not see who we *were* — He sees who we *are* in Christ.

A Life Ablaze

The moment the blood of Jesus washed you and the Holy Spirit entered your spirit, God *separated* you, *consecrated* you, and *set you apart* for Himself. My friend, you are the home of the Holy Spirit — and as such, you are *holy*.

A Life Ablaze

Just because you live in the last days does *not* mean that you should be affected by a moral downslide. By making God's Word your standard and upholding it in your life, you can stay free from the spiritual corrosion that is eating away at the world today.

Last-Days Survival Guide

Holy Spirit

The Holy Spirit indeed *is* the fire that keeps the Church — and its individual members — strengthened and ablaze with the glory and power of God.

A Life Ablaze

Jesus knew the Holy Spirit inside and out. In His earthly ministry, He was dependent upon the Holy Spirit, and He knew that He could do nothing of Himself — independent of the Spirit's power. Since that was true of Jesus, how much more is it true of all of us today?

Apostles and Prophets

As the Inspirer and Author of Old and New Testament Scripture, the Holy Spirit is the ultimate Teacher. No one knows the Bible better, and no one can teach it better than the One who inspired it and imparted it to the hearts and minds of men so that it could be recorded or written down. The Holy Spirit — our great Teacher!

The Holy Spirit and You

The Holy Spirit is a Gentleman and does not *force* you to obey Him. He prompts you, tugs on your heart, and pulls on your spirit to get your attention. Sometimes His tugs can be so gentle that you can miss them if you're not sensitive to them. But if you'll develop your sensitivity to the Holy Spirit, He will gently lead you exactly where He wants you to go with your life. But don't demand that the Holy Spirit tell you the whole story first before you obey Him! *Trust Him!*

Unlikely

The Holy Spirit is *not* a passive Partner. He aggressively and actively pursues you. He fiercely wants more of you. When you give part of yourself to something or someone else's control, the Holy Spirit wants to seize that part of your life and bring it back under His divine control. He even has malice toward your preoccupation with things in this natural realm. Make your relationship with the Holy Spirit your top priority. Don't give Him a reason to feel betrayed by or envious of other things in your life that have taken His place.

Sparkling Gems From the Greek, Volume 1

You and I can be assured that the Holy Spirit will *never* fail at His job as it pertains to our lives. Whatever form of help we need at any given moment, the Spirit of God is ever within us and alongside us to be the help we need, right at the time we need it!

The Holy Spirit and You

Wherever people make room for God's Spirit, He *always* moves.

How To Keep Your Head on Straight in a World Gone Crazy

Early believers knew the Holy Spirit so well that even if they didn't receive a specific word from Him, they were able to make necessary decisions because they personally knew what He liked, and they knew what He didn't like. They had more than an intellectual knowledge of Him, they shared a real communion with the Holy Spirit.

The Holy Spirit and You

When the Holy Spirit is given liberty to move as He wishes, He comes with all kinds of signs, wonders, and powerful spiritual gifts. When these spiritual manifestations are loosed among God's people, it literally ignites a *fire* that exposes sin, drives out darkness, brings answers to seeking hearts, and liberates people from all types of captivity.

A Life Ablaze

Honesty

Honesty is a big issue in the Body of Christ. Many believers are dishonest about what they really think and feel. Inside they seethe with anger toward someone about a perceived offense. Yet on the outside, they smile and pretend as if everything is all right. This dishonesty divides believers and keeps God's power from freely flowing between members of the Body of Christ.

Sparkling Gems From the Greek, Volume 1

When you are truthful, people will know you are being straight with them. Even if they don't like everything you say, they will know they can always depend on you to tell the truth when they need to hear it and not "fudge" about it. If you are truthful, you will set the standard for integrity, truthfulness, and *trust* with whomever you are dealing with.

Sparkling Gems From the Greek, Volume 2

You may not deliberately set out to be dishonest, but anytime you misrepresent the truth about your abilities, say something about another person that you don't know to be true, slightly twist the facts to your advantage, or trump up a story about yourself or your past deeds to make yourself look better in the sight of others — you have fully entered into what the Bible views as a dishonesty.

Sparkling Gems From the Greek, Volume 1

Honesty might be difficult, but it's not more difficult than living with a bitter spirit and a bad attitude. Being honest with the one who hurt you may seem difficult in the moment, but when forgiveness clears the breach in the relationship, you are *free*. Holding on to silent resentment makes you a prisoner in your own mind and emotions.

Sparkling Gems From the Greek, Volume 2

Hope

People are looking for hope — *and you have hope to give them!*

Last-Days Survival Guide

If you have been knocked down by life — if your emotions have been crushed, if your finances have been negatively impacted, if you're down in *any* area of your life — the resurrection power of Jesus can cause you to stand up again!

Build Your Foundation

For believers who have made the egregious error of tolerating and yielding habitually to sinful behavior — there is *hope*. If they will acknowledge how far they've strayed and become willing to repent, the Holy Spirit will rise up like a mighty force from deep within to invade their thoughts and begin the process of renewing their minds, once again, to the truth.

**How To Keep Your Head on Straight
in a World Gone Crazy**

Although we don't like to admit it, we all occasionally have times in our lives when we hit a brick wall, so to speak. We don't know what to say, what to do, where to turn, or even how to pray. Sometimes it seems as if we've hit a dead end and everything is *finished, over,* and *done with*. If you've ever been in a place like that, you know what a hard place this can be! These feelings usually arise when we think that we've failed, that people have misunderstood us, or that we've been unfairly judged. However, even when we've made serious mistakes, these setbacks are rarely as irreparable as they seem.

Sparkling Gems From the Greek, Volume 2

Hopelessness

If you've been tempted to fear or to feel hopeless about the changes happening in this age, it's time for you to tell fear to *leave* in Jesus' name! Then ask God to help you allow His delivering power to work through you to bring freedom to people who are confused or gripped with fear. The world is looking for hope — and you have a great hope to give them!

The Will of God — The Key to Your Success

It may seem like we live in an age of hopelessness amidst a fallen world that has run amuck, but these are the days we were appointed by God to live in, and He has not abandoned us to turbulent times. We have the Word of God to keep us firmly founded and the Holy Spirit as our Teacher, Mentor, and Guide. We even have brothers and sisters in the Christian community upon whom we can lean for support and receive help when it is needed, so that with all that God has provided, we are well able to live victoriously for Him in these last times!

Last-Days Survival Guide

In God, there's no such thing as *a hopeless situation*. That dead-end place you may be facing right now can become a place of new beginnings. This is *not* the end for you! God has a marvelous plan for your life, and the devil simply doesn't have the power to hijack what God has planned.

Sparkling Gems From the Greek, Volume 2

When you don't know what else to do and when you have no one else to turn to, that's usually when God's resurrection power begins to operate in you to the greatest measure! You see, there's no such thing as *no hope.* As long as there is a loving Heavenly Father you can call on, there is still hope for you!

Sparkling Gems From the Greek, Volume 1

Humility

Being aware of your limitations is just as important as knowing your potential.

The Point of No Return

The scriptures show over and over again that unhealthy pride is *fatal* to man's spiritual, mental, and emotional well-being — and often even fatal to his physical life. It is the root of rebellion and is always accompanied with catastrophic results. For this reason, God always has been and always will be against pride. God actually *resists* the proud, but He *gives grace* unto the humble.

A Life Ablaze

As long as we think we can handle an assignment by ourselves, we will be limited to our own ability. But when we realize that our new assignment in life is just too big to handle on our own, we have no choice but to move beyond ourselves into the dimension of God Himself.

The Point of No Return

Think of the humility that was required for God to shed His magnificent glory and lower Himself to become like a member of His own creation!

A Light in Darkness

Don't get into the business of exalting yourself. Let that be God's job. Self-exaltation is the fruit of pride, but God-exaltation is His response to humility.

A Life Ablaze

Although Jesus is now exalted — sitting at the Father's right hand and arrayed in splendor beyond human imagination — His humility still remains intact, consistent, and unchanged. It is one of the chief characteristics of His nature. He *was* humble, He *is* humble, and He *will always be* humble.

A Light in Darkness

I

Idolatry

Where idolatry is practiced, the spiritual floodgates of evil are opened, allowing a deluge of moral filth and depravity to pour out.

No Room for Compromise

The act of idolatry transpires when an individual gives his complete and undivided attention, devotion, passion, love, or commitment to a person, project, or object other than God. When something other than God takes first place in that person's mind, he has entered, at least to some measure, into the sin of idolatry.

Sparkling Gems From the Greek, Volume 1

In the early days of the Church, when pagans converted to Christ, one of their first actions was to destroy every remnant of their ancestral in-home shrines and altars, removing all idols and cleansing their homes of every shred of occult activity. There was good reason for this cleansing process, because turning to Christ entailed much more than a philosophical shift or a mere change in one's lifestyle. To acknowledge Jesus as Lord meant that a person had to reject all other gods and confess that Jesus was Lord over all. This conversion necessitated the confession of sin and severance from all previous spiritual and moral defilements — including every form of idolatry.

No Room for Compromise

Illumination

God gave you a marvelous mind, and He *wants* you to *use* it. He also wants you to yield to the work of the Holy Spirit within you, who is always endeavoring to bring enlightenment, revelation, insight, and illumination to your mind.

Life in the Combat Zone

As we study the Word of God, the Holy Spirit causes our understanding of God and His Word to be marvelously expanded. Just when I think that I have unearthed every gem that can possibly be found in a particular verse of the New Testament, the Holy Spirit wonderfully *opens my eyes* and *illuminates my mind* to show me truths that I previously didn't see!

Sparkling Gems From the Greek, Volume 2

A fight will always follow illumination.

Life in the Combat Zone

Satan hates it when you stand strong on God's Word. He will do everything within his ability to knock you off your stance of faith. He will use family members, friends, associates, and circumstances to thwart the plan of God for your life. And once you are "illuminated" regarding God's perfect will for you, you must determine that you won't budge an *inch* off the path of pursuing His will — regardless of any demonic opposition you encounter!

Life in the Combat Zone

Immorality

In the day we're living in — the very end of the last days — people's minds are being inundated with false information and a celebration of various forms of immorality, including a deluge of false propaganda about human sexuality. This last-days attack of seducing spirits is bent on modifying the collective mind of society and creating a way of thinking that is free of moral restraint, and this modification process is spreading its tentacles into every sector of society. Unfortunately, even people who grew up in church are now becoming affected and changed in how they view issues that *should* be set in stone in their lives.

How To Keep Your Head on Straight
in a World Gone Crazy

Largely unaware of the danger, people of this age ingest unrelenting mental bombardment from every aspect of society by way of wrong people, wrong sources, wrong information, and wrong spiritual influences. It's all part of the satanic war being waged against the human race (including believers) to adversely affect people's thought processes, to undermine their core belief system, and to damage and disfigure their minds until they can no longer see what is *wrong* about *wrong*.

Last-Days Survival Guide

Incarnation

As unfathomable as it is, God Almighty reached into the material world, clothed Himself in flesh as He grew in the womb of the Virgin Mary and, finally, was birthed into the realm of the human race for a moment in time.

Christmas — The Rest of the Story

Jesus in His preexistent form had all the outward appearance of God, but He also existed in the exact form of a Man — appearing and living on this earth in the same way as any other man. For a brief time in His eternal existence, He emptied Himself of outward divine attributes and literally became like a Man in every way.

A Light in Darkness

Although God wanted to be in the midst of His creation, He could not come in His splendor and glory because it would be too great for human flesh to endure. So God *re-clothed* Himself to look like us and took on our form. God literally exchanged His royal, celestial robes for the "clothing" of human flesh.

Christmas — The Rest of the Story

Just think of it — Almighty God, clothed in radiant glory from eternity past, came to this earth formed as a human being in the womb of a human mother for one purpose: so that He could one day die a miserable death on a cross to purchase our salvation! All of this required *humility* on a level far beyond anything we could ever comprehend or anything that has ever been requested of any of us. Yet this was the reason Jesus came; therefore, He chose to be obedient to the very end, humbling Himself to the point of dying a humiliating death on a cross and thereby purchasing our eternal salvation.

Sparkling Gems From the Greek, Volume 1

Out of His deep love for you and me, Jesus left His majestic realm of glory to enter the realm of humanity. Shedding all His visible attributes that were too much for man's flesh to endure, He dressed Himself in the clothing of a human being and was manifested in the flesh. That little Baby in Bethlehem was the eternal, ever-existent God Almighty, who came to us in human flesh so that He could dwell among men and purchase our salvation.

Sparkling Gems From the Greek, Volume 2

Inclusivity

We live in a day when diversity of beliefs, an ever-changing moral code, and an acceptance of moral perversion is seeping into the mainstream — and often these are encased within the noble-sounding ideas of *inclusivity* and *open-mindedness*. Many influential people in positions of visibility have even "jumped on the bandwagon" to promote these views.

Signs You'll See Just Before Jesus Comes

In order to meet the new cultural norms that exist in modern society, some denominations have gradually moved in the direction of modifying the Gospel wherever needed to avoid controversy or to better "fit in." This trend has gone so far that the early apostles would be hard-pressed to recognize the Gospel message at all in what is preached from the pulpits of many churches. The pure truths of Paul's epistles have largely been replaced with a gospel of inclusion that emphasizes social justice and social action on wide-ranging subjects.

How To Keep Your Head on Straight
in a World Gone Crazy

It is right to abhor doctrines that encourage believers to embrace compromise with the world. Messages that promote moral relativism and inclusiveness over absolute truth dilute the message of the Gospel and strip it of its life-saving power.

No Room for Compromise

The need to be washed in the blood of Jesus and transformed by the power of the Holy Spirit is not even on the radar in some denominations. This ominous departure from the truth of Jesus Christ has swung so far that now these denominations are promoting *inclusivity* as if *that* is the message of the Church in this hour.

Last-Days Survival Guide

Inclusiveness, negotiation, and accommodation with the world have the power to pollute a holy lifestyle with sin and corruption. Therefore, they are in direct opposition to Christ's call to the Church to be vigilant.

No Room for Compromise

Infilling of the Spirit

God has designed our lives in Christ in such a way that it would be very difficult for us *not* to freely receive an impartation of superhuman, supernatural strength for the fight. However, if we are to experience this ever-available, ever-near power, we must open our hearts to it, ask God to release it into our lives, and then by *faith* we must reach out to embrace it.

Sparkling Gems From the Greek, Volume 1

One infilling of God's Spirit may last for a while, but soon we must be replenished with a fresh infilling. This can only happen as we allow the Holy Spirit to drench our spirit in times of private fellowship with the Lord and then to set us ablaze with His fire.

A Light in Darkness

In the book of Acts, speaking in tongues was the norm, not the exception — a common practice that was expected to occur in the life of any person who was filled with the Spirit. And just as the early believers freely and fluently prayed in the Spirit, God has enabled us to do the same, *if* we will but open our hearts, open our mouths, and let our spirits speak to God.

Sparkling Gems From the Greek, Volume 1

God's intention is to water, irrigate, imbibe, soak, and saturate each one of us with the Spirit until we are *full* — regardless of our ethnicity, class, gender, or race — to bring us into spiritual growth and to demonstrate the glorious fullness of Christ in the Church.

Apostles and Prophets

It is God's desire for every believer to be so saturated with the Spirit that he can be set ablaze to shed light into the darkness of a lost and dying world, just as a lamp lights up a room. And the amazing news is that the Church has a whole reservoir of the Spirit at its disposal — so it's possible for every believer to be drenched with the oil of the Holy Spirit!

Sparkling Gems From the Greek, Volume 2

As long as there is still grace, there is still a free, supernatural inner strengthening available to you — *if* you reach out and take it. You have to receive a new touch of God's power *freely* — by means of God's grace. The devil will always be around to tell you that you're not good enough, not worthy enough, not faithful enough to deserve anything from God, but who said you have to deserve anything God gives you? Because Jesus died for you and washed you with His blood, you are a candidate for everything that God possesses!

Sparkling Gems From the Greek, Volume 1

Influence

As you press into God and put your wick down deep into the oil of the Holy Spirit, you'll become so saturated with His presence that you'll begin to burn brighter and brighter for Jesus. Just let your gifts flow and become the influence He intended you to be! *Believe me, friend, you've got everything it takes!*

Sparkling Gems From the Greek, Volume 2

If your light is going to be a blessing to the world, you must dare to lift that light high and put it on a pedestal where people will see it and be affected by it. Those who have influence — such as those who write the songs you sing, the books you read, or the sermons you hear preached on TV — are not necessarily the most gifted, talented, or anointed people. But they had the nerve to step out by faith and obedience to elevate their God-given abilities. Regardless of how good or seemingly inferior their abilities were, today they are renowned and influential because they had the guts and gumption to get their light out from under a bushel and to *let it shine.* A great part of their success is due to their willingness to step out from obscurity and let their light begin to shine to others.

Unlikely

It doesn't matter how much Gospel you preach to non-Christians, how many tracts and books you leave on their desks, or how much literature you send them in the mail — unbelievers are affected by what they *see, hear, smell, taste,* and *touch.* This means *your life is your primary pulpit.* That is why it's so important that your "curb appeal" be Christ-honoring and spiritually appealing to people who are watching you.

Sparkling Gems From the Greek, Volume 2

Your specific assignment is to reach every person in each group where you have influence. This means you needn't buy a plane ticket and fly to the other side of the world to do this job. Mission trips are great experiences, but you have a mission field right where you work, where you attend school, where you purchase your groceries every day — in every place where you have some level of personal influence.

Sparkling Gems From the Greek, Volume 1

Influential People

It is important that Christian leaders remember that *words have consequences.*

How To Keep Your Head on Straight in a World Gone Crazy

The Holy Spirit forewarns those with spiritual influence that they will ultimately be scrutinized by God Himself, who will watch to see if what they endorse or teach is in agreement with the entire body of Scripture. This means that every word, every phrase, and every nuance that is spoken in a public forum by a spiritual leader is significant to God.

Apostles and Prophets

Those with spiritual influence over others will be held accountable for what they say, what they endorse, and what they serve to saints who are gathered at their table.

How To Keep Your Head on Straight in a World Gone Crazy

What do you know about those voices you've allowed on your TV, computer, or other devices? Who is really speaking into your life? Do you know where they stand on matters that are (or *should* be) non-negotiable to you? Are you allowing someone who is safe to speak into your spiritual life, or are you permitting someone who is possibly spiritually corrupted to influence you? Always do your due diligence in these matters, ensuring that you really know who is speaking to you.

Last-Days Survival Guide

Initiative

It takes only a few personal experiences with desireless people to make it perfectly clear why God puts desire at the top of the list of character requirements for leaders. There is nothing more dreadful or irritating than to work with someone who is gifted and talented but who doesn't even possess enough initiative to get up and do his job!

Sparkling Gems From the Greek, Volume 1

How much time do you waste watching television when you could be reading, studying, working, and developing yourself into someone better? You'll never become someone great or achieve anything special by doing what everyone else does. If you want to stand above the rest of the crowd, you'll have to do more than what others do. If you don't have desire, you'll never make it!

Sparkling Gems From the Greek, Volume 1

It is frustrating to try to help, nurture, and develop people who have great potential but are apathetic about life. Desireless people stroll through life at their own pace, accepting standards and practices that would *never* be accepted in the business or secular world. They are like *dead people!*

Sparkling Gems From the Greek, Volume 1

Injustice

You cannot avoid the fact that you will sometimes face unpleasant situations in which you feel mistreated, abused, or discriminated against. As long as you live in a world where the devil operates and unsaved people have their way, evil and injustice will touch your life from time to time. So when you find yourself subjected to a situation that seems unfair and unjust, you must ask, *How does God expect me to respond?*

Sparkling Gems From the Greek, Volume 2

Knowing He was in the Father's will, the Lord yielded Himself to the One who judges righteously when He found Himself in the unjust situation of facing death on a cross. In that difficult hour, Jesus drew close to the Father, fully entrusting Himself and His future into His Father's hands and leaving the results in His control.

Paid in Full

If you are in a situation that seems unfair or unjust and there is nothing you can do to change it, you must draw as close to the Father as you can and commit yourself into

His loving care. Even though you have found yourself in a predicament that seems so undeserved, you still know that God wants the best for you. Your options are to get angry and bitter and turn sour toward life, or to choose to believe that God is in control and working on your behalf, even if you don't see anything good happening at the present moment.

Paid in Full

Intellectual Elitists

In the very end of the last days, there will be those who claim to be intellectually advantaged above the rest of the crowd with the right to decide what is right or wrong or what should be viewed as antiquated and out of fashion.

How To Keep Your Head on Straight
in a World Gone Crazy

The Holy Spirit warns us that *many* people within several spheres of society will emit a proud, God-defying attitude. This is especially true of those who fit the category of intellectual elitists — those who show disdain for others who hold to the immutable truth of the Bible. God's Spirit warns that this intellectually snobbish attitude will try to blast onto the scene in full strength, much like the dark clouds and destructive winds of a typhoon.

Last-Days Survival Guide

From their public platforms in the media and in Hollywood, their podiums in courtrooms, and their lecterns in university classrooms — those who scorn Bible believers haughtily mock, sneer, disdain, disparage, and scorn them as relics of the past simply because they stay true to their biblical convictions.

Last-Days Survival Guide

"Agenda-setters," or those who claim to be intellectually elite, see anyone who holds fast to past moral codes and beliefs as a hindrance to the new world they want to create. In truth, this is because we who refuse to budge from our Bible-based convictions are part of the restraining force that the apostle Paul referred to in Second Thessalonians 2:6,7.

Last-Days Survival Guide

Intercession

Nearly 2,000 years ago, Jesus died for you — but today He lives to intercede for you and to fight for your every need.

Paid in Full

The Holy Spirit intercedes for you when you are at a loss for words and don't know how to pray, or when you feel trapped and don't know what to say or do. Suddenly and supernaturally, the Holy Spirit falls into that place of helplessness with you to join you as a Partner in prayer in the midst of your circumstances.

How To Receive Answers From Heaven

Jesus has faced every temptation that any human being has ever encountered in life. This means He has experienced every temptation *you* face. He was personally tempted when He walked the earth, and He personally understands what you're going through. This means He is qualified to intercede on your behalf.

Paid in Full

If you will go to Jesus, your Great High Priest, and present your case to Him, He will intercede for you — rising up like a Mighty Warrior who is ready to go into battle to fight until you are delivered, free, and safe!

Paid in Full

Intimacy With God

Prayer brings us to a place of intimacy with God. When we pray, we face God. Our prayer brings us into the presence of God, and this is particularly important when we fight our spiritual battles to break through spiritual barriers.

How To Receive Answers From Heaven

Our intimacy with Jesus and our personal knowledge of Him is what will make the difference and serve as our sustaining force in the days that lie ahead.

Last-Days Survival Guide

Jesus is seated right now at the right hand of the Father on High, but you can know Him intimately through the ministry of the Holy Spirit, for the Holy Spirit is the Great

Revealer of Jesus Christ. Just ask the Holy Spirit to show you Jesus, and He will make Jesus more real to you than your natural mind can even imagine!

Paid in Full

Can you say that you are totally, unalterably, and irreversibly addicted to the presence of God?

Dream Thieves

Intolerance

Just as it occurred in the Early Church, whenever believers take a firm stand on absolute truth, they are viewed by the world as intolerant.

*How To Keep Your Head on Straight
in a World Gone Crazy*

To our natural eyes, it seems like society is degenerating at an ever-increasing rate. Laws are being implemented that are antagonistic toward people of faith, and Christians are increasingly labeled as *intolerant* because they refuse to endorse the activities of a morally bankrupt world. Therefore, it is important for us to remain aware that Christ is still seated on His throne in Heaven, ruling over the affairs of mankind, and no matter how turbulent the waters around us may seem, Christ has never moved from His highly exalted seat of authority.

Sparkling Gems From the Greek, Volume 2

The day the prophet Isaiah forewarned about is here — when what was once viewed as wrong by the culture has become right and is *even celebrated* (*see* Isaiah 5:20). To speak or act in any way cross-grain to this new norm is now considered by many to be unjust, bigoted, and intolerant.

Signs You'll See Just Before Jesus Comes

In the First Century, the issue pagans had with Christians wasn't that they believed in Jesus Christ; there was room for many gods in that society. The problem lay in what believers proclaimed as absolute truth: that Jesus' name was above every other name and that there was no other name by which men could be saved. This was simply too offensive and exclusionary for pagans to tolerate. Although early Christians were called intolerant, it was pagans who killed them, not vice versa, for pagans had no tolerance for anyone who stepped out of their pantheistic belief system or who adamantly upheld that their faith was true above all other faiths. By contrast, Christians loved, forgave, and prayed for those who persecuted them.

No Room for Compromise

Itching Ears

The words "itching ears" is used figuratively to depict a person (or a crowd of people) who wants to hear something *new* as compared to what he has already heard and known. Having his "ears" filled with something he wants to be told is the only thing that relieves this "itching-ear" syndrome. The craving and demand for these fanciful messages by those with "itching ears" will produce large numbers of newly fashioned teachers with *restyled* messages. The mixture of truth and falsehood these teachers deliver will eventually lead a large segment of people into a distorted perception of who the Christ of Christianity really is.

Sparkling Gems From the Greek, Volume 2

We must pray for God to raise up skilled, solid Bible teachers who will feed the pure Word of God to people whose hearts are crying out for it. God's people need good teaching, so let's be united in prayer for God-sent leaders who will not twist or alter what the Bible says in order to appease a crowd with "itching ears." We need bold preachers who will refuse to deviate from preaching the Word of truth, for absolutely *nothing* is more powerful than truth mixed with the anointing of the Holy Spirit.

Sparkling Gems From the Greek, Volume 2

Isolation

Isolation does not heal pain; in fact, it usually creates more problems by making you an open target for the enemy's emotional and mental attacks.

Dream Thieves

You may be tempted to feel isolated and alone, but if the eyes of your spirit were opened for just a moment, you'd see that you're not alone! God is surrounding you with the Holy Spirit's power, with angels, and with everything else you need to keep going forward.

Paid in Full

To allow yourself to become isolated and separated from the rest of the Body of Christ or from spiritual authority under ANY circumstances can be deadly to your walk with God and to the ultimate fulfillment of your dream.

Dream Thieves

Jealousy

Not only does it infuriate the Holy Spirit when believers turn their devotion to the world, but it drives Him to intense *jealousy*. When this happens, He will release His full rage against that unholy relationship, moving on the scene like a Divine Lover who has come to defend and rescue the relationship He holds so dear. This is something you can be sure of: If you commit more of your heart, soul, and attention to worldly things than you give to the Spirit of God, He will *not* take it lightly.

Sparkling Gems From the Greek, Volume 1

Jealousy and covetousness in others is an unfortunate reality that often manifests when God opens a door of opportunity for you. That's why it is so imperative that you learn how to be discerning. Those with impure motives have a way of showing up wherever people are being blessed, so don't be surprised if it happens to you. If you're not careful, these individuals will try to steal the victory away from you after you have worked hard to achieve it.

Sparkling Gems From the Greek, Volume 1

Jesus' Birth

Jesus is God's Gift to the world — truly the greatest Gift ever given to mankind!

Christmas — The Rest of the Story

The existence of Jesus Christ did *not* begin at His birth in Bethlehem. Rather, His birth simply initiated His temporary manifestation in the earthly realm — one that lasted for 33 years. But before that, the preincarnate Christ eternally coexisted with the Father and the Holy Spirit.

A Light in Darkness

At Jesus' birth as a Babe at Bethlehem, angels came in massive numbers to witness Him and to behold the face of God *for the first time ever*. In Christ, for the first time — angels and mankind were able to look into *the very face of God.*

Christmas — The Rest of the Story

People love to sing the song "Silent Night," but the holy moment of Christ's birth was probably not as silent as the song claims. Jesus was born in a cave filled with noisy animals and possibly other travelers who were also seeking refuge. It was probably downright *noisy* in that cave because there were animals all around, along with shepherds, and possibly other weary travelers.

Christmas — The Rest of the Story

In the years leading up to the time of Jesus' birth, there was a growing belief that a long-anticipated world leader was about to be born. This belief was so widespread that even the ancient writers Virgil, Horace, Tacitus, and Suetonius wrote about an expectation of a coming golden age and of a great deliverer who would soon be born.

Christmas — The Rest of the Story

That little baby in Bethlehem was the eternal, ever-existent God Almighty, who dressed Himself in human flesh so that He could dwell among men and purchase our salvation on the Cross as the Lamb of God who would take away the sin of the world and render its punishment *powerless*.

Christmas — The Rest of the Story

Jesus Is Coming

The Bible says that at the end of this age Jesus Christ will return personally and visibly — the dead will be raised, Christ will judge all men in righteousness, the unrighteous will be consigned to hell, and the righteous will receive their reward and will dwell forever with the Lord.

How To Keep Your Head on Straight in a World Gone Crazy

Jesus stated that no one but the Father knows the exact day or hour when Christ will return, but He said it's possible for us to know when we're *approaching* the outer boundaries of the age by looking at the *signs* (*see* Matthew 24:4-7). There are many such indicators to alert us that we have already entered the territory of the closing of this period in history.

Last-Days Survival Guide

Peter warned that in the last days, there will come scoffers who will mock and say, "Where is the promise of his coming?" In other words, they'll mockingly chide, "*Come on*...people have been saying that Jesus is coming again for 2,000 years, and He hasn't come. This is just a fairytale." Thus, the Bible tells us when people begin talking like this, we need to take it as a sign that we are living in the last days.

Christmas — The Rest of the Story

Only when every prophecy as yet unfulfilled has finally been fulfilled will Jesus return — and when He does return, it will be exactly in the same way He ascended nearly 2,000 years ago, but this time He will return as the King of kings and the Lord of lords!

Paid in Full

One of the ministries of the Holy Spirit is to reveal things to come so we'll know what to expect as we move forward in time (*see* John 16:13). Armed with this knowledge, it means we can protect ourselves, our families, and our loved ones from the destructive trends that will be associated with the closing days, and we can resolve to stand strong and do the will of God, shining as lights in the darkness that will certainly increase just before Jesus returns.

Signs You'll See Just Before Jesus Comes

We must be attuned to hear the voice of the Holy Spirit in our time and live in anticipation of Jesus' next coming, for a day will soon come when Jesus will penetrate the stratosphere to gather His people who are anticipating His return. *Jesus is coming soon!*

Christmas — The Rest of the Story

Joy

Happiness is based on circumstantial pleasure, merriment, hilarity, exuberance, or excitement and can disappear right before a person's eyes — but *joy* is unaffected by outward circumstances. In fact, joy usually thrives best when times are tough! Joy is God's supernatural response to the devil's attacks.

Sparkling Gems From the Greek, Volume 1

If you are in the will of God, it is likely that you're going to experience joy, peace, and fulfillment, even in the midst of hardships. But if your life is generally joyless and frustrating — if it seems like you go through one defeated experience after another — there's probably an adjustment that needs to take place in where you are or in what you're doing.

The Will of God — The Key to Your Success

If you're filled with the Holy Spirit and the power of God, you *can* do your job with joy, no matter what circumstances surround you! You can be victorious in any environment, even in working conditions that aren't exactly what you wish they could be. Besides, if you can't handle tiny inconveniences, how in the world do you ever think you'll be able to stand against the devil and the strategies he will try to use to assault you when you step out in faith?

Sparkling Gems From the Greek, Volume 1

When we get too busy, it is often the case that we give the daily intake of the Bible a lower priority in our lives than we did in the beginning of our Christian walk. And when that happens, our power and joy will begin to wane.

Last-Days Survival Guide

If you're *not* a generous giver, your joy in serving God will eventually wane. But when you live a life of generous giving, you are continually throwing another log into the fire of your heart — and it will cause you to burn ever more brightly for the Lord.

A Life Ablaze

Judgment

You and I must use *judgment* about the things we do or say in the presence of unbelievers. We must use *prudence, caution, good sense, carefulness,* and *good ol' common sense* in the way we conduct ourselves, and we should be *distinguishably different* from the lost world around us. Unbelievers are watching and are monitoring our actions, and by living upright lives before them, we can make a godly impact on them.

Sparkling Gems From the Greek, Volume 2

Be diligent to rid yourself of judgmental attitudes so you can remain a clear channel that God is able to continually work through to bring help and deliverance to others.

Last-Days Survival Guide

No matter how carefully or how slowly Jesus proceeds in correcting His Church, there is no way to avoid the painful effects of judgment against sin or erring leadership. Correction is always a painful procedure, and often it is bitter to the taste. But to reveal Jesus' compassionate heart and His desire to alleviate His people's pain during this ordeal, His divine sword carries the *anesthesia* of the Holy Spirit to numb the pain of the procedure.

A Light in Darkness

We will all stand before God and give account for what we have taught, shared, or allowed to occur in our midst.

Testing the Supernatural

"Fire" is an important symbol in Scripture and frequently represents *purification* and *judgment*. Which effect of divine fire we experience depends wholly on our response to God. If we as individuals, or as the Church at large, submit to the pleadings of the Holy Spirit and "hear what the Spirit saith unto the churches," we will experience the *first* type of fire — a holy fire intended to purify and to make us more like Christ. But if we resist the pleadings of the Holy Spirit and stubbornly continue to act in ways that are contrary to Christ's character, there is a *second* type of fire that burns up chaff and consumes everything that stands opposed to God. How we respond to the dealings of God determines which kind of fire we will experience.

Will it be a fire that purifies and takes us to a higher level in the Lord, or will it be a fire that burns up the chaff in our lives that we haven't been willing to surrender on our own?

Sparkling Gems From the Greek, Volume 2

Having sound and reasonable *judgment* is not the same as being *judgmental*. If you are going to be a person God uses to help others, you must be able to *judge* a situation without being *judgmental* about it.

Last-Days Survival Guide

God is not slow regarding the promises He has made. He is "longsuffering" for the sake of those who still need to come to repentance, just as He was longsuffering in the days before the Flood. God is not in a rush to judge and does not wish for anyone to perish. But the end of this age will come the *instant* the last person who is going to be saved is brought into the Kingdom — and then we will be miraculously transformed and translated to meet the Lord in the air.

Fallen Angels, Giants, Monsters,
and the World Before the Flood

Judgment Seat of Christ

When we stand before the Judgment Seat of Christ, we will not be shamed for our past sin. The Judgment Seat of Christ is *not* a place of shame, nor is it a place of embarrassment. We will *not* grovel in His presence — we will *stand* before Him as those who are washed in His blood and robed in His righteousness.

Build Your Foundation

When we stand before the Judgment Seat of Christ, He will assess our obedience to Him after we received Him as our Savior and Lord. It will be a place of evaluation, and on the basis of that evaluation, rewards will be given and our position of service in the Millennial reign of Christ will be revealed, and right now, we are in a qualification period for the next age.

Build Your Foundation

Our approach to life changes dramatically when we live with the awareness that one day we will stand before the Lord "eyeball to eyeball" and answer for how responsibly or irresponsibly we lived our lives. There will be no fast talking on that day, because every excuse will evaporate in His glorious light. This judgment will not be in regard to our salvation, for if we are at the judgment seat of Christ, we are already eternally saved. However, that day *will* determine our reward. Those who fulfilled the assignment Jesus gave them will receive a reward. Those who were *not* obedient will still be saved, but they will have no reward to show for their lives.

Sparkling Gems From the Greek, Volume 1

Remember that when you stand before the Judgment Seat of Christ, Jesus will reward you for what you built *correctly* and for that which passes the test of time.

Build Your Foundation

The Judgment Seat of Christ is a place where we will not be able to escape the facts as Jesus reviews our level of obedience after we were born again and evaluates us on how well we truly ran our spiritual race. Did we do what He asked us to do? Did we complete our role in the "games of the Kingdom" during our time on the earth? This absolutely means a factual report is in my future — and it is in your future as well.

Build Your Foundation

Judicial System

The last season of the age will be a time when the legal system will become *overloaded* with lawsuits of all kinds as more and more people refuse even to *attempt* reconciling their disputes or differences.

Last-Days Survival Guide

We are living in a day when the devil is in the court system — weaponizing the law to accuse, attack, slander, vilify, and ravage others financially.

Last-Days Survival Guide

Satan's goal is to poison systems of education, entertainment, politics, science, medicine, the courts, and even our churches, using the world system and the morally deteriorating culture that surrounds us.

How To Keep Your Head on Straight in a World Gone Crazy

Justice

God is not a respecter of persons, nor is He a respecter of civilizations. God's justice is so steadfast that when the world of Noah's day persisted in their egregious sinful behavior and refused to repent, God judged that entire ancient civilization. In fact, He judged it so entirely that He wiped it out — leaving only a handful of Noah's family surviving.

Fallen Angels, Giants, Monsters,
and the World Before the Flood

God is *fair* and *equitable* in His dealings!

Sparkling Gems From the Greek, Volume 1

The Bible teaches that it is God's habitual practice and normal behavior to be just and fair, so you can be sure people who have wronged you will get exactly what they deserve. He will see to it that they are reimbursed and that they receive a full settlement of trouble for the traumatic circumstances they have put you through. Those who have afflicted you will receive a full measure of affliction in return.

Sparkling Gems From the Greek, Volume 2

K

Knowledge

Satan knows that empty heads are easy to deceive.

You Can Get Over It

My God-appointed pursuit is to grow ever deeper in my understanding of God's Word, to never depart from the eternal truths contained in it, and to convey to others its life-giving, transforming power through the work of the Holy Spirit.

A Life Ablaze

Like a researcher who commits and focuses himself to serious exploration and research of a certain topic, the Body of Christ is to never stop its search of Christ until we are *intimately acquainted* with Him. God's call is for the Body of Christ to engage in a lifelong exploration of researching the riches of Christ and His Word until we have mastered professional knowledge of Christ — to know Him so intimately that we are *on top of this subject* and know Christ *inside-out*, as *experts*.

Apostles and Prophets

A battle will occur wherever God has told you to take a stand of faith. It is certain that this is precisely where Satan will show up to resist you. When you take a stand of faith and put your knowledge to work, that's when the battle really begins and the devil starts throwing darts at your life!

Life in the Combat Zone

God's plan is for the Church to finally come to a new spiritual destination, where it is so consumed with Jesus that all doctrinal differences melt away and we come into a supernatural harmony as we focus on Christ. This lets us know that God will never be satisfied with the Body of Christ living on a superficial level. He is still calling the Church to set itself on Christ Himself and to move upward into higher realms of the knowledge of Him.

Apostles and Prophets

L

Lance of Prayer

It is true that our victory has already been won through Jesus' death and resurrection, but regardless of how skilled, bold, and courageous we think we are when it comes to the issue of spiritual conflict, we simply cannot maintain a victorious position apart from a life of prayer.

Dressed To Kill

Never forget that prayer is a vital piece of your spiritual weaponry. If you neglect this strategic piece of weaponry, you will find that the enemy keeps attacking you from up close. But as you learn to pray with authority, you will develop the ability to strike the enemy from a distance and therefore maintain a victorious position in your life.

Sparkling Gems From the Greek, Volume 1

Paul tells us, "Anytime you get a chance, no matter where you are or what you are doing, at every opportunity, every season, and every possible moment — SEIZE that time to pray!"

Dressed To Kill

Language

Language is the cornerstone of human understanding, so it naturally played an immense role in the spread and dispersal of the Christian faith. From the earliest beginnings of the Church, Christianity, like Judaism before it, has always been a text-based religion. The books of the Old Testament and the inspired writings of Early Church leaders, such as the epistles of Paul and Peter and the four gospels, formed the very essence of Christian belief. Those writings that were considered to be Scripture became an infallible voice of authority by which all doctrine and heresy could be judged against, and the insights, revelations, and wisdom contained therein provided a solid foundation for a believer's faith to be built upon.

No Room for Compromise

Christianity at its core is text-based — centered on the belief that the Bible is the unadulterated Word of God and that the truths contained therein are final and not subject to change.

No Room for Compromise

Making teachings universally accessible in the early centuries of the Church was almost an impossible task, for texts were all written or copied by hand, and even among the major cities, illiteracy was common-place and writings were scarce. Congregations often relied on a few educated, literate believers to interpret and relate the available Scriptures and to communicate with church leaders in other cities in order to expound their limited knowledge. This led in part to a centralization of churches around centers of culture where resources such as libraries, schools, and an educated class were more readily available. In the countryside, illiteracy could be nearly universal, and believers who possessed a developed understanding of the written Word were far rarer. So consequently, Christianity generally penetrated these rural societies at a much slower rate. Communities might hear the Gospel and even embrace it, but if a dedicated missionary wasn't present to water the seeds by establishing a local church and patiently explaining the revelations of God's Word, the message could easily fall by the wayside, unable to take root and effect significant change.

No Room for Compromise

Last Days

We live in a remarkable time — certainly a time like none other behind us. We are living in the very final "minutes and seconds" of this present era, and we are gearing up for the climax of the greatest spiritual contest of the ages: *evil versus good — darkness versus light.*

Signs You'll See Just Before Jesus Comes

Out on the front lines — the cutting edge — Satan hits hard and often, trying to drive back the Lord's brave soldiers who are storming hell's gates and taking new ground for His Kingdom. As the end of this age approaches, the severity of these attacks is becoming more acute.

Life in the Combat Zone

A massive undertaking is being executed to lead the world into a state of epic lawlessness so that it will more readily embrace the antichrist. The world is unaware of it, but it is being primed and prepared at this very moment for that time.

How To Keep Your Head on Straight
in a World Gone Crazy

As time passes, society will begin to see true Christianity as being completely out of sync with the times. If this regressive trend continues, it is only a matter of time before the Bible is relegated to simply being "just another book," a relic of a bygone era collecting dust alongside a host of texts representing other religions. When this occurs, the authority of Scripture in society and the Church will be lost — which is precisely what the devil wants to achieve.

No Room for Compromise

Satan's early attack upon the Church failed miserably, for the harder the devil hit the Early Church, the faster the Church of Jesus Christ grew and multiplied. If the devil sends a new army of innumerable wicked spirits against the Church in these last days, the Church will once again grow, thrive, multiply, and overcome!

Dressed To Kill

We were born at this time for a reason, and we are chosen, anointed, and called to live for Jesus in these perilous times. We must lay hold of God's promises and rise up in this hour to let our light shine. We must wake up and realize that we are closing the age! We were chosen for this hour — *it is our destiny!*

The Will of God — The Key to Your Success

Now at the end of the age — when lawlessness in society is throwing off all forms of authority and is screaming for independence — God is calling His people to come back into alignment with spiritual authority. He knows that when His house is in order, *increase* will come, *promotion* will come, *protection* will come, and *provision* will come — and the Church will come ablaze with the power and the fire of God!

A Life Ablaze

Law of God

When people have a knowledge of God's law, such as the Ten Commandments, that knowledge makes them aware that they have fallen short of the glory of God and are therefore lawbreakers and sinners. The law of God is a major instrument by which the Holy Spirit convicts people of sin. This is one reason why the devil has worked so hard to remove the Ten Commandments from today's society.

Sparkling Gems From the Greek, Volume 2

Lawlessness

As a part of a last-days scheme, society will be seduced by demonic influences to construct a new world order that has few, if any, hard-and-fast rules of what is morally right and wrong. In essence, this will be *a lawless world* — that is, a world free from the "outdated" voice of the Bible.

***How To Keep Your Head on Straight
in a World Gone Crazy***

Lawlessness is spreading like gangrene in society today — and it has scattered its poison so widespread that we are now even living in a season when some children insist that their parents have no legal right to exercise parental authority over them!

A Life Ablaze

The biblical word "lawlessness" refers to the actions of an individual, a group of people, a nation — or even an entire society or culture — that has chosen to live apart from God's laws and principles. Although this person or group previously followed biblical laws and principles *in general*, they elected to forge their own ways of doing things that are *not* founded on the principles of God's Word, and thus, they have become *lawless*, or they are living by their own newly evolving principles that are not based on established truths so vividly portrayed in Scripture.

Signs You'll See Just Before Jesus Comes

The current trend toward lawlessness — that is, the construction of a new world order with morals contrary to those stated in God's Word — will eventually produce a collective mindset in society that no longer feels the pain or conviction of sin and is numb to its consequences.

Last-Days Survival Guide

As the last days unfold before us and we draw near to the Lord's return, the powers of darkness are putting forth their best efforts to throw the world into an ever-deepening downward spiral of spiritual darkness and confusion. The enemy is aggressively working to set the stage for an earthly, wicked leader who will one day exercise control at the end of the age. This "mystery of lawlessness" has been working for 2,000 years, preparing the unsaved world to receive the "man of lawlessness," who Paul foretold would be revealed in the immediate years preceding Christ's Second Coming.

A Light in Darkness

Noah's day — the time before the Flood — was a time when immoral behaviors were prevalent in the world, and it wasn't just a few who were affected in that climate of overflowing iniquity and lawlessness, for the entire population of that time was morally affected — and Jesus foretold that as we entered the wrap-up of the last age, it would be once again as it was in the days of Noah.

Signs You'll See Just Before Jesus Comes

Lawsuits

Accusing and *being accused* is getting so out of control that it truly seems as if Satan himself has fallen into the courts.

Last-Days Survival Guide

There has been a descent into indecent behavior and the loss of the ability to negotiate, to come to terms, to settle differences, or to decently solve disagreements with others.

People now freely and readily turn to the courts almost without hesitation.

Last-Days Survival Guide

We should be able to work out any differences between ourselves, but in today's modern society, even believers often turn to the courts as a first recourse. It's true that heart-wrenching times do occur in which no other option is available but to turn to the courts for help — but this should never be a Christian's first choice or course of action!

Last-Days Survival Guide

God wants us as serious believers, to the best of our ability, to learn how to come to terms with others and settle differences maturely.

Last-Days Survival Guide

Laying on of Hands

From the very beginning of time, God has used the laying on of hands for the supernatural transfer of power, blessing, spiritual gifts, and authority. Of course, hands have no magical qualities in and of themselves. But God in His wisdom designed for hands to be the means of transfer for spiritual goods. The divine transaction takes place when a believer lays hands on another person in faith and the Holy Spirit then imparts whatever is needed to the recipient. This includes healing, deliverance to the sick and the oppressed, and so much more.

Build Your Foundation

If you'll get your hands out of your pockets and start laying them on people, you'll begin to see supernatural activity, because God works through the laying on of hands.

Build Your Foundation

The apostles, who had been taught by Jesus, continued in the pattern of their Master, for they understood that through the laying on of hands, spiritual power would be imparted. They knew it wasn't enough to pray for them, and that they had to get their hands on them.

Build Your Foundation

Through your hands, God stands ready to impart His blessing, power, healing, and deliverance to others. You simply must yield by faith and obey His command to lay hands on those who need His touch as His Spirit leads you.

Build Your Foundation

Laziness

One thing is certain: When God is looking for someone to do something significant, He doesn't choose lazy people who sit around doing nothing. Think about it. Why would He call someone to do *His* work when that person hasn't successfully done his or her own work?

Sparkling Gems From the Greek, Volume 2

My experience has shown me that most lazy people spend a lot of time fantasizing. They dream about their future, they dream about the day they will have more money, or they dream about having a big ministry. But this kind of dreaming is nothing more than escapism from reality and these people need to quit dreaming and get to work!

Dream Thieves

Think of how many people you know who were given a remarkable opportunity to do something tremendous but failed to take advantage of the moment. Because of laziness, hesitation, fear, or a "take it easy" mentality, the opportunity given to those people slipped away and was lost. *Don't let this describe you!* If God has given you a moment when you can work to achieve something tremendous — or if an exceptional prospect stands before you that will enable you to make a difference in someone else's life — you must give yourself *enthusiastically* and *passionately* to the task that lies before you. These kinds of opportunities are usually short-term, so you must seize the moment right now!

Sparkling Gems From the Greek, Volume 2

A major symptom of laziness is inaction. Instead of acting on God's Word and obeying the Holy Spirit, people who are lazy basically choose to do *what* they feel like doing *when* they feel like doing it.

The Point of No Return

In many ways, because many believers today have grown up in a period of peace and prosperity, the army of God has become lax. To a great degree, the Church is unprepared for war, despite all of its knowledge and teaching. Far too many believers have become weak-willed, untrained, spiritually fat, and lazy. Instead of viewing their walk of faith as a privilege, they see it as an uncomfortable, unwanted obligation.

Life in the Combat Zone

There is not a single example in Scripture of God *significantly* using a person who was idly sitting around and wasting time when He called him or her. All the men and women of God in the Bible were already busy doing something when God spoke to them.

Sparkling Gems From the Greek, Volume 2

Simply put, laziness is a subtle form of rebellion.

The Point of No Return

Leadership

No one has all the answers! The smartest leaders in the world are those who realize both their gifts and their limitations. A leader is wise when he recognizes his need for gifted, talented, willing-minded people to chip in and help him effectively do what he is called to do. No one can do it all alone.

Sparkling Gems From the Greek, Volume 1

Young leaders are often more open to new ideas and are flexible concerning a fresh move of God's Spirit, and as such, they bring a much-needed vitality to the Body of Christ. But on the other hand, older leaders often bring rock-solid stability, experience, and a firmer understanding of the Word of God. Balance is very important when it comes to spiritual leadership, for if there are too many young leaders in a church, that congregation can become imbalanced, unstable, and immature, but if there are too many older leaders, it can cause a church to become limited by a strict adherence to tradition and an unwillingness to change or try new things. Having the right mix of young and old leaders will bring life, vitality, and stability to a church, making it feel fresh, exciting, well-balanced, and doctrinally sound.

The Will of God — The Key to Your Success

One of the marks of serious upcoming leaders is they have "stepped up to the plate," accepted responsibility, and filled a vacancy that desperately needed to be filled. Their diligence to do a job well has made them so crucial that the organization would suffer great loss if they suddenly disappeared. They have made themselves essential to that organization.

Promotion

Excellence begins with an inward attitude — a determination to always do the best you can with who you are and with what you have.

Chosen by God: God Has Chosen You
for a Divine Assignment — Will You Fulfill It?

Prayer is essential to making your vision happen. Not only is it the only way you are going to know the specific boundaries and perimeters of your vision, but it is the only way you can find out how, when, where, and with whom you are to proceed.

The Point of No Return

Never forget that when you're a leader, the most important pulpit you'll ever possess is the testimony of your own personal life. Whether you serve in a leadership capacity in a church, business, or organization, your influence is only as strong as your personal life. If your personal life is suffering and people know it, your influence in their lives will be negatively affected. A leader's life and message must be backed up by his own personal life. Nothing is more powerful than a message backed up by a life.

Promotion

Leading of the Holy Spirit

As believers, we must learn to pay attention to the lack of peace we feel in our spirits. Sometimes a lack of peace or inward disturbance is God's way of alerting us to something important or of telling us that something isn't right, and God is trying to spare us from problems and catastrophes.

Sparkling Gems From the Greek, Volume 2

The Holy Spirit is a Gentleman and does not *force* you to obey Him. He prompts you, tugs on your heart, and pulls on your spirit to get your attention. Sometimes His tugs can be so gentle that you can miss them if you're not sensitive to them. But if you'll develop your sensitivity to the Holy Spirit, He will gently lead you exactly where He wants you to go with your life. But don't demand that the Holy Spirit tell you the whole story first before you obey Him. *Trust Him!*

Unlikely

We must learn to put on the brakes, stop ourselves for a while, and wait until the Holy Spirit speaks clearly to our hearts. It may seem as if this way of doing things takes longer, but when He does speak, the results will be more rewarding and longer lasting. If we do this, we can avoid pitfalls that would have cost us a lot of time and effort in the long run.

Sparkling Gems From the Greek, Volume 1

Many people are afraid to obey what the Holy Spirit puts in their hearts to do. Fearful that they will be led astray or that they will make a mistake, they sit on the sidelines and watch other people achieve success, while they remain right where they've always been. But let me assure you: *You can trust the leading of the Holy Spirit!*

Sparkling Gems From the Greek, Volume 2

If you haven't yet run into one of these moments in your life, there *will* come a time in your future when you'll have to step out and do what God is saying, even though you don't relish the idea of what He is asking you to do. In that moment, it is vital that you follow the guidance of the Holy Spirit so He can lead you into new realms of wonder and possibility.

Sparkling Gems From the Greek, Volume 2

Make it your goal to become the Holy Spirit's constant "tag-along!" Watch to see what He's doing, where He's going, and how He's leading, and stay sensitive to Him so you can pick up His "nudge" in your heart.

Sparkling Gems From the Greek, Volume 1

As you grow in your relationship with God, remember that He wants to meet you and escort you along every step of the journey. He doesn't just say, *"Here is what I want for you — now figure out how to get there by yourself."* God wants to step in front of you and lead you! If you'll listen, you'll hear Him say, "I'm here to lead you, so follow Me, and I'll lead your heart to the place where I want you to be!"

Sparkling Gems From the Greek, Volume 2

Light

From the very beginnings of the Church, the kingdom of darkness attempted to put out the light of the Gospel wherever it was preached, but in every place, the enemy's efforts were unsuccessful because the light of God *always* prevails — even in what seems to be the darkest hour or the bleakest situation. Darkness is ultimately incapable of suppressing the light or holding the light under its domain. Although darkness may try to prevent the light from shining, it can never permanently hold it back. Eventually the light always breaks through in all of its glorious brilliance.

No Room for Compromise

God's plan is for every believer to be so saturated with the Spirit that we can be set ablaze to shed light into the darkness of a lost and dying world, just as a lamp lights up a room. And the amazing news is that the Church has a whole reservoir of the Spirit, so it's possible for every believer to be drenched with the oil of the Holy Spirit!

Sparkling Gems From the Greek, Volume 2

If you place a lamp on a table, you'll illuminate the people sitting around the table. But if you elevate that same lamp by putting it on a pedestal, the light that previously only illuminated a handful of people will begin to impact everyone in the room. The amount of light produced is the same, but the elevated position of the lamp makes the light much more effective. Likewise, if the Church is going to shine its light as God intended, believers must dare to lift the message of the Gospel up high — to elevate it and put it on a pedestal according to His purposes. God is calling believers to extend their sphere of influence so they can make an eternal impact on an ever-increasing number of people who are lost and without hope.

A Light in Darkness

Darkness does not have the ability to suppress or to hold the light under its domain.

No Room for Compromise

When the Word of God is heeded, embraced, and believed, it continuously shines its brilliant light into the dark, murky places of our lives.

A Life Ablaze

Daniel was such a light in darkness that even though he served in a dark part of the world, his life and testimony was a bright and shining light that was never forgotten in Babylon.

Christmas — The Rest of the Story

The Church contains a reservoir of the Holy Spirit's oil, but each believer must allow his or her heart to become *soaked* in that oil before the Church can shine God's light into this world as He intended it to do.

A Light in Darkness

Allow the Holy Spirit to shine His glorious light into the crevices of your soul and let Him reveal those areas of your life where you need to yield to His cleansing work.

Paid in Full

The Scriptures are God's lamp, designed to give continuous light to a people or society that would lie in darkness if the source of that light was removed. Only the light of God's Word drives away spiritual darkness — which is why demonic forces hate the Light *and* the Light-bearers!

A Life Ablaze

As darkness continues to seep into every corner of our modern culture, Jesus is calling us to stay separate from the world — to resist the temptation to conform and instead to keep extending our light *further* and shining *brighter* as we represent Him on this earth.

No Room for Compromise

Listening

History bears witness that the Spirit of God always warns His people in advance when difficult times are coming. There are abundant historical records that relate accounts of believers in hostile nations throughout the world who were forewarned by the Holy Spirit of future hardships.

Such divine warnings prepare believers to face the impending challenges *if* they will hear and heed the voice of the Spirit.

A Light in Darkness

Learning to listen is a skill that must be developed. If your head is so busy that you can't hear what is being communicated, you will miss important facts and details. In the end, your inability to listen will cause you to make mistakes in your assignment. It's essential that you slow down to really hear what is being communicated to you.

Promotion

Remember that listening is the first step of communication, and communication is a prerequisite for success in your dealings with both God and man!

Sparkling Gems From the Greek, Volume 1

Learn to withhold your comments while others speak and give yourself the opportunity to hear the entire matter before you respond. Slow your mind down. Discipline your emotions to be quiet. Keep your mouth closed while others are making their point, and then once you have fully heard what they have to say, respond. Learning to listen is a major key to becoming a good communicator.

Promotion

Those who cultivate and develop the skill of listening make good team players because they're better able to understand other people's opinions and positions. These people have a good foundation for success because *listening is the first step of communication.*

Sparkling Gems From the Greek, Volume 1

Loinbelt of Truth

The loinbelt of truth is the written Word of God, and it is the only spiritual weapon that has taken on a physical, natural form and has passed tangibly from the spirit realm into our hands! It is the most important piece of weaponry that we possess.

Dressed To Kill

A belt seems to be an insignificant little thing — until you take it off. Without a belt, your pants might start falling down, your shirt may come untucked, and you'll likely look like a mess! You'll end up spending your time trying to keep your pants pulled up, you won't feel confident, and you certainly won't want to make any fast moves! That is precisely why the Roman soldier had a loinbelt — it held all the pieces of his armor together. Even if he had all his weaponry, if his loinbelt was not in place, everything else would fall apart. That's why it can be said that the loinbelt was the most vital part of all the weaponry the Roman soldier wore.

Dressed To Kill

As long as the loinbelt of truth — the Word of God — is central in your life, the rest of your spiritual armor will be effective. But the moment you begin to ignore God's Word or remove it from its rightful place at the very core of your life, it won't be long until you will begin to spiritually come apart at the seams!

Sparkling Gems From the Greek, Volume 1

Notice that the loinbelt covered the Roman soldier's loins, but why did the soldier have his loins protected so heavily? It was because he wanted to preserve his ability to reproduce. Because the loinbelt of truth is the Word of God and historically loinbelts were used to protect the reproductive abilities of a man, this tells us that our ability to produce for God is directly tied to our relationship with the Word of God.

Dressed To Kill

Loneliness

The Church today is filled with lonely people.

Last-Days Survival Guide

You may be tempted to feel isolated and alone, but if the eyes of your spirit were opened for just a moment, you'd see that you're not alone! God is surrounding you with the Holy Spirit's power, with angels, and with everything else you need to keep going forward.

Paid in Full

We never have to struggle alone, for at any time of the day or night, we can come boldly before the throne of grace to ask for divine assistance.

Paid in Full

What should you do if you ever come to a moment when you're all alone but you feel so elated that you just need to shout, dance, or sing to express yourself? I encourage you to go ahead and do it! The Lord is right there with you, and He'll be happy to share that moment of bliss with you. So don't waste time feeling sorry for yourself — just open your heart to the Lord and let out that shout!

Sparkling Gems From the Greek, Volume 1

Longevity

There is no reason someone can't live a long life if he or she does what is necessary to take care of his or her body to achieve a longer life.

Fallen Angels, Giants, Monsters,
and the World Before the Flood

It is a grave mistake for more mature people to wrongly believe they are irrelevant due to being older. How tragic to move off the playing field and to sit on the sidelines before they reach an age that holds greater anointing and revelation than they have ever known in the past.

Fallen Angels, Giants, Monsters,
and the World Before the Flood

I have nothing negative to say about anyone who plans to retire at a certain age in life, but for me, there will simply be no retirement. After gaining so much life experience, I believe it would be a grave mistake to move off the playing field to sit on the sidelines. One leader I deeply respect noted that God intends a person's *first* thirty years to be years of learning and preparation, the *second* thirty years to be a time to implement what he or she has learned, and the *third* thirty-plus years to impart what he or she has learned to others. *This is what I believe too!*

Unlikely

Longsuffering

The word "longsuffering" is a translation of a Greek word that depicts *the patient restraint of anger,* and it can be translated *forbearance* or *patience.* Longsuffering is likened to a candle with a very long wick that can burn for an extended period of time. A person who possesses this quality is ready to *forbear* and *to suffer long* as he *patiently waits* for an event or result to transpire.

Last-Days Survival Guide

Although it may appear that Jesus is *slow* or *tardy* in returning to the earth, the "felt" delay is actually because of God's longsuffering.

Christmas — The Rest of the Story

It is the Holy Spirit who *could* take revenge on a sin-ridden society, but who *utterly refuses* to do so. The delay of God's *judgment* is due to God's *longsuffering* and *patience* with those who are unsaved. Indeed, God is willing to wait for the redemption of that *one last person* who will repent. That is the longsuffering of God, and the reason why He has waited and waited to end this age. God is not tardy, delayed, or slow in fulfilling His promise. He is simply holding out for the last soul to be saved.

Fallen Angels, Giants, Monsters,
and the World Before the Flood

For those who still need to come to repentance, God is waiting. But a day will finally come when the last person who is going to be saved is brought into the Kingdom of God, and His wait will be over.

Christmas — The Rest of the Story

Lordship of Jesus

Paul declared that Christ's exalted rank is far above all *human rulers* and all *angelic beings*, which means the natural and spiritual realms are both under the dominion of Jesus Christ — and there is absolutely no one in any realm more highly exalted than Jesus. Although there are individuals who wield substantial power and influence in the affairs of the world, their authority pales in comparison to that of Jesus Christ.

Apostles and Prophets

A day is coming when every knee will bow and every tongue will confess that Jesus Christ is Lord. Philippians 2:10 unequivocally describes a day when every created being in Heaven, in earth, and in hell will all join together in one universe-wide proclamation as they *loudly yell, shout, blurt out*, and *publicly agree* that Jesus Christ is Lord. Even those in hell with no opportunity to repent will publicly *shout out* with the full strength of their voices that Jesus is Lord. Those who reject Jesus Christ and refuse to acknowledge Him in this life will finally fall to their knees and *shout forth* their acknowledgment of His Lordship. However, their confession will come too late to reverse their eternal condition.

A Light in Darkness

Where Paul described Christ as the "head" of the Church in Ephesians 1:22, it emphatically means Christ is the *chief* and *head* of the Church — so *central* that He is the *core* of it. His exalted position also means that God made His greatest spiritual investment in Christ's exalted position, and as such, our focus, affection, and treasure should likewise be invested in His lordship over our lives and over the Church.

Apostles and Prophets

Lot

The story of Lot is the story of a man who had a great beginning, but who later departed from the faith that had been imparted to him. He coaxed himself into believing it was all right to live in the midst of immoral lifestyles and perverse situations that were profane in the sight of God.

**How To Keep Your Head on Straight
in a World Gone Crazy**

In the example of Lot, we see that he veered off course from the walk of faith he knew to accommodate the world around him, and he compromised his experience of faith to adjust to his culture — just as the Holy Spirit warned that some will do toward the end of the Church Age.

How To Keep Your Head on Straight in a World Gone Crazy

Love

Divine love knows no limits or boundaries in how far, wide, high, and deep it will go to show that love to its recipient.

Last-Days Survival Guide

Agape occurs when an individual *sees, recognizes, understands, and appreciates the value of an object or a person,* causing him to behold this object or person in great esteem, awe, admiration, wonder, and sincere appreciation. Such great respect is awakened in the heart of the observer for the object or person he is beholding that he is *compelled* to love. In fact, his love for that person or object is so strong, it is *irresistible.* This kind of love knows no limits or boundaries in how far, wide, high, and deep it will go to show love to its recipient. If necessary, *agape* love will even sacrifice itself for the sake of that object or person it so deeply cherishes. *Agape* is therefore the *highest, finest, most noble,* and *most fervent* form of love.

A Light in Darkness

Nothing in this world has enough power to disconnect you from the love of God. No angel, no demon, no government, no creature — and no mistake of your own making — will ever be capable of cutting you off from the love of God.

God's love is greater than man will ever be able to comprehend. It reaches to the highest mountain, and it penetrates to the lowest parts of the earth. Regardless of what you are facing in your life today, God's love is with you — and nothing will ever be able to disconnect you from this awesome, powerful, all-consuming love!

Sparkling Gems From the Greek, Volume 1

Out of His deep love for you and me, Jesus was willing to leave His majestic realms of glory to enter the sphere of humanity. Shedding all His visible attributes that were too much for man's flesh to endure, He dressed Himself in the clothing of a human being and was manifested in the flesh.

Christmas — The Rest of the Story

When God looked upon the human race, He stood in awe of mankind, even though man was lost in sin. God admired man; He wondered at man; He held mankind in the highest appreciation. Even though mankind was held captive by Satan at that moment, God looked upon the world and saw His own image in man. The human race was so *precious* to God and He loved man so deeply that His heart was stirred to reach out and do something to save him. In other words, God's love drove Him to action.

Sparkling Gems From the Greek, Volume 1

God has placed His love deep inside your "heart-closet." But you are the only one with the power to open the doors to that place where it is kept, take it off the hanger, and put it on. Furthermore, when you are tempted to take that love off and put it back in the closet out of anger or disappointment, remember that you alone can decide to adorn yourself in this *agape* love of God. So open your heart, reach inside, pull it out, and be determined to stay dressed in the love of God!

Sparkling Gems From the Greek, Volume 2

Lovers of Pleasure

Seeking pleasure and having happiness are not God's greatest will for you. His greatest will for your life is that you truly love Him and are *obedient*. If you are wholeheartedly doing God's will, you will find joy that is longer lasting than fleeting happiness.

Last-Days Survival Guide

When Paul wrote in Second Timothy 3:4 that people would be "lovers of pleasure more than lovers of God," he was *not* saying these people wouldn't love God. His meaning was that their love of pleasure would have *a higher rank than* and would *exceed* their love for God.

Last-Days Survival Guide

I don't know any Christian who would openly confess that he loved pleasures more than he loved God — but *a person's actions speak louder than his words* — and actions reveal the truth about what a person loves and values most.

Last-Days Survival Guide

M

Magi

Magi were an elite, powerful, fabulously wealthy group of high-ranking priests who were devoted to interpreting dreams and studying the constellations. In fact, Magi gained an international reputation for being experts at studying the constellations, which was regarded as a science at that time. Thus, they were a combination of scientists, politicians, and religious leaders — and they were staggeringly wealthy.

Christmas — The Rest of the Story

Magi possessed so much might and political clout that, if they chose to do so, and if they, as a group, agreed to it, they had the ability to depose a king with a single word. Or with a single word, they could install a new king of their preference in the place of the one they deposed. Indeed, they were viewed as *king-makers* in Eastern lands. Without their endorsement, it would have been difficult for anyone to become or to remain a king.

Christmas — The Rest of the Story

When the Magi came to worship Jesus, the gifts they brought Him were so numerous that it required many animals and servants to carry the cargo that overflowed with these treasures. They knew they were coming to see a king so great that the constellations announced His birth, and they brought gifts commensurate with His heavenly status.

Christmas — The Rest of the Story

Manna

In order for us to do what God asks us to do, we must eat of God's table and receive of His grace. Just as manna was provided to sustain God's people in the wilderness and angels' food was provided to replenish and strengthen Elijah in his time of need, God has divine provision for us. We will be replenished, strengthened, and enabled to overcome the most difficult circumstances *if* we will draw near to His table and eat the heavenly bread He has set before us.

No Room for Compromise

Rabbinical literature asserts that manna fell in the wilderness each day in such abundance that one day's supply of manna would have been enough to feed the children of Israel for 2,000 years! But despite this overabundance, God forbade the Israelites to take more than one day's supply per person except in the case of the Sabbath, in which case they were allowed to collect two days at once in order to avoid breaking the Sabbath laws. If anyone gathered more than what God prescribed, the extra became filled with maggots. This was doubtlessly a great test of obedience for many people, since the human tendency would have been to hoard manna just in case it didn't fall again. However, hoarding manna would have caused the Israelites to trust in their *supply* rather than trust in *the God who supplies*. By gathering only a single day's ration, it meant that they had to trust God anew for His faithful provision each day.

Sparkling Gems From the Greek, Volume 2

Those who make the decision to break away from the world will reap a bounty of spiritual power, holiness, and eternal rewards. If they will come to His table, Christ will personally provide the manna they need — *a divine touch* — to strengthen and replenish them so they can finish their race and complete their divine assignment. *He will provide the manna needed to stay strong for the journey!*

No Room for Compromise

Mannequins (Spiritual)

We are living in a strange age when "spiritual mannequins" are all around us — whether dressed in religious garb or sitting in our pews. They speak in religious terms and use Bible language and symbols, but they have stepped away from the Scriptures and from the authentic power of God. They are not true, living witnesses of the Gospel of Jesus Christ but simply hollow shells that imitate the real Church.

Last-Days Survival Guide

Imagine a mannequin dressed like a minister — in religious attire with a gold-chained cross draped across its chest — posed with a Bible in its hands. A good mannequin artist could dress it to bear a striking resemblance to a real minister of the Gospel. In fact, someone might even actually mistake this mannequin for being a real minister.

It would certainly have all the right outward trappings, yet it'd be nothing more than a shell — a form dressed in religious clothes. Paul prophesied a time would come when some within the Church would dress themselves in religious paraphernalia or "look the part" — but, like mannequins, would be empty shells, inwardly lifeless.

Last-Days Survival Guide

No one is immune to becoming a mere "form of godliness." Even the most sincere and devoted believers can gradually become a spiritual mannequin over time.

Last-Days Survival Guide

Marriage

The union between a husband and wife is God's most precious gift of relationship besides the gift of a relationship with Himself through Jesus Christ.

Last-Days Survival Guide

God intended for marriage to be a joint venture. Whenever a spouse is treated as less than an equal partner, that spouse can become deeply discouraged regarding the marriage relationship. This discouragement, if not corrected, leads to bitterness, hurt, and hardness of heart. This is why it is so essential that a husband learn to esteem his wife as his partner in life, which is precisely who God called her to be. If the husband's perception of her is anything other than this, he must renew his mind to the truth of God's Word and learn to value and appreciate her. He also needs to find ways to show his wife that he counts her as his most valued partner and friend.

Sparkling Gems From the Greek, Volume 1

Most marriage problems are communication problems.

Promotion

All you can do is your best, so I encourage you to let that be your goal in your marriage. You cannot answer for another's heart or what your spouse is unwilling to do, but you *will* answer for your own heart and your own obedience to the Lord. So make sure you have done everything He has required of you so you are able to truthfully say you did all you knew to do to make your marriage work.

Last-Days Survival Guide

What you sow is exactly what you reap — and it is far better for spouses to sow mercy and forgiveness than to get into the business of sowing bitterness. Even though it may seem very difficult to forgive and to let go of an offense, it is far easier to take this route than to sow wrong seed and thus get trapped in a destructive cycle of sowing and reaping bitterness and strife that will ultimately hurt you, your marriage, and your children.

Sparkling Gems From the Greek, Volume 1

God's power is ready and willing *right now* to go to work on any marriage that is submitted to His Word, His authority, and His power — and never forget that God specializes in raising dead things back to life again.

Last-Days Survival Guide

Mental Laziness

Digital devices provide information so quickly that *thinking* is virtually no longer needed, and as people use their devices more and more, their minds are inundated with stimulating visual images and constantly updated information. A great deal of that information is unverified, yet largely believed, because easy access to information has resulted in *mental laziness*. After all, why should a person *think* when the device he is using can do the thinking and analyzing for him?

How To Keep Your Head on Straight
in a World Gone Crazy

Although digital advancements have brought positive changes to our modern society, these advancements have also been gradually crippling people's ability to think beyond a surface level — and this situation is becoming so serious that experts assert this may be the most gullible and easy-to-deceive generation that has ever lived. How ironic that the most brilliant, innovative engineers in history have created a digital world that is now producing what may be the most non-thinking generation in recent times — or perhaps ever!

How To Keep Your Head on Straight
in a World Gone Crazy

Mercy

Even Christians who spend hours praying, reading the Word, and seeking to live a holy life sometimes get in the flesh, doing and saying things they later regret. It's just part of being human. When we receive our glorified bodies and go to Heaven, all our inconsistencies, mood swings, and complex emotions will be gone. Until then, we have to stay in an attitude of forgiveness and extend the same mercy to others that we expect them to extend to us.

Sparkling Gems From the Greek, Volume 2

Take the route of mercy, and you'll never be sorry. Believe it or not, there are times when you're supposed to shut your eyes to what you saw someone else do and just let it go! *If you give mercy to others, you'll receive a harvest of mercy when you need it in your own life.*

You Can Get Over It

When you are tempted to be judgmental about other people's self-imposed problems, it would be good for you to remember the many times God's mercy has intervened to save you from messy situations that you created yourself. Even though you deserved to get in trouble, God loved you enough to come right alongside you and help you pull things together so you could get out of that mess. Now whenever you see others in trouble, you have the opportunity to be an extension of God's mercy to them.

Paid in Full

A good rule to live by is to give the same grace and mercy to others that you want them to extend to you!

Sparkling Gems From the Greek, Volume 1

Mind

The *mind* is an area that many Christians have never officially surrendered to God. They have given Him their heart in the new birth, but often their thinking remains in their own control.

Christmas — The Rest of the Story

Whoever controls a person's mind also controls that person's life, and the enemy knows this! Therefore, he seeks to penetrate a person's intellect — a person's mental control center — so he can flood it with deception and falsehood, for once this is accomplished, the devil can then begin to manipulate that person from a position of control.

Dressed To Kill

Have you ever said, "Lord, I officially present my mind as my sacrifice to You. It's Yours and no longer mine. My memory banks and thinking capacity are at Your disposal once and for all"?

Apostles and Prophets

Every moment of every day, we are called to keep our hearts sensitive and our minds engaged so we can keep our heads on straight!

How To Keep Your Head on Straight in a World Gone Crazy

Because the devil loves to make a playground out of your mind and emotions, you must deal with him like the enemy he is. Rather than fall victim to the devil's attacks, you must make a mental decision to seize every thought he tries to use to penetrate your mind and emotions. Rather than let those thoughts take you captive, you have to reach up and grab them and *force* them into submission! You must take *every* thought captive to the obedience of Christ!

Sparkling Gems From the Greek, Volume 1

Freedom becomes a way of life only as we replace our wrong thinking and wrong believing with what the Word of God declares about our new condition. If these "residual areas" from the past are not removed through the renewing of the mind by the Word of God, these strongholds can and will continue to exert power in the life of a Christian. And if these "residual areas" are not dealt with according to the Word, these are the very areas that Satan will use to wage warfare against that person's new life.

Dressed To Kill

Most of the attacks the devil wages against you will occur in your mind. By poisoning your mind with unbelief and lying strongholds, the devil can then manipulate not only your mind, but also your emotions and your body. There is no doubt about it — the mind is the strategic center where the battle is won or lost in spiritual warfare!

Sparkling Gems From the Greek, Volume 1

Once a mind has become *debased*, it takes a great commitment to renew it — but the good news is that God offers hope for a believer who has strayed from the clear teaching of Scripture. The Holy Spirit will do the miracle of taking his or her sin-damaged mind and renewing it to a right, holy, fit condition — a mind that is once again esteemed by God!

How To Keep Your Head on Straight
in a World Gone Crazy

There is no better mental protection against the enemy's strategies than to fill your brain with God's Word! It will strengthen you and keep your mind free from unbelief and lying strongholds.

Sparkling Gems From the Greek, Volume 1

Ministers

A minister speaks on behalf of Christ, and to accurately represent Him, he doesn't have the authority to mitigate the truth or to change the message to satisfy his listeners. Regardless of the people's response, he is required by God to lift his voice loud enough to make the Lord's message clearly heard and to accurately deliver the truth entrusted to him by Jesus Christ.

A Light in Darkness

Considering the myriad distractions of life, it can be a real challenge for God's spokesmen to find time to fully devour, consume, concoct, and digest the words God gives them to impart before their next meeting. As a result, many messages are delivered without the power of the Holy Spirit, even though they are delivered in a professional and timely manner. For a message from God to be preached in the power of the Holy Spirit, a prophet must fill his inner being with the word that God has imparted and let it affect him completely, for only then can he step into the pulpit and publicly deliver a word from God with authority and power.

Apostles and Prophets

The Holy Spirit forewarns those who claim to speak on behalf of God that they will ultimately be scrutinized by God Himself, who will watch to see if what they endorse or teach is correct and in agreement with the entire body of Scripture. This means every word, every phrase, and every nuance that is spoken in a public forum is significant to God.

Apostles and Prophets

Ministry

God expects us to be passionately committed to using the gifts He has given us in such a way that pleases Him and meets the needs of others.

Why We Need the Gifts of the Holy Spirit

We live in a day when Christianity has in many ways become computerized, highly mechanical, and mass-produced. Thank God for all of these technological advances — and because of them, the Gospel is being spread to every corner of the world — but we must never forget that the Gospel needs a personal touch. It's so easy to reach people through television, radio, satellite, the Internet, the mail, and so on, that some people have come to neglect the warm, caring, personal ministry that should *always* accompany the Gospel.

Life in the Combat Zone

Regardless of where you live or what you believe God has asked you to do, it is important that you give your whole heart and soul to your divine assignment. Even if it is difficult sometimes, you must keep pressing forward toward your God-given goal in obedience to the Lord. And whenever the way of obedience seems difficult, you need to remind yourself once again of His promise that "your labor is not in vain in the Lord" (1 Corinthians 15:58).

Sparkling Gems From the Greek, Volume 2

Public ministry begins in a person's private life.

Promotion

Most *calls to the ministry don't begin in the pulpit!* Do you think God is going to hand you the pulpit out of the clear blue and say, "There you go — now *preach*!" You'd better pray it doesn't happen that way, because you won't be ready!

Life in the Combat Zone

Make the decision not to permit yourself to be disturbed or disappointed because the number of people at a meeting is smaller than you anticipated. Even if the numbers are small, it may be that you have reached the heart of someone who will one day have great influence and power — and that would make your results very successful indeed!

Sparkling Gems From the Greek, Volume 2

Always remember — this isn't our work we're doing — it's the work of the Lord. No work we do is more important than what we do in His name!

Promotion

Miracles

If you want the supernatural power of God to be a part of your life, the Bible must be central — for wherever the Word is authoritatively proclaimed, embraced, believed, and acted upon, the power of God is released!

A Life Ablaze

Jesus' physical absence didn't stop early believers from performing miracles, raising the dead, casting out demons, healing the sick, or bringing multitudes to a saving knowledge of Jesus Christ. Because the Holy Spirit was with them, this meant the ministry of Jesus continued uninterrupted in their midst.

Paid in Full

For many Christians, the miracle working power of Jesus Christ is like a fairy tale. When they read about the miracles He performed, they relegate His miracle-working power to a limited historical time frame that is long past and to a people who are no longer alive. The only thing they really know regarding Jesus' power is what they have read in the Bible. Never having personally witnessed His miracle-working power, they can only fantasize and try to imagine what His miracles must have been like. But God never intended for Jesus to be only a historical figure who did something in the past. Jesus is alive *today*, and through the ministry of the Holy Spirit and His gifts, Jesus brings His supernatural reality right into the midst of the local church!

Sparkling Gems From the Greek, Volume 1

Early believers understood their complete dependence upon the Holy Spirit, and they lived *ablaze* with His power. They healed the sick, cast out demons, raised the dead, and testified to the living reality of Jesus Christ as the miraculous abounded among them.

A Life Ablaze

If you haven't been experiencing the supernatural in your life, it may be a signal that you haven't been releasing your faith to see signs and wonders follow you. Remember, these signs *always* follow wherever the Gospel is preached and believers are believing for them to occur. This was Jesus' promise! He guaranteed that God's supernatural signature would be on anyone who preaches the Gospel and who opens the way for the supernatural to come to pass *by believing*.

Sparkling Gems From the Greek, Volume 1

Think of the profound effect that a single miracle would have on your circle of friends and the people you know.

Sparkling Gems From the Greek, Volume 2

I have observed that people who regularly experience the miraculous are those who regularly expect to see it. Rather than being passive, they are very aggressive about pushing forward in the Spirit to see the miraculous manifested in their lives or ministries. Those who press forward and release their faith to see the supernatural demonstrated are the ones who often experience these divine demonstrations in their lives.

A Life Ablaze

You and I should never forget the marvelous things we have witnessed God do in our own lives so that we can share them with others too!

Christmas — The Rest of the Story

If signs aren't regularly following you, ask the Holy Spirit to reignite the flame of passion in your heart to see the supernatural signature of God on your life. He wants to show up when you preach or share the Gospel! He wants to authenticate and guarantee that the life-transforming message you share with those who need to hear it is truly Heaven-sent.

A Life Ablaze

Missions

Jesus provided everything needed for those of us who would follow His call to the ends of the earth. He supplied us with supernatural protection from disasters, calamities, snakes, scorpions, and all the works of the enemy. He also promised traveling mercies and protection from acts of injustice. He even guaranteed that if we accidentally consume bad foods or deadly substances, they wouldn't weaken us physically or injure our health. He covered the gamut of protection, provision, and prosperity as we obey His calling and do His will!

A Life Ablaze

Jesus sent his followers to the farthest ends of the world. To fulfill this assignment, they were required to eat foods they had never seen before. In fact, their journeys to pagan lands would have no doubt necessitated that they eat foods they previously considered to be dirty or unclean. For them to take the Gospel to new places meant they had to eat "mystery food" — not knowing where it came from, who killed it, how long it had been dead, who cooked it, how clean or dirty the kitchen was in which it was cooked, or what effect the food was going to have on their stomachs.

A Life Ablaze

If you want the promise of supernatural protection from bad foods or fatal substances to be a reality in your own life, you must release your faith and activate this promise. So before you sit down to eat, take a few minutes to bless that food. Call it sanctified, and speak health, wholeness, and freedom into your body. Then eat the food, believing that it will only bless you and that nothing negative can happen to you as a result of eating it!

A Life Ablaze

It's time for you to quit worrying and start believing that Jesus meant what He said. If God is giving you an assignment that takes you to a foreign state, a distant country, or an unfamiliar culture, just keep your eyes fixed on Jesus and start moving forward in that assignment.

A Life Ablaze

Mistakes

When a person has passion without knowledge, he makes passionate *mistakes*.

Build Your Foundation

Sometimes people are paralyzed by not knowing answers to issues of the past while God is endeavoring to simply give them the grace to move forward. Someday God will show all of us how we could have done some things differently, so don't be disturbed if you don't always know the reason for everything that happens or what should have been done differently. What's important is that if you have made a mistake and you've gotten off track, you repent and get back on track again.

Unlikely

Money

How you handle your finances is a very spiritual issue!

Sparkling Gems From the Greek, Volume 2

Jesus made it very clear that where a person's treasure is — where his money is — reveals where his heart will be also. So if you want to know where a person's heart is, follow his money, because *money tells the truth*! The way he spends his money will tell the whole story of what he prizes, cherishes, loves, and adores.

Promotion

Riches are uncertain. Just ask those who thought they were financially set for life but then lost almost all their fortunes through a sudden change in the stock market. There are many people who wake up in the morning rich but go to bed that same night financially insolvent. Paul tells us that instead of putting our hope in finances that are uncertain, we are to fix our hope "in the living God" (1 Timothy 6:17). If your sense of security rests in your financial portfolio and then your portfolio diminishes or disappears, you could be thrown into an enormous identity crisis that results in great fear, anxiety, and insecurity. But when your trust is in the Lord, you are never shaken no matter what happens in the material realm.

Sparkling Gems From the Greek, Volume 1

Over the years, we've rarely had money up front to start any project God has given us. It is just remarkable to me that when God has given us an assignment, He has never based that assignment on how much we had sitting in our bank account. But if we're really hearing from God — willingly doing what He says to do *when He says to do it* and refusing to budge from our task — He will richly provide *everything* we need to get the job done.

Unlikely

If you aren't faithful, responsible, and trustworthy with money, which is the lowest form of power in this earthly realm, why would God promote you into greater levels of spiritual power, responsibility, and authority? Your money — how you handle it, how you manage it, and what you do with it — is far more important than you've ever realized.

Sparkling Gems From the Greek, Volume 2

Moral Confusion

It is simply a fact that we are watching moral confusion rage among the civilized nations of the world as never before in our lifetime. This moral confusion is perhaps no clearer anywhere than in the debate over gender identity — a manifestation of confusion so severe that it stuns most thinking minds.

Signs You'll See Just Before Jesus Comes

As a result of abandonment of truth and throwing away of moral foundations, moral confusion abounds, and society is teetering on a treacherous path — just as Jesus prophesied in Matthew 24:4.

How To Keep Your Head on Straight
in a World Gone Crazy

Largely unaware of the danger, people of this age ingest an unrelenting mental bombardment from every aspect of society of wrong people, wrong sources, wrong information, and wrong spiritual influences — it's all part of the satanic war being waged against the human race (including believers) to adversely affect people's thought processes, to undermine their core belief system, and to damage and disfigure their minds until they can no longer see what is *wrong* about *wrong*.

Last-Days Survival Guide

Only an on-fire, committed remnant that fixes their eyes and their hearts on Jesus will avoid the moral debasement that will occur throughout a last-days society.

Signs You'll See Just Before Jesus Comes

Moral Degradation

Believers of *every* generation have had to deal with issues of moral degradation and societal ills in the world around them. The realization that the world is waxing worse and worse is certainly nothing new, but the *rapidity* and the *depth* of moral decline in modern culture over the last mere 100 years are significant. It seems as if all restraints have been thrown off, and we are galloping along on a collision course with the end of an era.

***How To Keep Your Head on Straight
in a World Gone Crazy***

Many areas of the world are embroiled in bloody, long-standing conflicts that are being fueled by a seemingly inexhaustible current of hatred, economic instability, poverty, and desperation on all fronts, and society continues to slide further into immorality as people chase hedonistic thrills and godless lifestyles as substitutes for truth, meaning, and purpose in life. While this degradation increases, Christians who are standing by their beliefs in God's moral absolutes are finding themselves increasingly marginalized and penalized for their faith.

Signs You'll See Just Before Jesus Comes

Mouth

The mouth is the great revealer.

The Will of God — The Key to Your Success

It is significant to note that light was produced at the *mouth* of oil-burning lamps. Similarly, a believer's mouth is the outlet for the Holy Spirit's fire and light to pour forth through the preaching of the Gospel. As dark as this world is today, it is difficult to imagine how much darker it would be if there were no faith-filled believers using their mouths to proclaim the life-giving truth of Jesus Christ.

A Light in Darkness

There simply is no spiritual "law of gravity" powerful enough to permanently hold down and confine what is at the core of a person's being. What is on the inside eventually comes out — and what lies at the core of an individual will ultimately come out of his mouth because *the mouth is the great revealer of what is at a person's core.*

Last-Days Survival Guide

We are all guilty of saying ugly things from time to time simply because we all have tongues! This "tongue" problem is a universal dilemma. The only way our tongue can be subdued, tamed, and brought under control is if we submit it to the control of the Holy Spirit. The Bible says no *man* can tame the tongue, but the Holy Spirit is *well* able to tame the tongue once it has been submitted to His sanctifying power. You don't have to be embarrassed by unruly words that come out of your mouth any longer! By committing your tongue and your mouth to the Lordship of Jesus Christ, you give the Holy Spirit the authority to penetrate this realm of your life with His power and control, and He will help you keep a tight rein on your mouth so you can keep from saying things you will later regret!

Sparkling Gems From the Greek, Volume 1

Move of God

A move of God keeps growing and gaining momentum and strength until it *bursts* into spiritual flames so fierce that darkness simply cannot quench it!

Unlikely

God wants to visit His people with amazing supernatural experiences, and He tells us clearly in His Word that this is a vital part of the working of the Holy Spirit in the Church.

How To Keep Your Head on Straight in a World Gone Crazy

It often happens that during a move of God the first generation of Christians experiences dramatic salvations as that segment of the Church is born in the power of the Spirit. However, the second generation, raised in a Christian environment, often doesn't experience the same radical deliverance their parents did. Of course, it should be the goal of all believing parents to raise their children in a godly environment; however, they can never stop working diligently to keep the fires of spiritual passion burning. As each successive generation becomes more accustomed to a Christian environment — learning to speak the language of the church, sing the songs of the church, and act the way "church" people should act — it becomes easy for the younger generations to slip into a mindset of familiarity. Too often this produces apathy in people's hearts, ultimately leading them to take the redemptive work of Christ for granted. Therefore, the potential for spiritual fires to die down and become a pile of smoldering embers increases dangerously with each new generation. The only way for each local body and its members to avoid that process is to become unrelenting in their commitment to retain their spiritual passion for Christ.

Sparkling Gems From the Greek, Volume 2

I have experienced the book of Acts in all its aspects — miracles, signs, wonders, and mighty deeds — as God has moved upon these precious lands. When modern Church history is recorded, I am confident that what has occurred in the lands of the former USSR will be memorialized as one of the greatest advancements of the Gospel to ever occur in such a brief window of time.

How To Keep Your Head on Straight
in a World Gone Crazy

As faith-filled believers, we have a victorious perspective of the signs we're seeing in the world today because they indicate Jesus will return soon! Indeed, we know that we are living at the very end of the last days — in the last "minutes and seconds" of the age — so with diligence and fervor, we are awaiting a last-days move of the Holy Spirit and the reaping of a great harvest of souls before Christ returns!

Signs You'll See Just Before Jesus Comes

Moving On

Just think what could happen if *you* moved into the next season of your life where God is calling you! You may be getting ready to move into the most miraculous season of your life. It may be that God has things planned for you that are beyond your wildest imagination. He simply needs you to be in the right place at the right time — and that depends on your willingness *to follow* and *to obey!*

Sparkling Gems From the Greek, Volume 2

Have you ever come to a place in your life when you knew that your present season was ending and that it was time to move on — no matter how glorious or wonderful that season had been? When a phase of your spiritual walk is finished, it can never be extended or repeated, and all you can do is move forward toward the next new assignment God gives you.

The Point of No Return

Every so often, occasions come to us in life — landmark moments when we must choose to make a break with where we are in order to move into the new place where God is calling us. Such moments can be difficult. However, just beyond our struggle is where we discover the greatest joy and power of God.

Sparkling Gems From the Greek, Volume 2

If we will listen to the Holy Spirit, He will show us when to speak and when to be quiet — when to stay and when to move on. We must learn to be sensitive to the voice of the Holy Spirit in every situation. Then we can know when we are to remain in the battle or when it is wiser for us to withdraw, break camp, and relocate to new territory where greater victories will be won. The Holy Spirit will lead us — *if* we will quiet our hearts and listen for His voice.

A Light in Darkness

Mutiny (Against God)

The Bible explicitly foretold of a worldwide mutiny against God that would eventually come. By observing the cultural changes that are developing all around us, we get an unmistakable feeling that we are already in the middle of this creeping rebellion.

How To Keep Your Head on Straight
in a World Gone Crazy

A worldwide mutinous attitude is developing toward God and His Word — and as before, it will eventually be met with a harvest of judgment.

How To Keep Your Head on Straight
in a World Gone Crazy

The radical changes in society that we are experiencing are just the tip of the iceberg — just the beginning of a worldwide mutiny that Paul prophesied about so long ago — and according to the prophetic teaching of Scripture, societal and cultural changes will worsen as time passes.

Last-Days Survival Guide

Just as the Holy Spirit foretold, we are witnessing an escalating mutiny against God and the voice of Scripture in our time, as the "mystery of iniquity" is being released with a vengeance and is working full steam around the clock to seduce the world into mass deception.

How To Keep Your Head on Straight
in a World Gone Crazy

Mythology

In nearly every early culture there are memories of a time when celestial beings entered the earth's atmosphere to philander with women who gave birth to demigods, hybrid creatures, and giants. When the fallen angels descended with their dazzling appearances into the atmosphere of the earth, it must have looked like gods had descended, thus the reason people at that time welcomed them and participated in their spiritually criminal activities.

Fallen Angels, Giants, Monsters,
and the World Before the Flood

Images of monstrous beasts can be found in cave drawings, primeval structures, formations, stone tablets, carvings, and in a sundry of ancient artifacts. Although they have different names in varying ancient religions, they are essentially the same creatures. The odds that these creatures would appear regularly in the remains and artifacts of nearly all ancient civilizations who had little contact with each other is statistically almost impossible. For these stories to be told so consistently without a thread of truth being behind them is nearly zero.

Fallen Angels, Giants, Monsters,
and the World Before the Flood

Name of Jesus

If you find yourself in the presence of evil, don't shrink back in fear! Release your faith, lift your voice, and take authority over the devil's strategies in the name of Jesus — and as you do, you'll send those evil, malevolent powers scurrying away in terror! Then release the peace and the love of God into the situation, and God's power will go into operation to calm those who had been adversely affected by that demonic influence and to turn that situation completely around according to God's purposes and to His glory!

Sparkling Gems From the Greek, Volume 2

I have occasionally found myself in a confrontation with a demonized person. Just like the stories referred to in the Bible, I have heard demons speak, and I have seen them exercise physical power beyond human ability. But in each case, I have also seen them *wilt* and *shrink* when the name of Jesus is employed against them!

Sparkling Gems From the Greek, Volume 2

The name "Jesus" was a name the Herod household had heard for *years*. As sons of Herod the Great, they had heard tales about Jesus' supernatural birth, the kings from the East who had come to acknowledge Him, the failed attempt of their father to kill Jesus by ordering the murder of all the babies in Bethlehem, Jesus and His parents slipping into Egypt and waiting for the right moment to return to Israel, and the ministry of Jesus touching the nation with healing and delivering power. Because these stories of Jesus were so very familiar to the Herod household, Herod Antipas wished to personally meet this famous personality.

Christmas — The Rest of the Story

The devil knows that he is a lawbreaker. He also knows that if a believer stands against him — in other words, if the believer resists the enemy by using his God-given authority in the name of Jesus and the Word of God — it won't be long until that believer begins to rule and dominate the devil. Instead of sticking around and trying hopelessly to defend himself against the name of Jesus and the Word of God, the devil tucks his tail and runs!

Sparkling Gems From the Greek, Volume 1

If the enemy has gained ground in your family, you can stand on God's Word and use your authority in the name of Jesus to *take back* that territory and recapture whatever has been lost!

Last-Days Survival Guide

Natural Catastrophes

Scripture clearly teaches that natural catastrophes of unusual proportions will be witnessed in the last of the last days.

Last-Days Survival Guide

We must weep with those who weep and do all we can to lift up and come to the aid of fellow believers who are downtrodden or struck by catastrophe — whether it occurs from natural disasters, outbreaks of sickness and disease, scarcity and hunger, or persecution.

Signs You'll See Just Before Jesus Comes

There's no way to avoid the end-time prophecies outlined in the Bible — troubles *will* increase on the earth in the days ahead. However, these troubles are prime opportunities for those of us who know God and are called according to His purposes. By God's power, we can walk in faith through every fiery trial and become sources of supernatural provision to meet the needs of those who are suffering, demonstrating His love, grace, and wisdom to those who don't yet know His saving power in their lives.

Sparkling Gems From the Greek, Volume 2

Needs

It is easy to think of your own needs and desires, but how often do you focus your prayers on the concerns of others? When you pray, does God hear you primarily praying for yourself, or does God hear you praying for other people too? *If God were to give a report about the things He hears you pray about, would He report that you are an unselfish person who is concerned about the needs and dreams of others, or would He report that you are concerned only about yourself and your own needs?*

Sparkling Gems From the Greek, Volume 2

There are so many human needs in this world, and no one person, ministry, or organization can meet them all. But we are each responsible to respond to the nudge of the Holy Spirit to help those He brings across our path. If we'll each respond to the distinct nudges we feel from Him — one by one, many needs will be met. And through those acts of goodness, Jesus will touch hearts in a very tangible way.

Sparkling Gems From the Greek, Volume 2

Look around you, assess the various needs you see, and decide which needs you may be able to help meet. Prayerfully determine how your talents, gifts, and money can best be used to help others. Then go for it "full throttle!"

Sparkling Gems From the Greek, Volume 2

Neutrality

When we're in neutral, it may outwardly look like we're going somewhere, but inwardly we are merely running in place.

Dream Thieves

Neutrality is one of the worst enemies you will ever face in this life. It is a thief that can insidiously worm its way into your life and overtake you without you even being aware of its presence.

Dream Thieves

The word "slothful" comes from a Greek word that describes *something that is dull, monotonous, or unexciting; something that is slow and sluggish*; or *something that has lost its speed or momentum*. This "something" is still moving, but it has lost the drive, thrust, impetus, pace, and speed it once possessed. This word presents the idea of someone who was once zealous about something but whose zeal has now dissipated and been replaced instead by *neutrality*. Thus, the word doesn't present the picture of laziness; rather, it speaks of someone who has lost his zeal or his intense conviction about a matter that once was of great importance to him. It denotes a person who has become *disinterested* and whose zeal has been replaced with a *middle-of-the-road, take-it-or-leave it* mentality.

Sparkling Gems From the Greek, Volume 1

Nicolaitanism

Jesus was *repulsed* by the teachings of the Nicolaitans and *loathed* their presence. While He loved them as individuals, He found their teachings to be *utterly objectionable*.

Sparkling Gems From the Greek, Volume 2

Christ *never* said He hated the Nicolaitans themselves. What He hated was their compromising influence that caused believers to be lured back into a relationship with the world and dragged down into the sin from which they had been delivered. Their defiling deeds and doctrines may have purchased a temporary truce with the world, but it would ultimately result in catastrophic consequences for Christians. Christ died for the Nicolaitans as much as He died for anyone, but He hated the destructive influence of what they were teaching within the Christian community.

No Room for Compromise

Modern Nicolaitanism dresses itself in the guise of being *open-minded*. It cries that it is unfair and unjust to assert that beliefs alone are the absolute foundation for truth. Even if we choose to believe what we believe, this way of thinking makes allowances that we could be wrong or that others are equally right but with a different approach. It leaves no room for there to be such a thing as absolute truth or absolute morality.

Sparkling Gems From the Greek, Volume 2

When Jesus addressed the Nicolaitan leaders in the Bible, He stated that He would make a direct path to them, and this can only be interpreted as *a direct threat*. For Christ to speak in such strong words reveals that He had already warned them and given them an opportunity to respond — and because they had repeatedly ignored His pleas, the opportunity to avoid judgment was swiftly coming to a close. By lifting His voice loud and clear, Christ was providing one last opportunity for these errant leaders to repent and thus avoid the repercussions of His discipline. This was an act of love and a merciful plea to those who were leading others astray to *change* before He was required to take a more severe course of action.

No Room for Compromise

No Compromise

Before the clock stops and time runs out on this present age, we as believers are to remain vitally connected to Jesus and refuse to compromise. We're called to strengthen the weak, mend the broken, heal the sick, and win the lost for whom Christ died.

Signs You'll See Just Before Jesus Comes

The issue of compromise is deeply disturbing because it is a trade-off with the world and a willingness to assimilate with pagan culture in order to avoid persecution. Compromise may seem like a smart choice in helping some weather the storm of opposition, but in truth, it jeopardizes the Church's holiness, weakens the power of the Holy Spirit among them, and nullifies their witness for Christ. It is absolutely essential that believers stand firm, steadfastly refusing to compromise in the face of worldly pressures.

No Room for Compromise

What happens when the Church ceases to stand for truth or to live holy lives separate from the world? It produces a weak Church so contaminated with spiritual sickness that very little power remains in it.

How To Keep Your Head on Straight
in a World Gone Crazy

The changes taking place in the world in the closing days will result in one of two choices for every believer: a decision to accommodate the world or a refusal to compromise — but *riding the fence will no longer be an option.* Those who make no room for compromise may face the backlash of a society that grows increasingly intolerant of those who stand for moral absolutes. Yet these faithful and unwavering believers can expect the empowering of the Holy Spirit to uphold them and cause them to triumph in Christ who gives them strength.

Signs You'll See Just Before Jesus Comes

Jesus does not tolerate those who propagate doctrinal error or teaching that leads to compromise. Jesus died for the Church, and as the Great Shepherd of the sheep, He will guard it and stand *against* those who jeopardize its holiness, power, and accurate representation of Him to this world!

No Room for Compromise

No Fear of God

If society respects, recognizes, and acknowledges God, it results in enlightenment — but the opposite is also true. When the fear and knowledge of God is diminished and society begins to move away from Him, this is a spiritual "chemical mix" that will always produce an environment where *intellectual nonsense* — conclusions that don't make either rational or spiritual sense — become the inevitable consequence.

How To Keep Your Head on Straight
in a World Gone Crazy

A *casual* approach to God is usually an *irreverent* approach that doesn't include the thought of accountability or eternity.

Last-Days Survival Guide

When the knowledge and fear of God is removed, a vacuum is formed, causing intellectual and spiritual darkness to flood in and fill the void.

Last-Days Survival Guide

When people turn away from God, rather than getting smarter, they regress and become more and more *preposterous* in their reasoning, deliberations, calculations, and thinking processes.

How To Keep Your Head on Straight
in a World Gone Crazy

When people lose their fear of God, they begin to *tolerate* what was once intolerable and ultimately *do* what they once condemned as wrong and displeasing to Him.

Last-Days Survival Guide

Nourishment

You may feel that insurmountable odds are arrayed against you but know that you are not the first person to feel this way. If you stay in faith and refuse to budge, it's only a matter of time until you will outlast the attacks of your enemy the devil. And God promises special supernatural nourishment for those who stay in the fight!

Sparkling Gems From the Greek, Volume 2

Regardless of the obstacle that challenges you, God's Spirit will empower you to stand strong until the fight is won. Not only that, but He will give you the fortitude to maintain the victory once it has been achieved. He's not interested in you merely winning a skirmish; He wants you to win the final victory and *maintain* that victory once it is achieved. If you'll make the decision to overcome, He'll provide supernatural nourishment to keep you strong all along the way!

Sparkling Gems From the Greek, Volume 2

Novices

Too often, the Church places its official mark of approval on people before they are ready, and new arrivals in a local church are quickly elevated into positions of authority because of their outward appearance or past accomplishments. But time and time again, this practice of quick promotion has been known to result in *catastrophe*.

Life in the Combat Zone

The word "novice" comes from a Greek word that is understood to mean *a new convert* or *a new Christian*, but this word can also refer to *an old plant that is new in your garden* — in other words, it can refer to *a transplant*. Although the newcomer may look good and sound good and their talents may be urgently needed, a hasty decision to promote them before they are really known can result in catastrophe. This means that even if they have years of experience, if they are new in *your* garden — your church, ministry, organization, or business — you need to take the time to know them before you give them vast amounts of authority and responsibility.

Sparkling Gems From the Greek, Volume 1

Obedience

When God asks you to strike out into uncharted territory and accomplish something new and difficult, it can be challenging to bring your will into compliance with what He is asking you to do. Your mind will try to argue as if it knows best, and your flesh will try to drag its feet every step of the way. In these moments, you are faced with a defining moment in your life when you must place your trust in God's plan for your life and obey Him unconditionally.

Sparkling Gems From the Greek, Volume 2

Your obedience to God doesn't guarantee you a trouble-free life. You will always have to stay alert to thwart the attacks of an enemy who continually looks for ways to derail or discourage you as you seek to fulfill what God has asked you to do.

The Will of God — The Key to Your Success

We must not be afraid of the vicious winds of opposition, and neither can we wait until the winds have ceased to plant our seed. If we wait, we will undoubtedly lose our opportunity for harvest. Thus, no matter what winds are blowing, we must seize the opportunity, get out into the field of our God-ordained purpose, pray over our seed, and plant it in the ground of people's hearts. We *cannot* allow the winds to dictate our obedience!

Life in the Combat Zone

A life of obedience is never without cost.

Paid in Full

The longer you walk with God, the more you learn that He foots the bills when you are where He has asked you to be, doing what He has asked you to do. That doesn't mean you won't ever face financial challenges, but when you are doing what God has asked, your obedience opens the door to greater favor and provision.

The Will of God — The Key to Your Success

Never minimize what you are doing *right now*. It is likely that God has not shown you the full picture yet of what He will ask you to do in the future. But what God has asked you to do right now is critically important for your future success. Every single step of obedience builds upon previous steps of obedience. If you don't obediently do what God has assigned to you right now, you will not be prepared for things He will ask you to do in the future.

Unlikely

Obstacles

You will run into many obstacles in life that no one prepared you to face. Most likely people did not deliberately deny you the information — or they may have assumed you already understood, or they may have wrongly believed that you were more prepared than you actually were. But if you have the inward desire to achieve your goal, any obstacle can be overcome, any challenge can be conquered, and any mountain can be successfully climbed. If your level of desire is strong, it doesn't matter if you're ill-equipped or uninformed in certain areas. You *will* complete your assigned task because your inward determination and resolve will not let you give up!

Sparkling Gems From the Greek, **Volume 2**

Don't despair — the story isn't over yet! Don't throw in the towel and give in just because you've hit some kind of impasse. The devil has never had the last word on anything, and he isn't going to have the last word on this situation either. *Regardless of what the devil has tried to do, it's time for you to remember that what God promised SHALL come to pass as you hold fast to your faith in Him!*

Sparkling Gems From the Greek, **Volume 1**

The Bible is packed full of examples of those who heard from God, who took His Word deep into their hearts, and who refused to stop until they saw the fulfillment of what God had promised them. Like you, they faced hardships and challenges, but no matter what obstacles stood in their way, they kept going and never stopped until God's plan for their lives was accomplished. Don't let the devil tell you that you're the only one who has faced this kind of circumstance, because many have gone before you who have faced the same battles and won great victories.

Sparkling Gems From the Greek, **Volume 1**

Over the years, we have faced a lot of bizarre obstacles and challenges as we have followed the call of God on our lives. We learned that the devil is a real enemy who never wants the Kingdom of God to advance and often tries to thwart the plan of God at every turn. That's why anyone who dares to obey God and forges into new territory must determine that he or she is going to get the job done, regardless of the opposition.

Unlikely

Occult

The word "occult" is associated with *secret knowledge*. Nearly all occult practices are designed to enable one *to pry his way* into the spirit realm and, apart from God's help, access the spiritual world in order to obtain information and knowledge. In short, the occult is man's attempt to obtain insights about the future or to access the spirit realm on his own initiative, but one should never forget that if you cross a threshold that is not opened by the initiative of God, it will likely open the door to evil dimensions. If one chooses to open the door to another realm by his own volition, he needs to know that the devil is happy to provide him with an experience that is diametrically opposed to the teachings of the Bible.

Apostles and Prophets

If you are in Christ and walking in obedience to God's Word, you are safe, secure, and sealed in the protective blood of Jesus — and the power of that divine protection can never be breached by someone operating under, or in cooperation with, the powers of Satan. You need never be fearful of any curse assailed against you or your loved one, no matter how dark or "powerful" the vessel through which the curse tries to come. The occult has never been, *and will never be*, a match for the power of God that is inside a believer.

Sparkling Gems From the Greek, Volume 2

Offense

Part of living life victoriously is learning how to refuse to allow offense to sink its stinger into our souls and negatively affect us.

The Will of God — The Key to Your Success

Millions of Christians are held captive by bitterness, resentment, and unforgiveness because they will *not* determine to do what is necessary to live free of offense, and as a result, they have no joy, no peace, and no victory in their lives. They're miserable because they haven't made the choice to jump through the escape hatch God has provided for them and leave all that negative garbage behind.

You Can Get Over It

When you get offended or you find yourself wanting to nitpick someone about what you perceive to be his or her failures, take some time to get quiet before God and ask Him what to do. It may be that His highest will in that situation is for you to simply show forbearance and let go of the matter. Although loving confrontation is needed at times, it is not *always* the right course to take

Sparkling Gems From the Greek, Volume 2

Most grievances are more imagined than real.

You Can Get Over It

The next time you hear that someone has a wrong perception about you, don't let it ruffle your feathers too much. Remember all the times you've had a wrong perception about someone else! You were just so sure that your opinion about that person was right, but then you discovered you were so wrong! If you've perceived others incorrectly at times, why should it surprise you when the same thing occasionally happens to you?

Paid in Full

As long as we live in this world, we're going to have to deal with the potential of being offended. We can't prevent offenses from happening, but we *can* avoid taking offense and getting bitter.

You Can Get Over It

Oil

Oil itself has no healing properties, but in both the Old and New Testaments, it is used symbolically to depict the Presence of the Holy Spirit. By anointing the sick person with oil, the elder uses a tangible substance to declare that the Spirit of God is coming upon the infirmed to bring His healing power. Although the oil itself doesn't heal, the moment it is applied in prayer is the critical moment for the sick person to believe that God's Presence is coming upon him to bring healing to his sick body.

Sparkling Gems From the Greek, Volume 1

Just as oil-burning lamps contained oil, the Church is the container of the Holy Spirit in this world. Although it is true that the weaknesses of God's people are evident, it is even more true that He has graciously chosen to deposit the oil of the Holy Spirit within them — and He has provided a sufficient measure of that divine oil for His Church to extend His life-giving light to the very ends of the earth.

A Light in Darkness

Open Doors

If you sense a door is closing or a season is ending, it may turn out to be one of the best things that has ever happened to you. It may not be comfortable to go through this change, and it may be one of the most difficult things you've ever done. But *if* you put your eyes on the Lord and trust in Him, you'll discover that He is working behind the scenes to prepare the next place for you.

Sparkling Gems From the Greek, Volume 2

When God opens a door of opportunity before you, He also provides sufficient grace to escort you through it. On the other hand, when you presumptuously try to break open a door for yourself, you will quickly discover that ill-timed, forced opportunities are not fruitful.

The Point of No Return

You and I are not brilliant enough to figure out the right timing for everything by our own logic. The timing of our actions must be directed by the Holy Spirit, not by us. If we learn to depend on the Spirit's leading, we will walk through many strategic doors at key moments. But it is imperative that we understand this: When He says *NOW*, He really means *NOW*!

Unlikely

You may not feel ready for your next new assignment from God, but that's all right. When *God* thinks you're ready, He provides the grace and power to *make* you ready. He will mature and equip you for the task. God just wants to hear your heart say *yes* to the next exciting phase of life and open door He is placing before you.

The Point of No Return

Opinions

Being overly concerned about what people think of us and fearing their possible rejection of us is actually a dangerous trap of the enemy that he uses to try to control us. It will either muzzle and silence us from speaking the truth when necessary or provoke us to say what people want to hear!

Sparkling Gems From the Greek, Volume 2

Sometimes the enemy will use people to try to pressure you out of the will of God. If you are overly concerned or driven by what other people think of you, you can become very vulnerable in your Christian walk.

The Will of God — The Key to Your Success

It is what Jesus Christ knows about us that is most important — *not* what we think about ourselves or what others think and say about us.

A Light in Darkness

If voices of unbelief and adverse circumstances try to deter you from your objective, you must *refuse* to let yourself get distracted and veer off course. Keep your attention focused on what *the Lord* has told you to do so you can make it all the way to the end!

The Will of God — The Key to Your Success

Whether you and I like it or not, when we take a step of faith, it almost always puts us "center stage"! Our faith confession or our announced plans will become the dinner conversation among friends, family, associates, and foes. Everyone will seem to develop an opinion as to whether we are overstepping our boundaries by taking on something too big for us, or whether we will be able to fulfill our dream! Many of the people you thought would believe in you and support you instead buy a ticket to the show along with everyone else to watch how well you fare with your new, grand announcement. There will always be spectators who eagerly anticipate the moment they can laugh at you or say, "We told you so!" It's unfortunate — but many times these spectators are not unbelievers, but *believers*!

Sparkling Gems From the Greek, Volume 1

Opportunity

Many people are afraid to obey what the Spirit puts in their hearts to do. Fearful that they will be led astray or that they will make a mistake, they sit on the sidelines and watch other people achieve success, while they remain right where they've always been. Let me tell you something — you can trust the leading of the Holy Spirit! If you will let the Holy Spirit become your eyes and ears, you will learn to recognize key moments and divine opportunities for your life, family, business, or ministry.

Sparkling Gems From the Greek, Volume 1

You will never know what God can do unless you do something that gives Him the opportunity to show you!

Sparkling Gems From the Greek, Volume 2

The time in which we live is your opportunity to shine the light of Jesus into the darkness that has beset so many you meet every day in life. People are looking for solutions to their deeply embedded moral dilemmas, and *you* have the answers they need.

Last-Days Survival Guide

One day when I was praying, the Holy Spirit said: *"Tell people to get the word 'crisis' out of their mouths. Their mouths will either bless them or defeat them — so if they keep saying the word 'crisis' over and over again, they will become ensnared and defeated by the words of their own mouths. They need to start declaring, 'OPPORTUNITY is all around me! There's never been a time of greater opportunity! This is the long-awaited time I've been praying and waiting for. I will be supernaturally blessed, supplied, and provided for in this season!' Again, tell people to get 'crisis' out of their mouths and to begin to say that this is their time of OPPORTUNITY!"*

The Will of God — The Key to Your Success

Time and opportunities that are lost can be *redeemed!* If you are willing to do whatever is needed to make it happen, God will enable you to regain and recoup time that was previously squandered. He can give you more time and another opportunity so wonderful that it makes up for what you previously lost!

Sparkling Gems From the Greek, Volume 2

God has great plans for you. You may not see it right now. In fact, you may be going through a hard time, and it may feel like God has forgotten you. But rather than look at your circumstances, ask God to open your eyes to see His *opportunity*.

The Will of God — The Key to Your Success

Opposition

Satan doesn't hide in the closet and pop out at night to personally attack us while we're sleeping! Because he is the "god of this world," he uses the world to do battle with us. In other words, he uses people, events, situations, circumstances, and difficult dilemmas to obstruct us from reaching our goals.

Sparkling Gems From the Greek, Volume 1

As you dash out of the prayer closet with your word from God and collide with "the patience zone," you'll also become entangled in the wrestling match of your life. Just because God spoke to you about your business, talent, or career, that doesn't mean the dream He planted in your heart will burst onto the scene without resistance or adversity.

Dream Thieves

In the Early Church, believers faced unremitting opposition and were confronted by a host of hostile powers that were arrayed against them. The immoral culture, pagan religions, government, unsaved family and friends — all of these external forces put constant pressure on the early believers to forfeit their faith and return to their old ways — but they firmly believed that if they had endurance, they would survive and outlast all the opposition. They believed that if endurance was operational in their lives, the question was no longer *if* they would overcome their battle — only *when* they would overcome.

A Light in Darkness

Satan comes to challenge you when you are gaining new ground. He waits until growth has begun; then he strikes with an unrelenting force to shove you back into spiritual despair. He wants you to retreat and back off from the frontlines of battle!

Dressed To Kill

To push the forces of hell out of the way, you have to be more determined than hell itself.

Sparkling Gems From the Greek, Volume 1

The path to the fulfillment of dreams is often fraught with difficulties, challenges, and even outright opposition — but at the end of every struggle is a breakthrough, if we're doing God's bidding and staying unflinchingly in our place of faith.

Unlikely

Outpouring of the Holy Spirit

There will be a great outpouring of the Holy Spirit in the last part of the last days — a move of the Spirit like we have never seen before. Those who maintain hungry hearts for the things of God — who are ready to be His hands and feet *and His voice* to a last-days generation — will participate in this great move of the Spirit!

Signs You'll See Just Before Jesus Comes

A huge number of spiritual leaders and Christian believers — like faithful warriors — are digging their heels into the bedrock of Scripture. They are *refusing* to bend with the times, they have determined that they will not accept a watered-down, diluted version of the Bible, and they are holding fast in prayer for a mighty outpouring of God's Spirit upon the Church.

***How To Keep Your Head on Straight
in a World Gone Crazy***

I believe that a great outpouring is not far away, and it will be the most glorious event imaginable! It will be so glorious that masses of people will be converted as a result of God's glory on the Church! This will be *revival* on a scale that causes every previous revival to pale in comparison. This is the last great move of God's Spirit that our hearts have been waiting for!

The Will of God — The Key to Your Success

Overcomers

You and I have been chosen by God to live in this crucial hour — and as part of His Church, we have a spiritual inheritance to lay hold of that will empower us to live as overcomers in the midst of the storm. As we listen to what the Holy Spirit is saying and prepare ourselves by standing on the promises of God's Word, we can expect to experience the empowering strength of the Spirit of Might upholding us and seeing us through to victory in every situation.

Last-Days Survival Guide

Even if it seems like the entire world is trying to wipe you out, you can hold on to the promise that Jesus *has overcome* the world, He *is overcoming* the world, and He *will always overcome* the world. So regardless of what you are facing today, you can hold fast to the truth that Jesus has already overcome the world. He is with you to help you enforce victory in the midst of *whatever* you are facing!

Sparkling Gems From the Greek, Volume 2

When no one else is faithful, you can be sure that God is *always* faithful. He will see to it that you receive the strength and power you need to overcome and triumph in every circumstance.

Paid in Full

We can live as overcomers if we will keep ourselves pure in God's love, maintain the moral code of God in our hearts and homes, watch over our mouths, diligently teach the Word to our children, and shine the light of Jesus into the darkness that has flooded nearly every corner of society.

Last-Days Survival Guide

P

Paganism

Paganism at its core is *religious pluralism*. Its very nature staunchly opposes any message that preaches a single absolute truth above all others.

No Room for Compromise

Early Christians were surrounded by a sea of rampant paganism that frothed all around them. As they sought to live for Christ, these believers faced continual confrontations with the powers of darkness that resulted in bullying, persecution, prejudice, imprisonment, and even death.

No Room for Compromise

Pagan beliefs today are creeping back into homes through education, television, Hollywood, government, and the courts. Since this trend is having such a dangerous impact on our modern society and affects our children and grandchildren, it is vital that we also understand what modern paganism is and how to recognize it.

No Room for Compromise

Parental Authority

A child needs training and guidance from his parents — and believe it or not, he actually craves it!

Last-Days Survival Guide

You have a God-given parental *responsibility* to raise your children in the way they should go — and according to Proverbs 22:6, when you do this, they will not depart from it when they get older. Your God-ordained authority in your home is not just a *right*, it is your God-given *duty* and *responsibility*.

Last-Days Survival Guide

If you know a parent who is leading his children astray by a wrong example, pray for him to change. God can change even the hardest heart. And if you are a father or mother of this next generation, make it a matter of serious prayer and determine to wake up to the awesome responsibility God has charged you with to lead and provide a godly influence for your children and the younger generations in your life. You have the potential of changing young lives as you lead others through your authentic and godly example.

Sparkling Gems From the Greek, Volume 2

Isn't it true that when you're trying to teach a child discipline, it is often the moment when wills collide and that innocent-looking little child can put up the fight of a lifetime! *Isn't it amazing to see how strongly a child can resist your instructions!* At that moment, the conflict between parent and child may seem unending, but the truth is, it is *fleeting* and *temporary*. As tough as it can be to win the battle of wills and teach a child who's in authority, it is necessary for the parent to endure that moment in order to establish who's in charge and teach that child the need to obey and submit to parental authority.

Sparkling Gems From the Greek, Volume 2

Parenting

If you consistently plant the Word into the hearts and minds of your children or grandchildren, it will produce a harvest in every area of their lives and in the lives of those they touch. It is the parents' job to create an environment conducive to training up their children in the ways of God.

Unlikely

Never forget that respecting and appreciating the church — and experiencing the rich blessings it brings — does not come automatically to children. If you don't impart this and reinforce it as they are growing up, it is likely they will not have these values when they are older. Such values must be intentionally imparted and reinforced by example!

Christmas — The Rest of the Story

When God says, "Train up a child in the way he should go: and when he is old, he will not depart from it" (Proverbs 22:6), He is actually saying, "Give your children an appetite for the things of God when they are young, and when they are older, they won't depart from it." What you condition their spiritual taste buds to eat when they are young is what they will continually be drawn to when they are older.

Unlikely

Let your children know they have been consecrated and dedicated to God's service. Instill in them that God has a special purpose for their lives. Demonstrate to them by your own example the importance of living according to the Word of God and the need to regularly participate in God's house. Teach them and reinforce your teaching by your personal example.

Christmas — The Rest of the Story

Partnership

We must have a revelation that every person is essential in accomplishing the work of God — that those who water the work with their prayers and finances are just as important as those who do the actual work of tilling the soil and planting the seeds. If the first group tries to do their job without the assistance of the other group, failure will be the inevitable result. On the other hand, if both work together as a team, appreciating and valuing each other's role in achieving their common purpose, the result will be a great harvest.

Sparkling Gems From the Greek, Volume 1

When you go out of your way to meet the needs of the Gospel, God will go out of His way to make sure *your* needs are met. It is the law of sowing and reaping restated in another way. In other words, when you meet the needs of God's Kingdom, He will see to it that your needs are met — *but* when God meets *your* needs, He will do it *lavishly, abundantly, excessively,* and *richly!*

Sparkling Gems From the Greek, Volume 2

Mere words cannot express how very thankful I am to God for assembling people to complement my gifts, for without them, I wouldn't have been able to accomplish all that we have done over the years. I had the passion and impetus to start many projects, but the advances we have made in so many realms of ministry wouldn't have been possible without the divine connections that God had prearranged.

The Will of God — The Key to Your Success

When there is uncertainty and instability in world financial markets, you must lay hold of this promise and believe God to release a divine supply of provision that is reserved especially for givers. This heavenly reserve has been set aside and kept for *you.* God is ready to open His heavenly account and lavishly demonstrate that He will be faithful to you, regardless of what is happening in the world markets. His goodness and His faithfulness are not affected by world economies — *and if you are a giving partner with a church or ministry, you qualify for God to meet your needs right now!*

Sparkling Gems From the Greek, Volume 2

There is a precious group of people whose faith is remarkably seen in our ministry, and that is our ministry partners. They didn't hear it when Heaven resoundingly issued the command and call for us to take the Gospel to the nations of the world. But they believed that *we heard it* — and they have not only seen the fruit that has been borne as a result of our obedience, but they hold that fruit in their own hands as a result of *their* obedience. It is laid up to their account, too, for participating with the call of God on our lives through their giving.

Unlikely

Pastors

Raw stones need a specialist to chisel, cut, trim, sand, grind, buff, and polish them to snugly fit next to other stones in the building. This brings us to the Christ-given fivefold ministry gift of pastor. In God's great building program, pastors are specialists who are anointed to carry out the nitty-gritty business of chiseling, cutting, trimming, sanding, grinding, and polishing all the souls or "living stones" that the evangelist gathered in the field and brought to the building site. A part of a pastor's function is to prepare all those living stones to be fitted into their respective places in God's House.

Apostles and Prophets

Pastors are held firmly in Christ's right hand and are under His custodial care. They are *answerable* and *accountable* to Jesus for delivering His message to the churches under their oversight. Jesus calls the Church to heed the message, but He holds *pastors* accountable for delivering the message accurately on His behalf. They are to be the *vocal instruments* through which He, as Head of the Church, speaks to His Church.

A Light in Darkness

The Bible makes it abundantly clear that the chief call of a pastor is to provide the teaching of God's Word to his congregation. If he does not do this, he is failing at the most basic level, as the most basic meaning of the word "pastor" is *to feed*. It is imperative for pastors to never be sidetracked by other things or forget that it is the anointed exposition of the Bible that will bring spiritual health, healing, and numerical and spiritual growth to their flocks.

Apostles and Prophets

What transpires *at the core* of a pastor's life is what determines his or her *brevity* or *longevity* in the ministry.

Sparkling Gems From the Greek, Volume 2

A pastor must come to grips with the fact that he is preaching at all times. Whether he or she recognizes it or not, people watch how pastors speak to their spouse, how they react in difficult situations, how they give and spend money, how they pray, and how they worship. Pastors are on full display to people who are watching all the time. Pastors are to live so godly, stable, strong, and faith-filled that those in the congregation will want to duplicate the life they see in their pastor.

Apostles and Prophets

Jesus *is* the Chief Shepherd of all God-called shepherds. One day when pastors stand before Him, Jesus will reward those pastors who have executed their ministries faithfully, and He will give them a special crown, and this should be the greatest motivation for obediently serving Jesus in pastoral ministry.

Apostles and Prophets

Patience

The Early Church called patience the "queen of all virtues" because they knew that as long as they had this character trait working in their lives, it wasn't a question of *if* they would win their battles — it was only a question of *when* they would win.

How To Receive Answers From Heaven

Don't budge an inch, and don't give in to the devil's attacks! Stay in the place God has called you to. *Refuse to be moved*, even if the load seems as if it has become too much for you to bear. Patience and endurance will put you over and put Satan under! *Satan has no counterattack for patience!*

Life in the Combat Zone

If your roots are securely fixed in Jesus Christ, you'll outlast every dry season, every foul climate, and every storm — and eventually, you'll enter into the fruit-producing season of your life, your ministry, your family, or your business.

The Point of No Return

In earliest years of the Church, believers knew that to survive the unremitting pressure and persecution that was methodically conducted against them, it was essential to have *patience* — the persistent, steadfast, tenacious spirit that refuses to crumble or concede to defeat. And because they possessed this quality of patience, they never surrendered in the face of pressure or capitulated to the forces that attempted to stamp them out.

A Light in Darkness

We all need a good dose of patience — a fruit that can only be produced in us by the Spirit of God.

Paid in Full

Just as a husband and wife must come together to produce a child, faith and patience must come together to produce the promises of God.

Dream Thieves

Peace

Nothing compares to the *powerful, protective, guarding* peace that God has positioned to stand at the entrance of your heart and mind! When this peace operates in you, it dominates your life. It stands at the gate of your heart and mind and disables the devil's ability to disturb you by preventing his attacks from bypassing and slipping into your mind. The devil may try his best to find access to your mind and emotions, but this guarding peace paralyzes his efforts.

Sparkling Gems From the Greek, Volume 1

Don't ignore a lack of peace in your heart!

Sparkling Gems From the Greek, Volume 2

It is imperative that we fill our hearts and minds with the Word of God in order to maintain peace in our lives so that we can be instruments of comfort, healing, and deliverance to a wayward generation. This is not a time for us to cower in fear — *but it's a time to be filled with the Spirit of God and to reach a generation that desperately needs the Good News of the Gospel.*

Signs You'll See Just Before Jesus Comes

When peace is in place in your life, it gives you the assurance you need to step out in faith and make the moves God is leading you to make. But before you take those steps, you need to be sure His peace is operating in your life. This mighty and powerful piece of your spiritual weaponry is essential because, without it, the devil can try to kick, punch, pull, and distract you. But with that conquering peace firmly tied to your mind and emotions, you will be empowered to keep marching ahead, impervious to the devil's attempts to take you down!

Sparkling Gems From the Greek, Volume 1

If we'll yield to the peace of God, it will stand at the door of our hearts and minds to block the entrance of any toxic intruders that try to enter in. God's peace — if it is permitted to do its job — prohibits fearful thoughts from entering our minds, upsetting our emotions, and causing us to turn aside from our steadied position of faith, peace, and rest.

Signs You'll See Just Before Jesus Comes

Persecution

The Christian faith was *scandalous* in the First Century when believers lived by a solid biblical foundation in a tossing sea of philosophy that held no moral absolutes — very similar to what is developing today when Christians are viewed as bigots and narrow-minded simpletons just for standing true to their faith.

Signs You'll See Just Before Jesus Comes

Jesus promised, "…The gates of hell shall *not* prevail against it [the Church]" (Matthew 16:18). Although brutal waves of persecution have come and gone many times over the past 2,000 years of Church history — even right up to this present day — every turbulent episode has proven Jesus' words in Matthew 16:18 to be true.

No Room for Compromise

Before us have been generations of persecuted saints who sowed the first seeds for a move of God — with their prayers, and often with their very lives — for a harvest that would occur in our time. As they lay in prisons and died, they released their faith that a day would come when those hard times would be recompensed with change — with *reformation.*

Unlikely

We must not forget that approximately 75 percent of the world *right now* lives in situations that are precarious for believers. *In fact, it is only a small fraction of the world that knows no Christian persecution.*

Signs You'll See Just Before Jesus Comes

Today there are situations where spiritual leaders are being bullied by people in congregations for fulfilling the divine command of God to reprove and rebuke when it is required — but God's requirements don't change. He has commanded His spokesmen to speak the Word without compromise, regardless of the consequences.

How To Keep Your Head on Straight
in a World Gone Crazy

If early believers could survive victoriously in the midst of utter darkness, then committed Christians today can be assured that they, too, can withstand the forces of evil surrounding them and be sustained by the glorious light of truth.

A Light in Darkness

Jesus promised that if we find ourselves in places where adversaries are trying to corner us, accuse us, and charge us, we can rely on the Spirit of God to give us "…a mouth and wisdom, which all your adversaries shall not be able to gainsay nor resist" (Luke 21:15).

Signs You'll See Just Before Jesus Comes

The world may accuse you of being *antisocial, contrary, noncompliant, intolerant, narrow-minded, nonconformist, inflexible, obstinate,* and *uncompromising,* but regardless, stick with your commitment and *refuse* to be contaminated by the spirit of the age.

Last-Days Survival Guide

Pluralism

The trend toward pluralistic thinking is increasing so rapidly, even among young people who attend church regularly, that many are wavering on the most basic tenets of the Christian faith. Foundational beliefs, such as the virgin birth, the sinlessness of Christ, the need to repent, moral rights and wrongs, and a literal Heaven and hell — are all on the table with a younger generation.

How To Keep Your Head on Straight
in a World Gone Crazy

What was at the *beginning* of the Church Age is attempting to arise again at the *end* of the Church Age. Although our society today is filled with new technology and sophistication, the pluralistic, inclusive view that dominated the First Century is once again lifting its ugly head. Certain key elements of paganism that dominated the First Century — such as its diversity of beliefs, its ever-changing moral code, and the acceptance of moral perversion — are seeping back into its mainstream, encased within the noble-sounding ideas of *inclusivity* and *open-mindedness*. There is no question that we are witnessing a return to paganism right before our eyes.

No Room for Compromise

To experience the religious pluralism and inclusiveness that is reemerging in these days, you simply have to take an absolute moral stance on sex, abortion, or other hot issues for which the Bible provides solid answers and then witness how those around you react.

No Room for Compromise

Politics

Although wicked rulers and evil governments may rail against the Church and cause temporary discomfort and pain, it is Christ who sits on the highest throne of judgment. Just as precious believers were brought before a Roman proconsul to be judged during the days of the Early Church, a day will ultimately come when every person will stand before Jesus Christ, the One to whom the Father has committed all judgment.

No Room for Compromise

When ungodly men run the affairs of state and government, we must be cognizant of the fact that God's Word promises a day will come when every man will stand before the throne of judgment. We must pray for ungodly men to repent and to come to the knowledge of the truth, but we must also never forget that those who resist and oppose the truth will not escape the consequences of their wicked actions. A time will inevitably come when every man will be called into Christ's high court of reckoning.

No Room for Compromise

Regardless of the power any human leader may try to exert in the world, Jesus Christ is the Ultimate Authority; He is the One who has the final say in matters of life and death. Although wicked rulers and evil governments may rail against the Church and cause temporary discomfort and pain, it is Christ who sits on the highest throne of judgment.

No Room for Compromise

Power

We are specially designed by God to be the receptacles for His divine power. God is the Giver of this explosive power, and we are the receptacles into which this power is to be deposited.

Dressed To Kill

Anytime the devil tries to insinuate that you're not a serious threat to be feared, you need to rise up and remind him that the Holy Spirit lives in you and He is your *Power Source!*

Paid in Full

Although we may not always be mentally aware of it, we are constantly rubbing elbows with this divine power of the Holy Spirit on a day-to-day, hour-to-hour, and minute-to-minute basis. This means we are never far away from a fresh surge of superhuman power into our own human spirits — and, in fact, a new release of God's power within us is as accessible as our very next breath of air!

Dressed To Kill

If we stay ablaze with the Holy Spirit's power, the Gospel will be established in the hearts of those we come in contact with who were once gripped by the power of darkness. We will heal the sick, cast out demons, raise the dead, and testify to the living reality of Jesus Christ as the miraculous abounds among us and through us to a dying world!

A Life Ablaze

You can be assured that Satan was watching with great concern as the Holy Spirit's power came upon the believers gathered in the Upper Room on the Day of Pentecost. With the emergence of the supernatural Church of Jesus Christ in Jerusalem, the devil knew — beyond any shadow of doubt — that his earthly domain was no longer secure. If Jesus could single-handedly defeat him so thoroughly, how could he now stand against multitudes of people filled with the same Spirit who raised Jesus from the dead?

Dressed To Kill

We must arm ourselves with God's Word and the weapons of warfare He has provided. Then we must allow the Holy Spirit's power to flow through us so we can each run our race with endurance all the way to the end! And before we conclude this spiritual race and make the big exit, we must do all we can to tell the Good News of Jesus Christ to people we encounter so we can take as many people with us to Heaven as possible.

Last-Days Survival Guide

Never forget that you have the power of the Holy Spirit within you, and if you'll surrender to His indwelling presence, He will give you the strength needed to remain faithful and unwavering in the face of any situation you are facing!

Signs You'll See Just Before Jesus Comes

Praise

If you are in a tough spot in life and do not "feel" like offering audible praise to God, you must push your soul and flesh to the side and choose to do it anyway. In such moments, your praise becomes a *sacrificial offering* that you bring to the Lord. God knows when it's difficult for you to lift up praise, and He is honored when you bring a "sacrifice of praise" to Him.

Apostles and Prophets

As you take a stance of faith, lift your voice to thank God *in advance* for the answer you are seeking! *Thanksgiving is the voice of faith that thanks God for the answer before it comes!*

Sparkling Gems From the Greek, Volume 2

It may cost you something to offer praise, especially when your soul argues that there is nothing to praise God about — or when you have a bad attitude, are in a foul mood, or are in the midst of a challenging situation that makes it difficult to praise God. When your soul is uncooperative, but you chose to push through it all and praise God anyway, it is a sacrifice that is well-pleasing to God.

Apostles and Prophets

Prayer

When we enter into prayer, it should be done at a place and time when we are not interrupted so the Holy Spirit can speak to our hearts and we can bare our hearts to Him. It is to be a mingling together of human spirit with divine Spirit in sweet communion.

The Holy Spirit and You

Perseverance is one of the most important qualities of prayer!

How To Receive Answers From Heaven

When we "come to the altar" to pray, our prayers arise like incense, and the sweet aroma produced by prayer reaches the nostrils of God as a well-pleasing aroma that invites face-to-face communion, the blessing of His presence, and a divine exchange of our lives for His life.

Apostles and Prophets

We need never fear that we are *too frank, too bold, too forth-right, too honest, too outspoken,* or even *too blunt* as we bear our hearts to Him or request His help. While we should never be irreverent, neither do we need to be ashamed to speak exactly what is on our hearts.

How To Keep Your Head on Straight in a World Gone Crazy

Never forget that prayer is a vital piece of your spiritual weaponry. If you neglect this strategic piece of weaponry, you will find that the enemy keeps attacking you from up close. But as you learn to pray with authority, you will develop the ability to strike the enemy from a distance and therefore maintain a victorious position in your life.

Sparkling Gems From the Greek, Volume 1

We must learn to press into the realm of the Spirit and to continue in prayer — *robustly, steadfastly,* and *tenaciously* calling out to God for Him to answer us in great and mighty ways (*see* Jeremiah 33:3).

A Life Ablaze

Preaching

Preaching God's Word is the highest form of spiritual warfare, for the mighty two-edged sword that is the Word of God has the greatest power available in this life to banish the forces of darkness from any environment.

A Light in Darkness

There is nothing more powerful than the anointing being passed to others through our lives. Regardless of the spiritual climate or the difficulty of the hour, we must be directly, personally involved when it comes to planting the Gospel seed into the hearts of men.

Life in the Combat Zone

We must let the Bible speak for itself, and our role as God-called ministers is to study the Bible, to see accurately what it teaches on every subject, and then to present truth as it is presented in God's Word.

How To Keep Your Head on Straight in a World Gone Crazy

Only preaching and teaching that is Word-based, precise, anointed, and straightforward has the dual power to shake people from slumber and keep them tender of heart yet strong in spirit.

Signs You'll See Just Before Jesus Comes

Unfortunately, *reproving* and *rebuking* have largely been put aside, and as a result, the deeper issues of the heart that need to be addressed and corrected — *which are so vitally important* — are often ignored. Although it is not always the case, it's true that much preaching and teaching today consists of *exhortation* to stir the saints with a positive message, and while this is good, it leaves out the other two vital elements that are so essential for people's hearts to be convicted and changed by the power of the Holy Spirit.

Signs You'll See Just Before Jesus Comes

Pride

If you find even a hint of pride in you, it is in your interest to *eradicate* it from your life!

A Life Ablaze

Let's face it — the flesh delights in deceiving itself into believing that it is better, more spiritual, or more enlightened than anyone else. It thrives on being puffed up, prideful, and boastful. It enjoys thinking too highly of itself. It adores being selfish, self-consumed, and self-focused, and it takes pleasure in caring for its own selfish interests. And if allowed to do so, flesh will separate into a faction, a division, or a sect. It will gravitate to others whose flesh also wants to believe they are better than others. When all that flesh gets together in one place, they will inevitably form a super-elite clique inside the church that is so tight no one else will be able to get in it — including the pastor!

Sparkling Gems From the Greek, Volume 1

The scriptures show over and over again that unhealthy pride is *fatal* to man's spiritual, mental, and emotional well-being — and often even fatal to his physical life. It is the root of rebellion and is always accompanied with catastrophic results. For this reason, God always has been and always will be against pride.

A Life Ablaze

Satan's ultimate goal with unhealthy pride is to see that we make destructive choices and behaviors that will lead to our *elimination* from our God-appointed positions. He wants us to be ejected from the game so that we are no longer a threat to his plans and no longer usable in God's Kingdom.

A Life Ablaze

The biggest open door to pride is *offense*. An offense may be rooted in a real or a perceived issue. We feel personally insulted, overlooked, taken for granted, or mistreated, or we feel these emotions on behalf of someone else. If we hold on to the hurt rather than surrender it to Jesus, it grows into bitterness and resentment — the perfect breeding ground for pride — and becomes an open door for the devil to gain access and sow seeds of his slanderous accusation into our hearts and minds.

A Life Ablaze

Don't let pride get you stuck in its poisonous thought pattern that inevitably leads to dissatisfaction. That toxic way of thinking will sour you until you've set yourself up for possible elimination.

A Life Ablaze

Priesthood

The word "priesthood" is a translation of a rare Greek word that denoted *a priesthood with all its priestly functions*. The New Testament uses the word "priesthood" to depict an entire royal kingdom of priests in which every member in the Kingdom is a priest with priestly functions and responsibilities. This was a radical concept because there had never been *an entire kingdom of priests* in any kingdom anywhere in human history. In the Old Testament, certain God-chosen groups had priestly functions, but there simply had been no kingdom *ever*, in which every member in it was a priest. But God's Kingdom is a Kingdom in which *every believer* is a God-called priest with priestly functions and responsibilities.

Apostles and Prophets

Not only is *every believer* a "living stone" in the Temple of God — the Church — but *every believer* is, without exception, a God-called priest with priestly functions and priestly responsibilities. The Church is a "holy priesthood" in which every redeemed member has become a God-called priest engaged in offering spiritual sacrifices to God!

Apostles and Prophets

Priests

Although physical sacrifices in the Jerusalem Temple eventually ceased, the act of sacrificing actually never stopped in God's mind, because Christ has called every believer as a member of a brand-new holy priesthood to offer up sacrifices of a *spiritual* nature. Physical, bloody sacrifices ended, but other sacrifices continued and do continue — today each believer is simultaneously a *temple* and a *priest*, meaning any believer can offer up a "spiritual sacrifice" at any time and in any place.

Apostles and Prophets

Just as temple priests followed a protocol of offering sacrifices each day, God calls on us to follow a *daily protocol* of offering ourselves to Him. This is where priestly service begins, and it cannot be sidestepped if we are to be faithful priests. The business of offering ourselves as a living sacrifice is a lifelong priestly occupation.

Apostles and Prophets

As believer-priests, we are called by God to prayer and to the altar, where the Holy Spirit may convict our hearts concerning areas that need to be surrendered to His sanctifying power. He will never forcibly take these things from us; *we* must surrender them. Prayer brings us to a place of decision and consecration — to an altar where we freely vow to give our lives to God in exchange for His life.

Apostles and Prophets

Productivity

Try to put together a list of people who were doing *nothing* when God chose them for a big assignment. I actually tried once to compile one, and I couldn't think of anyone who was used significantly by God but was doing nothing when He called him.

Sparkling Gems From the Greek, Volume 2

I have learned that I cannot have productive days without time with the Lord. During those early morning times, I pray and I pour out my heart to God with thanksgiving for all He has done in my life. I pray fervently for partners and for others who are on my prayer list. I virtually never start a day at home without sitting in my silent place to seek the face of God and to allow God's Spirit to search my heart and bring me to a more intimate experience with Jesus. And after that quiet time, I am refreshed, reinvigorated, filled with new ideas, and empowered for my day. *Such moments of solitude with God are critical to the daily victory of every believer!*

Sparkling Gems From the Greek, Volume 2

It is possible to "multi-task" ourselves into a state of unproductiveness as a result of nearly nonstop activity.

Dream Thieves

Sometimes when you are working hard to do what God has asked you to do, it can seem overwhelming, but progress is gained one step at a time. The increments of forward movement might seem tiny, but no matter how big or small the steps, remember that you are inevitably progressing toward the goal that God has set for your life!

Sparkling Gems From the Greek, Volume 2

Productivity for God must never take the place of passionate love for Him. Christ requires us to be both productive for Him *and* passionate about Him.

Sparkling Gems From the Greek, Volume 2

Promotion

How you perform in what you are doing right now may be the factor that determines whether or not God will call you to do something greater and more significant later. If you prove yourself faithful, God will know He can trust you with the next big promotion. Thus, the outcome of your future has a great deal to do with your present attitudes and job performance.

Dream Thieves

Sometimes God takes a little longer than we might like to promote us in order to make sure we're really ready for that next big assignment. It's hard on the flesh while we wait, yet it is actually the mercy of God at work. You see, during that time of waiting, the imperfections that would have ruined us are exposed so God can remove them. Then He can move us up into the new position with no concern that a hidden flaw will cause us to fall flat on our face!

Sparkling Gems From the Greek, Volume 1

One of the saddest things I see on a regular basis is talented men and women who have been promoted too quickly and thus lack the spiritual roots and depth of character needed to sustain them.

The Point of No Return

Do not jockey for position or try to prove your importance to others with a lot of hollow, empty boasting and self-promotion. Instead, have a modest opinion of yourself, and learn to recognize the outstanding contributions that others have to impart.

Sparkling Gems From the Greek, Volume 1

Promotion to a leadership position most often comes only after years of learning submission, faithfulness, and hard work. Normally the new leader who seemed to "step out of nowhere" into his role of authority actually came up through the ranks, putting in long hours over a long period of time. After years of diligence, he finally attained this position of influence and authority, and he earned it through the sweat of his brow.

The Point of No Return

Prophets

Often prophets operate like anointed building inspectors who are divinely enabled to *see* what others may not see, including what is done correctly or incorrectly. With Christ-given insight, Christ-given prophets impart courage to build correctly and at times to address issues that need to be fixed in the building process.

Apostles and Prophets

The first divine assignment for a prophet is to be *before* God's presence, to hear His message, to capture His heart, and to devour, consume, and digest what God speaks to him. The prophet is to allow God's words to go down deep into his belly — his spirit man — that he might be changed, corrected, and nourished by them — and he is to swallow the *entire* message given to him, for he has no right to eat of it selectively. God expects him to put aside his own feelings and thoughts so God's words can be fully ingested, assimilated, understood, and then delivered in power.

Apostles and Prophets

All prophets are eventually expected by God to speak what they have either heard or seen. In the Old Testament, there were various levels of prophets — major prophets, minor prophets, well-known prophets, unknown prophets, speaking prophets, and seeing prophets — but there were primarily two categories: *hearing prophets* and *seeing prophets.*

Apostles and Prophets

A prophet — like a ship — is dependent on the wind of the Spirit. There is nothing he can supernaturally *self-produce* — by himself — and he cannot even accurately speak with power until the Spirit moves across his spirit. Therefore, he positions himself *before* God's presence and waits for the wind of God's Spirit to move upon him. The prophet sets his spiritual sail to catch the wind of the Holy Spirit, and once he is aware of the Spirit moving across his spirit, then — finally — he is in a position to turn toward the people and move into the public phase of his prophetic ministry.

Apostles and Prophets

Nearly every genuine prophetic word will give *a call to action or ask the listeners to respond in some way.* For example, if a prophetic word says there is "sin in the camp," it will follow with a call to repentance. If a prophetic word forewarns of hard times, it will follow with a call to face the enemy in the power of the Spirit and to endure until victory is achieved. Prophetic ministry is never simply foreboding but is filled with practical instruction and a call to action — a way to respond to what God is saying — that will equip those who have an ear to hear with the power to overcome.

Apostles and Prophets

Protection

God is your Divine Protector! He is your *Hiding Place*, your *Strong Tower*, your *Shield*, and the *Mountain* that surrounds your life! He promises to be with you at all times and to *never* abandon you. All He asks is that you "stay put" in the center of His will where He has called you — *refusing* to move or give up and rejecting every scare tactic of the enemy to abdicate your post.

The Will of God — The Key to Your Success

Evil is always lurking in the shadows — waiting for us to drop our guard or to fall asleep on the job. In those vulnerable moments of lethargy, the enemy is positioned to seize his opportunity and attack, often with devastating consequences. Therefore, it is essential that we are always on guard — diligent, wide-awake, and doing our part to protect ourselves from the evil that is in the world.

No Room for Compromise

Divine protection is activated in those of us who *believe* that God's promise of protection will work for us. When we enter dangerous territory in fear, doubt, and unbelief, we are likely to get in trouble. But if we will go into that space believing and claiming that God's protection is ours and that the enemy can't do anything to hurt us, our faith in this promise will activate it and cause it to be manifested in our lives — it will even activate the ministry of angels to keep us safe!

Unlikely

We can claim God's power to protect us when He calls us to carry the Gospel to parts of the world that are considered to be unsafe. We may not deal with serpents and scorpions like the early believers did, but there may be times when we are required to fly on rickety airplanes, drive on dangerous roads, pass through highly volatile areas, or work in regions that are considered dangerous.

A Life Ablaze

God is good and His hand of protection, provision, and safety is all around us!

Paid in Full

If you are in Christ and walking in obedience to God's Word, you are safe, secure, and sealed in the protective blood of Jesus — and the power of that divine protection can never be breached by someone operating with the powers of Satan. The occult has never been — and will never be — a match for the power of God inside a believer.

No Room for Compromise

Jesus provided everything needed for those of us who would follow His call to the ends of the earth. He supplied us with supernatural protection from disasters, calamities, snakes, scorpions, and all the works of the enemy. He also promised traveling mercies and protection from acts of injustice. He even guaranteed that if we accidentally consume bad foods or deadly substances, they wouldn't weaken us physically or injure our health. He covered the gamut of protection, provision, and prosperity as we obey His calling and do His will!

A Life Ablaze

Provision

If you do what is right and obey God's command to give, you needn't worry about the future because the law of sowing and reaping *works*. This universal law assures a harvest of provision for you, for your family, and for your business, regardless of what happens in the world around you!

Sparkling Gems From the Greek, Volume 2

You may ask, "How many needs does God want to meet?" Philippians 4:19 states that He will meet "all" of them. In the original language, this is an all-encompassing word that leaves nothing out and means whatever the need is, God intends to meet it.

Christmas — The Rest of the Story

It's important to remember that we cannot always measure success by finances. Sometimes when we are exactly where we're supposed to be and we're doing what God has asked us to do, the devil tries to resist us in the financial realm, and that's when we have to determine to stick with God's plan regardless of the resistance we are bumping into at that moment. Ultimately financial provision will come, along with favor and countless other blessings, if we stay in agreement with God's will and hold fast to our trust in Him.

The Will of God — The Key to Your Success

Jesus promises to provide *spiritual provision* and *replenishment* to every one of us who will come to His table with faith to receive. He is sufficient to provide the spiritual refreshment and nutrients needed to strengthen us through tough times to accomplish our assignment. God's grace is available to us, just as daily manna had been available to the children of Israel during their trek across the desert.

Sparkling Gems From the Greek, Volume 2

God's people need to upgrade what they think about God meeting their needs. God does not want to give just enough for you only to skimp along in life. God wants to lavishly meet the needs of His people until they are totally filled, packed full, and overflowing to the point of bursting at the seams and spilling over.

Christmas — The Rest of the Story

Purity

You may sometimes feel disheartened by what you see or know about the Church. You may even be tempted to think that the modern Church is in such an irreversibly sad condition that it will never turn around for the better. But whenever your mind is bombarded by such thoughts, it is vital to remember that Jesus loves His Church, that He bought it with His own blood, and that the Holy Spirit is still actively working to purify it.

A Light in Darkness

We must choose to yield to the fiery effect of God's Word working in us — because even though the process is not always comfortable, to say the least, it blazes a fire so strong that it incinerates those things that are displeasing to the Spirit and need to be removed.

A Life Ablaze

You need to know that God has plenty of time, and He is not in a hurry, nor is He focused on the clock as we usually are. He is more concerned about character, integrity, faithfulness, and purity of heart than about the calendar.

Sparkling Gems From the Greek, Volume 2

Not one of us is exempt from the purifying process. Each of us must allow the Holy Spirit's fire to expose our weaknesses, impurities, and defects so Jesus can scrape them away. This removal process is painful, and just when we think the task is finished, the Holy Spirit turns up the blaze another notch and the process is started all over again! But the heat of the refining fire is *essential* for us to be purified and strengthened to fulfill the Master's will!

A Light in Darkness

Purpose

All those who are born into God's Kingdom by accepting Jesus Christ as their Lord and Savior receive a specific purpose for their lives — and you are no exception. You were born again by the Spirit of God not only to be a child of God, but to be a child of God with *power*!

Dream Thieves

Each one of us has been given equally unique and important gifts. Your grace defines your place, so discover your grace, embrace it, and then allow it to dominate your life! When you reach this point, you no longer feel threatened by or envious of the grace of anyone else. You are able to confidently say, "This is my grace! Other people can't do what I do, and I don't have to do what they do because that is their grace." Thank God, we're not all the same!

Sparkling Gems From the Greek, Volume 2

Just as a rudder steers the course of a ship, your divine purpose provides a sense of direction to steer the course of your life. Are your habits and immediate goals consistent with your life's purpose? If not, those habits and goals, although well-meaning, can pull you off course.

Dream Thieves

Get quiet in God's presence and humbly ask, "Lord, what do You see in my character, my abilities, and my heart that has caused You to include me in Your purposes? And what do You see in me that needs to change or be perfected so that I can serve You with excellence and longevity?"

Christmas — The Rest of the Story

Are you clear about the plan of God for your life? If you do not yet know your life's purpose and priority, then ask the Holy Spirit to help you discover God's will for your life and make the decision to do it — no matter the cost.

Paid in Full

Those who contribute nothing to life are usually the ones who struggle with a sense of purposelessness. A person's life becomes *pointless* when he or she contributes nothing to life. God didn't bring you into the world so you would live a pointless and inconsequential life! He has a purpose for your life and wants to reveal it to you!

Sparkling Gems From the Greek, Volume 1

Quench

The word "quench" is taken from a Greek word that means *to extinguish, smother, suppress, douse, put out, snuff out,* or *to quell.* It most often means *to extinguish a fire by dousing it with water.* In some places, it means *to evaporate* or *to dry up.* Thus, if we ignore the Holy Spirit's voice long enough and often enough, eventually we will become spiritually hardened and will no longer be able to hear Him when He does try to speak to us. It will be like His voice *evaporates* or *dries up,* and we will hear it no more.

Sparkling Gems From the Greek, Volume 1

Instead of continually shutting your ears to the Holy Spirit's voice and dousing the flames of the Spirit in your heart, it's time for you to say, "Yes, Lord, I'll do what You say. I'll go where You send me. I'll obey what You tell me to do!" When you adopt this attitude, *you start putting fuel back on the fire again!* Every time you say, "Yes, Lord," *and follow through with obedience, you stoke the coals of your heart and cause the Holy Spirit's fire to burn more brightly in your life.*

Sparkling Gems From the Greek, Volume 1

Quiet

If we will listen to the Holy Spirit, He will show us when to speak and when to be quiet — when to stay and when to move on. We must learn to be sensitive to the voice of the Holy Spirit in every situation.

Sparkling Gems From the Greek, Volume 2

I am convinced that the failure to be quiet is one reason people get confused in life. They get so busy that they no longer are in touch with themselves — what they believe, what they need, and what they feel. Instead, they just keep moving through life like robots. You need times of deep contemplation in order to stay in touch with your own heart.

Sparkling Gems From the Greek, Volume 2

If we will listen to the Holy Spirit, we can know when we are to remain in the battle or when it is wiser for us to withdraw, break camp, and relocate to new territory where greater victories will be won. The Holy Spirit will lead us — *if* we will quiet our hearts and listen for His voice.

Sparkling Gems From the Greek, Volume 2

Quiet Time

As a believer, it is absolutely essential that you spend time in the Presence of the Lord so you can hear His Word and capture His heart. You should never think of the time you must spend in God's Presence praying or reading the

Word as laborious or dreadful. It is a *high honor* that God has given you. He beckons you to come into His throne room so He can speak to you, share His heart with you, and then empower you with His Spirit to take the message to people who are desperately waiting for it. Never forget that you possess a position of great privilege.

Sparkling Gems From the Greek, Volume 1

Don't just run in and run out of the Lord's Presence. Plan to settle down and stay there long enough to get everything you need to carry on. Once you've stopped long enough to really rest in His Presence, you're finally in a position where you can start receiving from Him. Don't move too fast! Just hang around in God's Presence as long as you possibly can.

Sparkling Gems From the Greek, Volume 1

When we enter into a time of prayer, it should be done at a place and time when we are not interrupted so the Holy Spirit can speak to our heart and we can bare our heart to Him. It should be a time of a sweet mingling together of human spirit with the divine Spirit. Each of us should make it a daily priority to have this special time of communion with the Father through the Holy Spirit. It doesn't matter *where* you and I spend this private time with God; it just matters that we actually do it. Of course, it is best to find a time of the day when we can put everything else aside and concentrate only on Him, for the time we give to seek God is sacred time.

Sparkling Gems From the Greek, Volume 1

If God is calling you to set aside some extra time for Him, you need to be prepared for your flesh to put up a fight! That's why it's going to take determination to do it. When other things try to scream for your attention and pull you out of that consecrated place, you have to be determined to stay there unmoved, because that is where your source of strength, your peace, and all your answers will come from.

Sparkling Gems From the Greek, Volume 2

Quitting

There are many things Satan can do to try to elbow us out of the race, but the only one who can decide to *quit* is you or me. *Satan can't make us quit.* That choice lies in our hands alone.

Sparkling Gems From the Greek, Volume 1

Have you ever tried hard to do what is right, but felt crushed or continually resisted by some circumstance or person? Has that opposition caused you to feel tempted to throw in the towel? In spite of the destructive forces that may have tried to rail against you or loom over your life — *don't quit*, even if you're facing a truly unjust situation!

Sparkling Gems From the Greek, Volume 2

It's naïve to think that the devil is just going to lie down and watch you flow from one victory to the next. He does *not* want you to succeed at fulfilling the will of God for your life. That's why you have to make the decision before it happens that you are never going to quit or bend to circumstances. You are required to have a mindset that says, *It doesn't matter what happens to me or what the devil says. I am going to do what God called me to do.*

Sparkling Gems From the Greek, Volume 2

People often quit when they don't see results as quickly as they want. If their prayers for healing aren't answered immediately, they allow their flesh to convince them, for example, that it is God's will for them to be sick. Or if they sow their finances and believe for a financial harvest but don't see that harvest in a matter of months, they are tempted to think that everything they have been taught concerning prosperity must be a lie. The problem is that these Christians want quick "microwave answers" to problems that probably took some time to develop. *They need to give their faith time to work!* If this sounds like you, don't quit before your faith has had time to fully work.

Sparkling Gems From the Greek, Volume 2

If a day comes when you let loose of your faith and back off your position, it won't be too long until a spiritual sadness comes over your life. Spiritually speaking, your shoulders will slope, your head will drop, and you'll feel like someone has pulled the plug on your energy level. Your eyes will drift toward the couch or bed, and soon you'll end up completely going to bed on your faith. *Don't let that happen to you!*

Sparkling Gems From the Greek, Volume 1

R

Rapture (of the Church)

The Rapture will occur the *instant* the last person who is going to be saved is brought into the Kingdom — and then we will be miraculously transformed and translated to meet the Lord in the air.

Signs You'll See Just Before Jesus Comes

Second Peter 3:9 states that God is "…not willing that any should perish…." Although it's true that not all will be saved, God is waiting for the Gospel to reach the ends of the earth and for that last person who will respond to His call. God is not tardy, delayed, or slow in fulfilling His promise — He is simply holding out for the last soul to be saved.

Signs You'll See Just Before Jesus Comes

Once the Gospel becomes available in every place, the conditions will be *finally, exactly* right for His return to "catch away" His Church (*see* 1 Thessalonians 4:17). So once the Gospel has reached every people group, Christ's catching away of the Church could happen at *any* time!

Signs You'll See Just Before Jesus Comes

Redemption

When we came into Christ, God deemed our old identity dead and powerless over us. Now there is a permanent disconnection from the old person we used to be and the things we once did. Christ rendered the old man dead, and He gave us a brand-new life!

Sparkling Gems From the Greek, Volume 2

Jesus Christ came into the world to untie and unloose Satan's binding powers over us — and at the Cross, Jesus unraveled Satan's power until His redemptive work was finally complete and our liberty was fully purchased!

Dressed To Kill

If we've lost precious opportunities in any area — including time lost with our families — we can *reverse* that condition. Through our recommitment to ourselves and to the Lord, we can buy back time that has been lost, wasted, or forfeited — and with the Holy Spirit's help, we can accomplish in *a short time* what we thought was forever lost. We really can *redeem time* and get back on course!

Last-Days Survival Guide

If old things from your past or former ways of thinking attempt to express themselves again, speak to those voices and remind them that they have lost their power over your life. If they try to wake up and act like they still have influence, your task is to reckon them lifeless — that is, keep them buried "six feet under" — locked away in a casket that is covered with the grace of God. Never — *not for a second* — allow your old memories to tell you they have the right to live. Christ has rendered them powerless, and you never have to return to who you were or to what you did.

Sparkling Gems From the Greek, Volume 2

God has a way of using the experiences of our early days — even our very bad experiences — and redeeming them as only He can. He forges them into a glorious purpose for our lives and uses our seasons of obscurity, loneliness, brokenness, clumsiness, and even *failure* to weave together a plan so *unlikely* that only He could bring it to pass. Our future doesn't lie in our own impressive resume or grandiose list of accomplishments, but in our faithfulness and consistency day to day as we walk with God and build a "resume" of accomplishments, exploits — *and even godly character* — with Him.

Unlikely

You don't have to keep being negative about yourself all the time, and you don't have to beat yourself over the head, constantly telling yourself how unworthy you are. In fact, you actually insult the power in the redemptive work of Jesus when you do that, for Jesus Christ *made* you worthy when He went to the Cross on your behalf and shed His own precious blood. He *made* you righteous! He *made* you a new creation in Him.

The Holy Spirit and You

In Christ, we are filled with the potential of the Holy Spirit inside us, and we are stronger, better, and improved because of what Jesus has done to *rescue* us, *redeem us,* and *restore* our lives to a state of wholeness in Him!

Sparkling Gems From the Greek, Volume 2

Refreshment

Allow yourself a little relaxation and time for recreation — time away from your problems. Then when you come back to face challenges and problems again, you'll be refreshed and recharged with renewed vision. You'll see that challenge with new eyes, and you'll face it with new strength. It may be hard to allow yourself the time to do what I'm suggesting, but if you don't take a break from that constant stress, it will keep wearing you down until you become easy prey for the devil. Take a break and allow yourself a little time to rest, relax, and recuperate!

Sparkling Gems From the Greek, Volume 1

One of Satan's greatest weapons is discouragement, and he knows exactly when to use it. He waits until you are tired, weak, and susceptible to his lies. Then he hits you hard in your emotions, trying to tell you that you are accomplishing nothing valuable in life. But if you will yield to the Holy Spirit who dwells in you, He will supernaturally revitalize you. He will rejuvenate you. He will refresh you with a brand-new surge of supernatural life. He will fill you with so much resurrection power that you will be ready to get up and go again!

Sparkling Gems From the Greek, Volume 1

Jesus never promised that He would take difficult assignments away from you. However, He did promise that if you come to Him, He would give you the rest you need in order to be refreshed for the continuation and conclusion of the journey. So when it seems like you've given all you have but there's still so much more for you to do before you're finished, just take a break from your journey and go to Jesus for some supernatural refreshing!

Sparkling Gems From the Greek, Volume 1

Regret

If you live in a state of regret, that negative emotion will only make things even worse, dragging you down into a state of discouragement and self-condemnation. It's so much better to just lift your hands and rejoice that you still have an opportunity to redeem the time that has been lost. Don't let the devil lie to you and tell you that it's too late. It's *not* too late!

Last-Days Survival Guide

Regret is self-pity that is focused more on your own personal loss than on the pain or loss you caused to others or to the heart of God, and it leaves you *unchanged.*

Repentance

Make the decision today that you're *finished* with fixing your mind on things that are in the past — things that you have repented about, that have been erased by the blood of Jesus, and that you can't do anything about now. You have the power to *turn away* from yesterday and start focusing on what is in front of you. Yesterday is done! The clock cannot be turned back, and living in regret will only keep you from moving forward into the future.

Sparkling Gems From the Greek, Volume 2

Relationships

When you step out to obey what God has told you to do, He will put you together with the right people. He will supernaturally establish *divine connections* with other believers assigned to help you fully accomplish His will.

The Will of God — The Key to Your Success

Relationships are like savings accounts; you have to put something *into* them if you expect to get something *out of* them. If all you do is *take*, eventually you will drain that relationship, like a bank account that gets drained and has nothing left in it. For your relationships to remain healthy and vibrant, you need to make many deposits into them. As you invest in the people in your life, they will grow, but if you put nothing *into* a relationship and keep expecting to take *from* that other person, you will eventually come to a point where that relationship will be drained and nothing will be left for you to draw upon. That's when you'll regret that you didn't make better choices and invest more into that relationship to make it the long-lasting blessing God intended it to be in both your lives.

Sparkling Gems From the Greek, Volume 2

If you have been personally disappointed or hurt by shallow relationships, ask the Holy Spirit to heal your heart.

God does not want you to live in brokenness for the rest of your life and wants to lead you to other godly people who, like you, are seeking deep and meaningful relationships.

Last-Days Survival Guide

God has divine connections awaiting *you* all along your life's journey. Sometimes when you least expect it, the Lord will surprise you by bringing you just the right person you need to help you do what He has assigned for your life.

The Will of God — The Key to Your Success

It is important to learn how to recognize those times when the devil is trying to inject a seed of division into your heart. You see, he wants to drive a wedge between you and the people you love. Rather than let him get away with this evil tactic, you must make a decision to resist every temptation to get angry and offended — and by resisting these thoughts, you will resist the devil and protect your relationships.

Paid in Full

If we lay down our weapons of war and suspicions of each other — and ardently follow after peace with each other, doing the things that make for peace and edification — the Holy Spirit will give us a divine plan about how to bring about peace in any relationship. Rather than tear each other down, the Holy Spirit — who is the Chief Architect and Engineer — wants to show us a plan that will build strong relationships for years to come!

Sparkling Gems From the Greek, Volume 2

You can't change history or go back and relive seasons that are long past, but you can pray for God's will to be fulfilled in the season you're in now — and you can expect that He will work to restore hearts and lives according to His design and plan.

Last-Days Survival Guide

Friend, *stay the course* God has placed you on, and don't deviate from His instructions. Let Him be the One to move you or adjust your assignment. Be willing to work hard to accomplish His will and thank Him for the people He has teamed you with to encourage you and lighten your load.

The Will of God — The Key to Your Success

Remembering

Sometimes when you are discouraged, it's good to hit the rewind button in your mind and drift backward to earlier experiences with the Lord when faith was simple and life was uncomplicated. Do you remember how precious those days were? Do you recall how changed you were by the power of God? Do you remember the laughter and joy you experienced? It's good for you to rehearse those experiences because they stir you up, encourage you, and summon your strength for the battle you are facing right now.

Sparkling Gems From the Greek, Volume 1

God has done so many miracles for you and me. Think of how God has delivered you, saved you, and rescued you from harm time and time again, yet you still tend to wonder if God is really with you or not. How in the world could you ever question the faithfulness of God after all He has already done for you?

Paid in Full

Do you treasure the things God has done in *your* life? What are you doing to ensure that you never forget what God has done, and how are you passing those memories on to others?

Christmas — The Rest of the Story

Remnant

God has always had His remnant who will not bow to external pressures, and in these last days, He will have that remnant once again. And those who refuse to fear or to compromise their faith in Jesus Christ will experience previously unknown levels of the power of God as a result of their commitment to stand by truth.

No Room for Compromise

Besides those who veer from truth, there will also be a different group of believers who emerge at the end of the age who will hold fast to the ageless Word of truth regardless of consequences or opposition and proclaim its timeless teaching, so let's make sure that *this* is the group *we* belong to!

How To Keep Your Head on Straight
in a World Gone Crazy

In our time and in the times to come, there is — and will continue to be — a remnant of believers who will not bow to the pressures of society, no matter how heavy those pressures become. Although some may collapse under the weight of these external forces, there are committed Christians who will not bow to the new cultural norms of compromise, nor will they succumb to the pressures and afflictions that are forced upon them.

Signs You'll See Just Before Jesus Comes

Remorse

Remorse expresses the *guilt* a person feels because he knows that he *has done wrong*, that he *will continue to do wrong*, and that he *has no plans to change* his course of action. He feels shameful about what he is doing but continues to do it anyway, which results in a state of ongoing guilt. This guilt produces *no change* in a person's life or behavior, but genuine repentance would fix this feeling of guilt and remove it completely.

Repentance

Remorse enslaves you in sorrow that engulfs you emotionally and leaves you feeling sad, depressed, hopeless, and *unchanged*.

Repentance

Decide today to stop wallowing in remorse concerning things that are in the past and are unfixable. If you made a mistake, learn from it and let the Holy Spirit lead you into the wonderful life that lies directly ahead of you.

Sparkling Gems From the Greek, Volume 2

Renewing the Mind

When a believer first accepts Christ as his Lord and Savior, there are areas in his life that need to be healed, restored, and changed. By walking in obedience to the Word of God and learning to serve in the local church, a person's mind can become conformed to the mind of Christ, and his life can gradually become transformed to reflect the excellence of Jesus Christ. However, for these changes to occur in a person's life, it requires his complete participation. These kinds of changes don't occur without hard work, commitment, and determination to make one's heart a place where God feels honored.

Sparkling Gems From the Greek, Volume 2

For believers who have made the mistake of yielding to sinful behavior for so long that it has spiritually damaged their hearts and minds, there is *hope* — for if they will acknowledge that they've strayed and are willing to repent (*see* 1 John 1:9) the Holy Spirit will rise up as a mighty force within and begin to invade their minds to renew them again to the truth.

Signs You'll See Just Before Jesus Comes

Transformation of the mind will require a person to absolutely *submit* his or her mind to the Word of God and the work of the Holy Spirit, and it will require courage and sustained commitment, for once a person's mind has been this profoundly impacted by sin and deception, it can be restored to its previous condition only as that person submits his or her mind 100 percent to meditating on and obeying the truth of God's Word.

How To Keep Your Head on Straight
in a World Gone Crazy

It is important that we keep our minds soaked with the Word of God, which renews us to right thinking in a world that has morally slipped in a wrong direction. It is imperative that we put the Word into our hearts — keeping it before our eyes and hearing it with our ears. It's equally important to verbalize the truth of God's Word to ourselves and to other believers, thus strengthening the truth *in us* and *between us* in a day when truth is slipping away.

Sparkling Gems From the Greek, Volume 2

Repentance

Repentance is the "birth canal" through which people enter the Kingdom of God, and it is the only way to truly be delivered from the kingdom of darkness and to emerge spiritually reborn and filled with the God-kind of life.

Repentance

Repentance is not just accepting what needs to happen. That's just an acknowledgment. Repentance is when you actually make the decision to *turn*. It is a conversion *so deep* that it results in a permanent life change. If there's no transformation — no change of behavior or desire — in a person who claims he repented, it's doubtful that genuine repentance ever took place.

Build Your Foundation

The changes we need to make will *not* occur accidentally. We must *decide* to change on purpose. We must decide *to remove, lay aside, and permanently put away* attitudes and actions that adversely affect our walk of faith.

The Will of God — The Key to Your Success

Emotions may accompany repentance, but they are not required to repent. True repentance is *a mental choice to leave what is displeasing to God, and to turn toward Him with all of one's heart and mind in order to follow Jesus.*

Repentance

If you've missed the mark in some area and deviated from God's plan, He will require you to do what is right before He will move you to the next phase in your life. If you're willing to repent and seek forgiveness from those you've wronged, God is so gracious that He can bring healing and restoration into even the most breached relationships, and He will likewise help you get back on track with His plan for your life.

Unlikely

Instead of trying to hide our sin, we must be honest before God, be willing to change, and confess sin to the Lord — and He will release forgiveness into our lives, which then releases the power of the Holy Spirit on our behalf to enable us to change and bring forth the fruits of repentance.

Build Your Foundation

Reprobate

We are living in a day when people's minds are being inundated with false information and a celebration of various forms of immorality, including a deluge of counterfeit propaganda about human sexuality. We are witnesses to a last-days attack of seducing spirits, bent on modifying the collective mind of society and creating a way of thinking that is free of moral restraint.

Last-Days Survival Guide

The word translated "reprobate" speaks of minds that have been seriously damaged by long-term, continuous exposure to evil influences and by a continual bombardment of wrong thoughts. A person's mind, created by God to gloriously function, can thus become *unfit* if it is regularly exposed to toxic environments and wrong types of thinking. It can lose its ability to discern what is morally right and wrong.

Last-Days Survival Guide

There is no doubt that we are witnessing a society lured into depths of degeneracy and depravity over this past century that have not been seen since the days when paganism ruled the earth. In fact, we may be witnesses to a pandemic of reprobate thinking on a level that no generation of any epoch in history has witnessed before.

How To Keep Your Head on Straight
in a World Gone Crazy

God's Spirit will plead with people not to abandon truth and go another direction, but if society chooses to do so, He will *release* them to follow their inclinations.

Last-Days Survival Guide

As people walk away from God's spiritual laws and His well-established biblical principles, they put themselves in a position to become reprobate.

*How To Keep Your Head on Straight
in a World Gone Crazy*

Reputation

You need to terminate contact with any place, action, language, or relationship that gives people the impression that you are doing something wrong. It doesn't matter what you think is acceptable; what matters is what other people perceive. So put a great deal of distance between yourself and anything you are doing that people could misinterpret and that could thereby stain your reputation.

Sparkling Gems From the Greek, Volume 2

When Paul told us, "Abstain from all appearance of evil" (1 Thessalonians 5:22), he was strongly urging you and me to *put distance between* ourselves and any appearance of evil. The Greek word for "abstain" used here demands that we do not allow even the smallest hint of inappropriate behavior or any act that could be misinterpreted or viewed as being immoral or unethical. There is no doubt about it — the word "abstain" calls for extreme caution and vigilance.

Sparkling Gems From the Greek, Volume 2

So many people have forfeited their testimony because they didn't use their head and think about how their actions might be perceived by others! Perception is often reality in the eye of the beholder. Even if you know that you're doing nothing wrong at all, the fact remains that people don't see your heart — they see your actions. If they see you do something that appears immoral or unethical, you will likely be judged by what they perceive.

Sparkling Gems From the Greek, Volume 2

Throwing one slanderous accusation after another at your mind, the devil will do everything he can to slander and belittle you. He will defame, malign, revile, and smear your faith in order to drive you back into the ditch of self-preservation where you never do anything significant in your life. Satan wants to ruin your effectiveness with deceptive suggestions and lying allegations!

Dressed To Kill

Rescue

We must do everything within our power to *snatch* people from spiritually dangerous predicaments. Although they may not feel the heat of the fire at the moment or realize the seriousness of their spiritual condition, we must speak forcefully and truthfully to them in order to *seize* their hearts and set them free. We're not in the business of kidnapping people or taking them out of situations against their will, but we can ferociously pray for fellow believers who are caught in sin and don't realize the dangerous nature of their situation!

Sparkling Gems From the Greek, Volume 1

The Holy Spirit feels everything you feel, He understands the complete inadequacy you are experiencing, and He knows about every battle you are facing. He willingly joins you in your circumstances, sharing your emotions and frustrations, and then He begins to put a supernatural plan of rescue into operation to get you out of your mess! So the next time you get into trouble, there's no need for you to sweat it out by yourself. The Holy Spirit is standing by, just waiting for you to ask for His assistance. Helping you is a part of His ministry, so never hesitate to say, "Holy Spirit, help me!" This is what the intercessory ministry of the Holy Spirit is all about!

Sparkling Gems From the Greek, Volume 1

Respect

When you treat people with heartfelt respect, it keeps the door open to relationship even when they don't agree with you. In fact, showing sincere respect is a door opener to *every* person's heart, regardless of culture, language, or skin color.

Sparkling Gems From the Greek, Volume 2

When we speak to people who are different than us or who lead a life far from the righteous standard God demands, we must remember the way we approach them could determine whether or not they ever hear a full presentation of the Gospel. Even if they are sinners, they are made in the image of Almighty God and demand respect as human beings. Rather than malign them with disrespectful or condemning words, ask the Holy Spirit to show you how to find common ground on which you can build a bridge into their hearts.

Sparkling Gems From the Greek, Volume 2

If you're in a situation in which you must confront someone with the truth, imagine how you would respond to that same truth if it were being presented to *you*. Then try to picture what would help you receive it in the easiest way that would bring growth to your life and be a blessing. As you ponder these ideas, what you discover will create a path for you to follow to speak the truth in love into someone else's life. As you follow that path, you will most likely end up treating that other person correctly — with dignity and respect — as you tell him or her what you perceive to be the truth.

Sparkling Gems From the Greek, Volume 2

Responsibility

It's crucial that we understand there is a future judgment of the unsaved — and the revelation of this truth will ignite our hearts to obey God more fully regarding our responsibility to share the saving news of Jesus Christ and to ask the Holy Spirit to open the eyes of the spiritually blind so they can come to Christ and avoid this final judgment.

Build Your Foundation

The Foundation under our lives is Jesus, but what we build on top of that Foundation depends on our personal commitment and the level of excellence we demand of ourselves in every area of our lives. So I ask you: Are you building something with your life that will be enduring — or are you building so hastily and poorly that everything you've built could go up suddenly in a puff of smoke?

Sparkling Gems From the Greek, Volume 2

Every single one of you without exception has received a grace-given gift from God. Embrace what God has placed inside you. Take ownership of it and do your best to use that special gift to meet the needs of one another. God has entrusted a lot to you by placing those special gifts in your life, and He is depending on you to be faithful with this great responsibility.

Sparkling Gems From the Greek, Volume 2

If you haven't discovered it yet, there are many freeloaders in the Body of Christ who would love to shirk these responsibilities and find someone else to do everything for them. If you know someone who shirks responsibilities, it's time for you to start helping that person accept responsibility for his own life! If you know someone who is freeloading on the goodwill of others, God may want to use you to tell him to stop it!

Sparkling Gems From the Greek, Volume 1

Rest

If you feel depleted and fatigued, is it possible that you need to get away for a little while? Could it be that the Lord is urging you to take a breather from the constant pace you're maintaining so you can shake off the problems and relax a little bit? When you're under constant pressure, it affects your ability to think right and see things clearly. We live in a world that is spinning faster and faster, so we have to learn how to keep our lives in balance so we can keep our focus clear.

Sparkling Gems From the Greek, Volume 2

The Bible declares that the people of God can rest in their salvation once they have given their lives to Jesus Christ. His work on the Cross was so complete, perfect, finished, and flawless that there is nothing anyone can do to add to it. A person isn't brought any closer to salvation by asking, begging, pleading, and imploring God to be saved or by trying to prove his sincerity so he can be worthy of salvation. If a person has given his life to Christ, he can "rest" in the fact that it is a done deal.

Sparkling Gems From the Greek, Volume 2

If you don't take a break from constant stress, it will keep wearing you down until you become easy prey for the devil. Take a break and allow yourself a little time to *rest, relax,* and *recuperate*!

Sparkling Gems From the Greek, Volume 1

Restoration

Within the covers of the Bible are all the answers for every problem man could ever face. The truths contained in the Bible bring new life to hearts, establish order to confused minds, and restore souls that are being rocked by life.

*How To Keep Your Head on Straight
in a World Gone Crazy*

People have been hurt *before* they came to Christ, and people have been hurt *after* they came to Christ, but believers' hearts and minds are to be infused with the Word of God — and as they let that Word work inside them. It doesn't matter how many times they've been knocked flat by life, Scripture has the power to restore them and put them upright on their feet again.

Last-Days Survival Guide

Jesus is earnestly seeking to perform a rescue operation in every area of your life where Satan has attempted to bring devastation and ruin. It doesn't matter how the destruction occurred — whether it was due to your own neglect, to the actions of others, to circumstances, or to an attack by Satan himself — Jesus is *still* pursuing you for your *rescue*, your *safety*, and your *recovery*! And if we participate with Jesus in what He is trying to restore in our lives, it is simply a fact that the process will be sped up as He restores us to the wholeness He originally intended for our lives.

Sparkling Gems From the Greek, Volume 2

When the Bible is applied to your life, it has the supernatural ability to get you ready to be a success in life. It doesn't matter how many failures you have experienced, or how many times you have faltered, if you are willing to believe, embrace, and act on the Scriptures, it will release all the power needed to set your faltering life back on the road to success.

Last-Days Survival Guide

Jesus paid the price for your salvation, your liberation, your physical healing, and for your *complete* restoration!

Paid in Full

Restrainer

Through the sacrifice of His Son, God established the Church on this earth with the intention that evil would *never* be left unchecked.

How To Keep Your Head on Straight
in a World Gone Crazy

The only reason Satan has not already brought the Antichrist onto the world stage is the active restraining force of the Church that has hitherto stopped this diabolical move.

Last-Days Survival Guide

God is calling His Church to take its place as His restraining force to enforce Christ's victory, slow down the advance of the enemy's evil agenda, and make way for the great end-time harvest of souls.

How To Keep Your Head on Straight
in a World Gone Crazy

A day is coming when the Church that has delayed the worldwide domination of evil and lawlessness will be removed. At that moment, the evil forces that have long been suppressed will suddenly be freed, and their wicked plans, purposes, and desires will be abruptly energized.

When the Church is removed, these events will quickly come to pass with no hesitation, for the Church — who is presently the Great Restrainer — will be out of the picture.

Sparkling Gems From the Greek, Volume 1

It's our responsibility to take an uncompromising stance on God's Word and to serve as the restraining force that impedes deception's forward progress in society so it cannot take hold and entrench itself in people's minds as "just the way things are."

How To Keep Your Head on Straight
in a World Gone Crazy

Resurrection

It is glorious to know that Jesus will one day raise you from the dead. But you also need to know that if you've been knocked flat by life, Jesus is your Resurrection *right now*. If you embrace Him and His grace, He'll lift you up and put you on your feet again!

Build Your Foundation

When Jesus came out of that grave several days after his death, it was no hoax or fabricated story. In addition to all the people who saw Him die on the Cross, there were many who verified that His dead body was in the tomb before the stone was permanently sealed by an officer from the Roman court of law. But even though his body was inspected and the tomb was legally sealed, it was gone!

Paid in Full

The resurrection of Jesus Christ is the cornerstone of our faith!

Build Your Foundation

The power of God exploded inside the tomb where Jesus was buried. It reconnected His spirit with His dead body, flooded His corpse with life, and He rose from the dead! So much power was released behind the sealed entrance of His tomb that the earth itself reverberated and shuddered from the explosion. An angel rolled the stone from the entrance and Jesus physically walked through the door of that tomb *alive*!

Paid in Full

When Christ was raised from the dead, He seized the keys of hell and the grave (*see* Revelation 1:18), and He conquered death once and for all (*see* Romans 6:10; 2 Timothy 1:10), never to die again!

Build Your Foundation

Retaliation

Any of us may be tempted to be vindictive from time to time — especially if someone has seriously disappointed us, harmed us or our families or friends, or tried to hurt our personal reputation. But no matter what evil others have done to us, we must remember what the apostle Paul wrote in First Thessalonians 5:15: "See that none render evil for evil unto any man; but ever follow that which is good, both among yourselves, and to all men." This makes it clear that Christians are to abstain from all acts of retaliation and self-vindication.

Sparkling Gems From the Greek, Volume 2

Never underestimate the importance of how you react to those who persecute you. Your words of blessing and forgiveness can put to bed forever all the past wrongs ever committed against you. On the other hand, your words of retaliation can reignite the fire of opposition so that the same kind of opposition keeps occurring again and again.

Sparkling Gems From the Greek, Volume 1

If you are surrounded by people who are angry and retaliatory, their words and reactions may incite you to react in anger or with other negative and non-productive emotions. Stomping, screaming, and making threats won't help you. In fact, that kind of behavior just makes situations worse!

Sparkling Gems From the Greek, Volume 2

Retribution is not the way we do business in the Kingdom of God. If there is any need for retribution, let it be something taken care of by God and not by you or me. Let's remember that we are in the business of redeeming the lost, *not* taking revenge or getting even with people when they upset us!

Sparkling Gems From the Greek, Volume 2

Revelation

There is no higher revelation available to mankind than the Word of God — and that Scripture needs no modifications, alterations, or additions to make it more relevant to a society in a constant state of flux.

How To Keep Your Head on Straight
in a World Gone Crazy

One of the ministries of the Holy Spirit is to reveal things to come so we'll know what to expect as we move forward in time (*see* John 16:13). Armed with this knowledge, we can protect ourselves, our families, and our loved ones from the destructive trends that will be associated with the closing days. We can resolve to stand strong and do the will of God, shining as lights in the darkness that will certainly increase just before Jesus returns.

Signs You'll See Just Before Jesus Comes

The Holy Spirit speaks privately to an individual's heart about sin, but if a situation has become so full-blown that it is affecting an entire congregation, it is not unusual for the Holy Spirit to address it publicly, either through an inspired message preached by the pastor, or through a revelatory gift of the Spirit. In such cases, the Holy Spirit's objective is to address the issue and thereby bring the congregation to a position of repentance and cleansing.

Why We Need the Gifts of the Holy Spirit

There was a time in the past when the eye could not see, the ear could not hear, nor could the heart begin to imagine all the amazing, wonderful things God had prepared for those who love Him, but when the Holy Spirit came, He removed the veil that once obstructed our view so now our eyes *can see*, our ears *can hear*, and our hearts *can fully comprehend* the specific, special plans that God has meticulously prepared for each of us!

Sparkling Gems From the Greek, Volume 2

Never forget the important spiritual truths that have been passed from one generation to the next, and the need for every one of us to pass insights to subsequent generations, and to treasure the precious revelations we have received.

**Fallen Angels, Giants, Monsters,
and the World Before the Flood**

Rewards

When we stand before Jesus, He is not going to whip us or castigate us for our failures. Instead, it will be a place of evaluation where Christ will weigh and assess our works, our efforts, and our faith. It will be a place of designation where He will determine the kind of reward that should be given to us for what we did in obedience to His plan.

Build Your Foundation

Skilled warriors *deserve* blessings, good athletes *deserve* recognition, and diligent farmers *deserve* to eat their crops. And if you are faithfully fighting a fight of faith, *you deserve a big victory*, not only a spiritual reward in Heaven, but also a tangible, measurable reward right now — just like any warrior, athlete, or farmer should expect!

Life in the Combat Zone

I've never hung on a cross as Jesus did, and I can't even imagine it. However, there have been times when God has asked me to endure some very hard things that I could escape only by disobeying His instructions. But regardless of how difficult it was to be obedient, I had to keep my eyes fixed on the prize before me and endure the moment. On the path of obedience, difficult or painful moments eventually come to a conclusion, and when they do, resurrection and exaltation follow.

Sparkling Gems From the Greek, Volume 2

A day is coming when Jesus will step forward, dressed in the regal splendor of the exalted King of kings, and place a crown of life upon the heads of those who have faithfully run their race to the very end. The Savior Himself will be personally involved in the giving of this priceless reward. There could be no greater reward than Jesus Christ Himself personally placing this victor's crown on the brow of Christians who have endured to the end and victoriously finished their race of faith.

A Light in Darkness

Religious thinking tries to delude us into believing that we should expect nothing in this life for our service. This thinking says that all rewards are spiritual only and bestowed only in Heaven. In fact, these same religious spirits tell us that if we expect to be rewarded now with temporal blessings for our efforts, our motives are wrong and we are in sin. This incorrect view says that we should never give tithes and offerings with a thought of receiving something in return and that we should never serve in any capacity with a hidden thought of being rewarded, but *this kind of thinking is completely wrong!*

Life in the Combat Zone

God's promise to you is that *anything* you do for Him is *never* a waste! So when your flesh or the devil whispers to you and tempts you to think that no one notices or appreciates your efforts, that your job is insignificant, or that you are wasting your time — *that* is the moment for *you* to remind yourself and the devil that nothing done for the Lord is ever a waste. Every effort, every deed — *everything* you have ever done in obedience to His instructions — will be accredited to your heavenly record!

Sparkling Gems From the Greek, Volume 2

Rhema

It's true that the Spirit of God can speak a lengthy personal word to our hearts about our lives, but this is the exception and not the rule. When you study history, you'll see that most great men and women of God who have earned a place in the pages of history have done so by obeying a single, simple word from God.

Dressed To Kill

We need to *stab* the enemy! And in order to do that, we will need a *rhema* — a *specific, quickened word* from the Scriptures — placed into our hearts and our hands by the Holy Spirit. Once we have a *rhema* word from God, we have the "sword power" to render the enemy *powerless* in his attempts to steal, kill, and destroy everything good in our lives!

Life in the Combat Zone

We must become "people of the Book," continually receiving God's *rhema* — *living words* — that He is speaking to us through His Word and His Spirit into our hearts and minds so the very substance of God can be released into our lives. We have to open up God's Word like we would open a treasure and allow *who* is inside the written Word to flow within us. This Word is the only thing that will heal us and make us whole, protect our families, and help set our children and our marriages on a blessed, right course.

Sparkling Gems From the Greek, Volume 2

The next time you find yourself in close combat with the enemy, take the time to get quiet in your heart and listen, and the Holy Spirit will reach up from within your spirit and *quicken* to you a scripture that has the exact power you need for the situation you find yourself in at that moment. The Holy Spirit will give you a *rhema* — a specific word for a specific time and a specific purpose — and when that happens, you have just received real "sword power"! Then it's time for you to *insert your rhema word, twist your sword,* and *do damage* to the devil!

Sparkling Gems From the Greek, Volume 1

Ridicule

In these greatest of days and most troublesome of times, your uncompromised stance for Jesus might put you on a roller coaster of opposites when it comes to man's acceptance of you. You might experience rejection and ridicule in one part of your day and then see someone's life changed forever by your godly influence in another part.

How To Keep Your Head on Straight in a World Gone Crazy

Escaping trouble was never promised in Scripture, but experiencing the overcoming power and presence of God *is* promised to those who trust Him as they hold fast to His revealed will for their lives. Times may be difficult, but those who stay on track and refuse to budge from their divinely assigned place will encounter the presence of God's power to sustain and undergird them, no matter what they face.

The Will of God — The Key to Your Success

Early believers endured bullying, ridicule, imprisonment, and were even put to death because they refused to conform to the world that surrounded them on all sides. Although some believers collapsed under this pressure, many steadfastly resisted this coercion to conform and held fast to their faith. God has always had His remnant — those who will not bow to external pressures — and in these last times, God will have that remnant once again. Those who refuse to fear or to compromise their faith in Jesus Christ will experience previously unknown levels of the power of God as a result of their commitment to stand by truth.

Sparkling Gems From the Greek, Volume 2

Hasn't the world always been harsh and bitter toward God's people? From the beginning of time, the lost world has ridiculed, made fun of, sarcastically accused, and debased the people of God. There is nothing new about this at all. Remember that Jesus was also "despised and rejected of men" (Isaiah 53:3). Rejoice — you are in good company with Jesus!

Unlikely

Roles

As you ponder your own role in God's house, it is important for you to remember that some people's roles are more visible, while others have a less visible part to play. Yet *everyone's* role is vital and of great consequence, for if those working behind the scenes didn't do their part, those with more visible roles wouldn't be able to do *their* parts.

Sparkling Gems From the Greek, Volume 2

Human beings tend to glamorize people who perform on the stage, but entertainers wouldn't seem so glamorous if they had no makeup artists to prepare them. They wouldn't shine so brightly if there were no lighting specialists to light up the stage. Their voices would be unheard if there were no sound technicians. The makeup artists, lighting specialists, and sound technicians are unseen, but I guarantee you that their absence would be noticed if they didn't do their jobs. *They are all vital for the show to go on!* So don't let the devil badger you into thinking your role is not important because it is less visible than others. Your part is very important in God's house!

Sparkling Gems From the Greek, Volume 2

There are many different roles in God's Kingdom, and each role is significant and important. Maybe your role is visible, or maybe yours is behind the scenes. Regardless of the role you have right now, consider it an honor that God would use you in His house, and say *yes* to the role God has given you at this time. Throw open your arms, embrace it, and hold it close. Take deep into your heart the place of service to which God has assigned you for this season. Master that position — fulfilling its responsibilities with an excellent attitude — and then watch God move you to higher levels of responsibility according to His will and His purposes for your life!

Sparkling Gems From the Greek, Volume 2

Rules

Just as my father reminded me that as long as I lived under his roof, I was going to live by his rules, God also expects us to live by the rules of *His* house. We must remember that we are His sons and daughters in the household of faith. It is our obligation and responsibility to live under God's roof according to His rules. I assure you that if we are out of sync with God's Word, He isn't going to bend to accommodate *us*. *We* are the ones who must change and conform to *Him*.

Sparkling Gems From the Greek, Volume 2

When God finds a man or woman who knows the Word, honors the Word, and follows the Word in every situation, He has found the type of person to whom He will give authority and responsibility. The fact that this individual knows the rules and lives by them demonstrates to God that he or she can be trusted with greater responsibility.

Sparkling Gems From the Greek, Volume 2

If you are sloppy about how you apply God's rules to your life, you need to be honest with yourself and realize that the big break you've been hoping for may still be very far away. *For God to give you a big assignment, He needs to know that He can trust you to live according to the rules of His house!*

Sparkling Gems From the Greek, Volume 2

Running the Race of Faith

Jesus has *appointed* a goal for your life and has even *pre-established* the course you need to run to get there! We're not smart enough to figure out how to reach God's goal for our lives, so Jesus has taken care of that part for us. He just needs our willingness to jump into the race and run with all our might — keeping our eyes on the goal!

Sparkling Gems From the Greek, Volume 2

When I am tempted to yield to weariness, or I know I'm looking at difficult times on the road directly before me — in those vulnerable moments, I lift the eyes of my faith and focus on the moment when the King of kings will place a victor's crown on my own head because He found me faithful. Thinking of that makes me want to stay in the race and *finish it all the way to the end!*

Sparkling Gems From the Greek, Volume 2

Do you see yourself as someone who is running the spiritual Olympic event of his or her life, or are you simply "jogging for Jesus?" If you're serious about fulfilling God's plan for your life, it's time to shift into high gear and to start putting all your spiritual, mental, and physical energies into getting the job done. You have to remove all distractions and commit yourself to a life of discipline, balance, and devotion.

Sparkling Gems From the Greek, Volume 1

Jesus is beckoning you to run your race with all your might. Your emotions may even tell you that the entire endeavor is just not worth it because it's so much more than you bargained for when you began — but quitting is *not* the answer. Jesus didn't give you a goal you can't reach, so shove your negative emotions out of the way, determine that you *are* going to stay put in the race, and *then make a run for it!*

Sparkling Gems From the Greek, Volume 2

S

Sacrifice

Bringing sacrifices to God existed since the time Cain and Abel (sons of Adam and Eve) brought their first sacrifices (*see* Genesis 4:3-5). Noah sacrificed animals to God upon leaving the ark (*see* Genesis 8:20,21). Abraham offered up various burnt offerings during his sojourning (*see* Genesis 12:7,8; 15:9,10). Then later, God stopped Abraham from sacrificing Isaac, and the Bible tells us Abraham instead offered a sacrificial burnt offering in the place of his son (*see* Genesis 22:13). And, of course, during the years Israel wandered in the wilderness, they offered sacrificial offerings and then continued that practice after they finally settled in the Promised Land.

Apostles and Prophets

The process of sacrificing to God was such a massive endeavor that to do it required long-term planning, complex organization, and the employing of a substantial workforce to slaughter so many animals in such a short span of time. Thus, presenting a sacrificial offering was much more than a mere casual, physical act. It was a plan conceived in the heart and mind and carried out purposefully and worshipfully.

Apostles and Prophets

Realize that whatever you're doing today may simply be the training ground for your future. Don't allow yourself to get so cemented in what you're doing that you can't move forward to the next step God has in store for you. And if it ever seems like God is asking you to make a huge sacrifice, remember this is just His way of freeing you so He can give you something better and greater and make you more productive for the Kingdom of God.

Sparkling Gems From the Greek, Volume 2

For the Jewish people, sacrificial rituals were *deeply personal* and were to be *deeply felt*. For example, if a worshiper was seeking atonement for sin, it wasn't sufficient to merely bring a physical offering. The one who brought it had to *feel remorse* for his sin as the sacrifice was slaughtered and offered on the altar. One Jewish scholar stated that to genuinely repent, the person offering a sacrificial offering for sin had to realize that what was being done to the animal essentially should have happened to *him* instead.

Apostles and Prophets

To become a living sacrifice, as God calls every believer to be, will require *a death to self.* Such a living sacrifice occurs when you bow your will, dethrone self, enthrone Jesus by choosing to submit to His lordship, and choose to obediently live to fulfill His commandments.

Apostles and Prophets

Salt

When Jesus taught that we are to be "the salt of the earth," it meant that through our *influence*, we should be a *preserving force* in a world that is filled with rot, spoil, and decay. God's Word working in our lives causes us to be like salt, and our very presence helps abate the corruption that is eating away at the world.

Sparkling Gems From the Greek, Volume 2

Salt was a very important ingredient for physicians and those employed in the field of medicine, for they used salt as a *healing agent*. If a person was severely wounded, salt was poured into the wound to sanitize it from germs, to stop the spread of infection, to stop the bleeding, and to speed up the healing of the wound. When Jesus said we are to be "the salt of the earth," it meant that we should be *carriers of physical healing* to a world that is suffering with all manner of sickness and ailments. Through the preaching of God's Word and personal ministry to those who are physically ill, we are to be "the salt of the earth" that brings healing to those who are physically suffering.

Sparkling Gems From the Greek, Volume 2

Salt was an important ingredient used by farmers to enrich and fertilize their soil in order to produce larger crops of a higher quality. Even a small amount of salt scattered sparingly on the ground could improve the quality of the soil and result in bigger harvests and healthier crops, so it was viewed as an essential ingredient in the farming industry. The words "the salt of the earth" could actually be translated "the salt of the soil" — and the implication is that our very presence should enhance life and make this world a better place to live.

Sparkling Gems From the Greek, Volume 2

At the time Jesus said we are to be "the salt of the earth," Israel was subject to Rome's rule, and because of this, the Israelites regularly witnessed the pagan practices of Roman religions. One practice of the Romans and other pagan religions of the time was rubbing salt over a newborn baby in order to protect that child from evil spirits. Pagans believed so wholeheartedly in the magical, protective powers of salt that they regularly administered heavy quantities of salt to the thresholds of their homes and businesses, believing it would create a strong barrier that evil spirits could not cross. When Jesus said we are to be "the salt of the earth," it meant through our *influence*, we are to be a source of spiritual protection, deliverance, safety, and freedom to people who have been assaulted by demonic powers. *We are to be carriers of protection, safety, and deliverance!*

Sparkling Gems From the Greek, Volume 2

Salvation

The Bible clearly teaches that people who trust in *any-thing* other than Christ will go to hell after death. It's that simple, so never let yourself forget that the only ones who go to Heaven are those who have wholly and completely put their trust in Christ alone.

Build Your Foundation

If you struggle with your salvation, wondering whether or not you are *really* saved, nail it down forever by praying one last prayer of repentance and surrendering your life to Jesus Christ. Then walk away from that place of commitment and *never* revisit it again. *Quit struggling and start resting in what Jesus has done for you!* It is high time for you to kick back and *rest* in the fact that Jesus saved you and that this work of redemption is utterly complete.

Sparkling Gems From the Greek, Volume 2

When a person is saved, his sins are removed, he is washed in the blood of Jesus — and in that moment — his nature is changed and his name is written in the Lamb's book of life. This is an event the entire spirit realm recognizes, including mighty angels who stand in the very presence of God, who get so excited when this mightiest miracle takes place that they stop everything to celebrate!

Sparkling Gems From the Greek, Volume 2

The Bible declares that the people of God can rest in their salvation once they have given their lives to Jesus Christ. His work on the Cross was so complete, perfect, finished, and flawless that there is nothing anyone can do to add to it. A person isn't brought any closer to salvation by asking, begging, pleading, and imploring God to be saved or by trying to prove his sincerity so he can be worthy of salvation. If a person has given his life to Christ, he can "rest" in the fact that it is a done deal

Sparkling Gems From the Greek, Volume 2

The moment Jesus became Lord of *your* life was the exact split second you *entered into* God's completed work of salvation. Regardless of what the devil may try to whisper to make you think that you must do more to *really* be saved, the fact remains that if your life has been given to Jesus Christ, you have already entered into the perfect, complete, finished, and flawless work of God. You can calm down, relax, and be at peace! *It's a done deal!*

Sparkling Gems From the Greek, Volume 2

That little baby in Bethlehem was the eternal, ever-existent God Almighty, who dressed Himself in human flesh so that He could dwell among men and purchase our salvation on the Cross as the Lamb of God who would take away the sin of the world and render its punishment *powerless*.

Christmas — The Rest of the Story

Sanctification

When God is working good things *into* you, He is simultaneously weeding bad things *out* of you.

The Point of No Return

Through the years, I have learned that it doesn't matter how much I surrender to God's sanctifying power today — by tomorrow He will be asking me to surrender more. Every second, every minute, every hour, every day, every week, and every year that passes by my eyes are illuminated to new areas of my life that have never been surrendered — and He asks me to yield those areas to His control.

The Holy Spirit and You

When the Bible is ingested into the soul, its divine fire identifies, ignites, and consumes debris that needs to be expunged from a person's life. That fire also ignites new life in areas of a person that have grown indifferent and resistant to God's will.

A Life Ablaze

We must never forget that if we don't deal with issues at the root, they will remain alive and will reactivate at a critical moment later in life.

How To Keep Your Head on Straight
in a World Gone Crazy

The Holy Spirit desires to possess *you* — *all* of you.

The Holy Spirit and You

Satan

Jesus stripped Satan of his legal authority over us, but his intelligence remains intact. It is that cunning, keen, sharp, wily, brainy mind that the devil uses against us today. Satan's power is no match for the all-surpassing power of the Holy Spirit, and he knows it, so he seeks to outwit our natural minds with malevolent strategies that he has invented with his incredibly intelligent mind.

Dressed To Kill

God lets us know that Lucifer became so inflated with pride and enamored with himself that he lost sight of the fact that he was only a mirror and began to wrongly believe that he was self-generating his own radiance.

A Life Ablaze

When Lucifer was cast out of Heaven, this once-dazzling archangel — created to be a reflector of God's resplendent glory — was reduced to an evil, monstrous figure that would eventually be laughed at by the nations of the world. The moment Lucifer was cast out, the light went out that once shone so brilliantly upon him, and his name was changed to Satan.

A Life Ablaze

Satan is terrified of the Body of Christ because he knows it is his greatest enemy in the world. And remember, you are a member of the Body — the devil is terrified of *you!*

Sparkling Gems From the Greek, Volume 2

Satan is not seeking just anyone to devour; he is seeking *those whom he may devour.* In other words, the enemy is looking for those who are weak in faith, ignorant of the Word of God, isolated unto themselves, and not mature enough to stand in the face of his constant, hassling allegations. These are the individuals that this "roaring lion" is seeking after, and his objective is to devour them.

Dressed To Kill

From the time he was kicked out of Heaven until the present day, Satan has been operating in darkness in a vain attempt to regain the glory he lost. Working through society, culture, and entertainment, he strives to get people to worship him. Preying on the hearts and minds of selfish men and women whose hearts are bent toward evil, Satan continues to attempt to steal God's glory. But it always was and always will be a vain attempt. Satan will forever be eliminated from his exalted position because of his pride.

A Life Ablaze

Self-Image

If you've been dealing with a poor self-image, grab hold of this truth, because this is the greatest self-image booster that exists! Inwardly you are so beautiful and magnificent that Almighty God wanted to live inside you! What kind of home do you think God would require? A shabby shack made of dirt and sticks? No! He has built for Himself a beautiful temple within your heart — and that is who you are right now! *Now live like the magnificently decorated cathedral of God's Spirit that you are!*

Sparkling Gems From the Greek, Volume 1

Rather than let other people affect your self-image and confidence, you need to know who you are in Jesus Christ and hold your head up high!

Sparkling Gems From the Greek, Volume 1

When I finally understood that *God* was the One who made me different, I began to see that I could shine His light in ways that others could not. What I thought would hold me back is actually what gave me my place in His plan, and when I began to accept who God made me to be, I began to step out of the shadows so God could begin to use me in a greater way. I was finally able to *embrace* my uniqueness that made me shine differently from others!

Sparkling Gems From the Greek, Volume 2

It is simply a fact that you will inevitably *project* what you feel about yourself to others. So this question about how you see yourself is very important. If you see yourself as a champion who wins every fight, that is exactly how others will see you. But if you see yourself as someone who struggles and wrestles with a bad self-image — that is precisely how others will perceive you. Such people feel so badly about themselves that they *exude* their negative perception of themselves and their sense of insecurity.

Sparkling Gems From the Greek, Volume 1

Quit seeing yourself as someone who is substandard, second-rate, low-grade, or inferior. You are filled with the Spirit of God and have the call of God on your life!

Sparkling Gems From the Greek, Volume 1

Sex-Reassignment Surgeries

Modern procedures are being performed on those who are most certainly in an extreme case of confusion both mentally and emotionally. For someone to willfully have an irreversible, maiming procedure performed on one's own body is itself a symptom of inner chaos and spiritual sickness — yet society has veered so far from biblical truth and is so affected by delusional thinking that more and more people are embracing the notion that gender is not determined at birth by the Creator and may be electively changed by surgery.

How To Keep Your Head on Straight in a World Gone Crazy

How I wish that someone could justly accuse me of exaggerating, but this travesty of gender reassignment surgery in Western society is being perpetuated against children more and more frequently and often with the endorsement of their parents and physicians. *How can this not be considered child abuse?*

> *How To Keep Your Head on Straight in a World Gone Crazy*

Our compassion must be extended to others, especially when we *know* that the actions someone has taken are to his or her own lasting detriment. These precious souls need answers from the Word of God. They need the Holy Spirit to heal their souls. They need the compassionate touch of Christ to be transmitted to them through non-condemning believers who themselves have been forgiven, delivered, and restored by the redemptive power of the Cross.

> *How To Keep Your Head on Straight in a World Gone Crazy*

Shield of Faith

There is no doubt that the devil will try to shoot his arrows in your direction. But having a shield of faith that is soaked in the Word of God gives you double protection against these attacks. It guarantees that the enemy's fiery darts will have little or no effect, even if they get close enough to strike your heart, mind, or emotions in the midst of the situations you find yourself facing today.

> *Sparkling Gems From the Greek, Volume 1*

Many believers are hit by the enemy's fiery arrows every day because they are not walking with their shield of faith held out in front of them where it belongs. Not only that, but they neglect their shield of faith, failing to keep it anointed by the Spirit and saturated with the water of the Word. If only they would do what they should to maintain and strengthen their faith, that invisible shield would keep those hellish arrows from getting through to harm them!

Dressed To Kill

Without a fresh touch of the Holy Spirit's power on your life, your faith can become hard, stiff, and brittle. If you ignore your faith and allow it to go undeveloped, never seeking a fresh anointing of God's Spirit to come upon your life, your faith won't be soft, supple, and pliable enough to stand up under attack when a challenge comes your way. Faith that is ignored nearly always breaks and falls to pieces during a confrontation with the enemy.

Dressed To Kill

Don't ever worry or fret that God has given others more faith than He has given you. Rest assured in the fact that He has imparted enough faith to you to make sure you are covered from head to toe!

Dressed To Kill

Our faith will work for us personally, but when we join our faith to the faith of others, we position ourselves to make some significant gains! Believers are called to march together side-by-side, holding their closely connected shields of faith out in front of them just as the Roman soldiers did on their way to meet the enemy army. When that kind of unity exists among believers who are walking together in faith, it doesn't matter how many demonic forces are out there to oppose them, because those unified believers will be able to steadily and aggressively move forward to put pressure on the enemy and to thwart all his strategies with the power of their unified, corporate faith!

Dressed To Kill

Shoes of Peace

"Shoes of peace" are both defensive and offensive. Peace protects you, but it also provides you with a weapon to wield against the enemy when he attacks. If you use the weapon of peace correctly, it will keep spiritual foes where they belong — under your feet! One good kick, and the enemy's strategies against you will be crushed!

Dressed To Kill

The peace of God gives you a firm footing! The devil may attack and attack, but when you have the peace of God functioning in your life, you will never be moved, because peace will hold you in place! Just as the roots of a tree hold the tree in place when strong winds come against it, God's peace will hold you in your stance of faith as well.

Dressed To Kill

If you make it past the rocky places in your life and are headed toward victory, the enemy may try to abort your victory by forcing you through a thorny situation. But when the peace of God is working in your life, you will also make it through those sticky situations. The prevailing, conquering peace of God will rule to such an extent that you can walk through those thorny places in life without receiving one poisonous prick to your mind or emotions!

Dressed To Kill

If the devil wants to stand in front of you and oppose you and the work of God in your life, then don't stop and ask him to move! Just keep marching, stomping and pounding as you move forward to obey the plan of God for your life — and as you move forward in faith, do as much damage to the enemy as you possibly can!

Dressed To Kill

Signs of the Times

When Jesus foretold events that will occur at the end of the age, He verbalized them in such a way that those times would be easily recognizable, not obscured or difficult to understand, and He gave concrete markers to let us know where we are on our journey — approximately how close we are to our destination — and what we need to know so we can remain safe and effective on the path. Although the Scriptures forecast that the times ahead will be fraught with difficulty, the warnings Christ revealed were intended to direct and instruct us, not send us "running for the hills"! As we lock our trust onto Him, we can be sure that He will enable us to safely navigate the road ahead of us and *pass with care* the dangers that would ensnare us or hinder our journey.

Signs You'll See Just Before Jesus Comes

In recent decades, the world has seen a variety of uprisings sweep across entire geographical areas, and in each place where these have occurred, it has resulted in disturbances, upheavals, political instability, and the spawning of more insurgencies and revolts — and this is what Jesus prophesied would be a sign of the end of the age.

Signs You'll See Just Before Jesus Comes

Jesus prophesied the stirring of *ethnic groups* — including racial, religious, and political groups and factions — would occur in the very last days. Regardless of the cause, it is clear that these contentions are happening with greater frequency in our day and stand as a clear signal that we are approaching the very end of the age.

Signs You'll See Just Before Jesus Comes

Jesus clearly stated that "pestilences" — whether they are outbreaks of old or new diseases — would be an indicator we are nearing the wrap-up of the present age.

Signs You'll See Just Before Jesus Comes

Jesus predicted a time of prolific seismic activity that will occur at the end of the age. In Luke 21:11, Jesus spoke of "great" earthquakes — which in Greek can depict something *large* in size or it can also mean *numerous* in quantity — but He added these earthquakes will occur in "divers places." This means the earth will be touched globally by increased seismic activity toward the end of the age.

Signs You'll See Just Before Jesus Comes

In Luke 21:11, Jesus said those who live at the end of the age would see "fearful sights." These words are translated from a Greek word that depicts *fright, horror,* or something *scary,* but ancient Greek writers used this word to describe *monsters.* What Jesus was referring to is not exactly clear, but it does mean that a last-days society will witness things that are "monstrous" in the eyes of God and the minds of men.

Signs You'll See Just Before Jesus Comes

Jesus forecast a time of persecution would come to His followers at the end of the age stating that many would be *afflicted* and even *killed* — and that many would be *offended* and would *betray* and *hate* one another for the Gospel's sake.

Signs You'll See Just Before Jesus Comes

According to Jesus' words in Matthew 24:7, there will be a scarcity of food in many parts of the world toward the end of this era just before He returns. Jesus prophesied a time of *great physical hunger* would develop in nations of the world toward the very end of the period.

Signs You'll See Just Before Jesus Comes

Jesus prophetically forecast that financial instability would become more and more common as we draw closer to the end of the age. In other words, the earth at that time in history would exist in a state of being *financially troubled, stirred up, agitated, anxious, and upset.*

Signs You'll See Just Before Jesus Comes

Iniquity abounding with the love of many growing cold (see Matthew 24:12) can occur in every single home, church, community, city, state, and nation on earth. In fact, Jesus said this would emerge worldwide as a societal occurrence, and because it will happen among "sinners and saints" across the board as the end draws near, it means even Christians around the world are susceptible to this phenomenon.

Signs You'll See Just Before Jesus Comes

Jesus warned that no one but the Father would know the exact moment when He would return (*see* Matthew 24:36). Those who have tried to fix dates on Christ's coming have embarrassingly learned that no one is able to pinpoint the exact day or hour of the Lord's return!

Signs You'll See Just Before Jesus Comes

Sin

Sin not only affects us, but it grieves the Holy Spirit in us!

The Holy Spirit and You

Having material possessions, social status, and so forth, in your hand is one thing — but having these things in your *heart* is another. When the things of the world get in your heart and you become preoccupied with them, you have crossed a serious line!

The Holy Spirit and You

When non-Christians or Christians knowingly living in sin are in our midst, we are obligated to make sure they understand that sin separates them from God. They are *not* all right with God. It may be painful for them to hear the reality of their situation, but we must not merely toss "painkillers" at people who are lost or out of fellowship with the Lord to numb them and keep them ignorant of the truth. We must ask the Holy Spirit to help us open their eyes to the root of the problem in their lives — their spiritual condition.

Repentance

Instead of trying to hide our sin, we must be honest before God, be willing to change, and confess sin to the Lord — and He will release forgiveness into our lives, which then releases the power of the Holy Spirit on our behalf to enable us to change and bring forth the fruits of repentance.

Build Your Foundation

Demon spirits cannot destroy a person unless there is already an area of sin in his life they can grab hold of and twist to that person's destruction.

Dressed To Kill

Compromise with the world or allowing a slack attitude toward sin are the most dangerous enemies of faith. It isn't acceptable to win a single battle and then lose the war because of a slack, unguarded attitude. Christ admonishes each of us *to be permanently and consistently undeterred in our efforts to overcome and to obtain a lasting victory over sin in our lives.*

No Room for Compromise

Imagine trying to run a race with hundreds of added pounds on your shoulders. You wouldn't be able to run very far, and this is exactly what sinful habits and attitudes do to your walk with the Lord. If you don't *remove* them, they will eventually *weigh* you down and knock you out of your race of faith, so we must take a good look at our lives and remove everything that weighs us down and keeps us from a life of obedience.

The Will of God — The Key to Your Success

As Jesus' strength continued to drain away and the full consequence of man's sin was being realized in Him on the Cross, the soldiers at the foot of the Cross unthinkably played a game to see who would get His finest piece of clothing!

Paid in Full

Slothfulness

The word "slothful" is taken from a Greek word that describes something that is *slow* or *sluggish*. This word isn't talking about laziness; rather, it carries the idea of something that has lost its speed or momentum. It is still moving, but not with the same velocity and aggression it once possessed.

Dream Thieves

Slothful people make excuses for themselves and rationalize why they don't keep promises or why they fail along the way. Instead of honestly admitting that they didn't do what was required, they attempt to hide their lukewarm,

"I-don't-really-care" attitude under a worthless heap of excuses. If you have failed in this area of your life, don't get depressed and beat yourself up — *just do something about it!*

The Point of No Return

If you are serious about serving and pleasing God, you must view the loss of your passion, momentum, and desire as totally unacceptable. If slothfulness has slowly wormed its way into your life, this spiritual problem can be corrected. You *can* get back on track again! By repenting and deciding to turn from slothfulness and neutrality, you can remove this hindrance from your life, but if you continue in that sorry state, it will only be a matter of time before you look back and realize how much ground you've lost.

Sparkling Gems From the Greek, Volume 1

Small Beginnings

Everyone has a small beginning, and you will not be the exception. Instead of bemoaning the fact that you feel so far away from doing what God has placed in your heart, *thank* Him for the precious time you're in now to grow, mature, and prove you are worthy of greater responsibilities. God needs to see this growth process in you.

Unlikely

I encourage you not to lament whatever "small thing" you may be doing right now as being too tiny or unimportant. Believe me when I tell you that nothing is being wasted in what you are doing right now. God is *committed* to training you now so you can be a success in the future!

Unlikely

My own beginning in ministry was so small it was almost unnoticeable, but it was a beginning! Everyone has to have a beginning — including you! If you know what God has gifted you to do, don't wait around and lose precious time as you wait for a hypothetical, fantasy-like "perfect moment" to get started. Instead, put your hand to the plow and begin to use your gifts right now. Once you take that step of faith, God will have something to bless, but as long as you do nothing, you're not giving Him anything to prosper!

Sparkling Gems From the Greek, Volume 2

Social Media

A modern-day trap of seeking popularity is the ever-broadening platform of social media in which success can be measured by how many "likes" a person receives. To garner more "likes," some use their social-media pages to get attention, often making outrageous statements just to create a buzz.

How To Keep Your Head on Straight
in a World Gone Crazy

People's desire and ability *to think* — to process, gather, and study information to ensure they arrive at an accurate conclusion — has been greatly diminished in our time due to a nonstop bombardment of visual messages on social media that has had the net effect of causing people's attention spans to be radically decreased.

How To Keep Your Head on Straight
in a World Gone Crazy

It is wise for spiritual leaders to deeply ponder the content of what they endorse, teach, or share in various media. It is a holy duty for any leader to think through a teaching all the way to its logical conclusion before they package and present it to those who listen to them.

How To Keep Your Head on Straight
in a World Gone Crazy

Because of this nonstop infiltration of information, we must use caution about "what" and "who" is channeled into our devices and into the privacy of our homes.

Last-Days Survival Guide

Society

More and more, society as a whole is rejecting the authoritative voice of the Bible and seems bent on embracing self-destructive and ungodly ways of thinking and behaving.

How To Keep Your Head on Straight
in a World Gone Crazy

Just as the human heart pumps blood into the various parts of the physical body, the heart of a wayward society pumps *foolishness* and *flawed thinking* throughout its "circulatory system" until eventually every stratum of that society becomes touched with the destructive effects of the foolishness produced and disseminated when man separates himself from his Creator.

Last-Days Survival Guide

If we want to know where society is headed, all we need to do is to look back at the past, for what once existed only in historical textbooks is reappearing before our eyes as society continues to turn from God.

A Light in Darkness

While society sinks deeper into deception and depravity, God's Word and His Spirit can enable you to rise above the downfall of the world, high above the "waters" of destruction that will cover the earth at the end of the age before Jesus returns for His Church.

Signs You'll See Just Before Jesus Comes

Before the "man of lawlessness" can be revealed, the world must first become a place where lawlessness abounds, for a world guided by God's Word would never tolerate a lawless leader. Therefore, the moral temperature of society must continue to decrease dramatically if the bulk of the population is ever to embrace a man of lawlessness. As time slips away and the deterioration of modern society accelerates, this will be a clear signal that Christ's return is at hand.

A Light in Darkness

Soldiers

When you examine the history of the Early Church, you find that the majority of early Christians were not nobility but were just regular people who were unspoiled by the luxuries of life, content with little, inured to fatigue, and accustomed to hard work — perfect soldiers in the army of the Lord!

Life in the Combat Zone

To a great extent, the Church at large is trying to affect a lost world without requiring any sacrificial effort from its ranks. Instead of being hard on slothfulness and undisciplined behavior, many churches choose to pamper their members and go out of their way not to hurt anyone's feelings. They make a great effort to not ask anything of their congregations that would require any extra effort on their part. While we are supposed to be the army of the Lord, the Church is full of complacent civilians instead of seasoned soldiers!

Life in the Combat Zone

As soldiers in the Lord's army, we must understand exactly what our role is in the Body of Christ. Once we know our God-appointed place, we must make every effort to get in formation, stand firm in our proper position, and learn to march to the Lord's orders — without being threatened by the position or authority of other people. *That's* when we will be able to inflict great harm upon the enemy!

Life in the Combat Zone

Many believers study books, listen to audio and video teachings, and receive what other men have to say, but their scriptural knowledge is only skin deep. When they get out in the heat of the conflict, they find out that they haven't truly absorbed the Word into their hearts, and, as a result, they're unprepared for the heat of the battle. We need to be ready to take some heat — and we must never be afraid of the heat!

Life in the Combat Zone

Today — *right now* — God needs a special brand of believers to boldly challenge the kingdom of darkness in the authority of Jesus Christ and to *storm* the gates of hell! God is looking for those special believers who will hear His voice, surrender to His call, and willingly enter the combat zone to do battle for the cause of His Kingdom.

Life in the Combat Zone

Sorrow

Have you ever felt sorrow because of a sin you committed that grieved the heart of God? Did you allow that godly sorrow to do its full work in you and produce a desire to change within your heart — resulting in a change in your character, behavior, and lifestyle? Or did you merely brush off that sorrow and thereby resist God's dealings with you *and* His grace to help you grow?

Repentance

If you are overwhelmed with sorrows, remember that Jesus carried *your* sorrow. And if you are consumed with grief, remember that Jesus bore *your* grief.

Paid in Full

As we approach the end of the Church Age, Jesus said the world will begin to feel stress and pressure like a woman preparing to give birth to a baby. Let's think for a moment about that. A woman's pain starts slowly then gradually grows stronger and stronger. Finally, her whole body is pushing downward to deliver that child. At the last moment, the pain comes quickly and intensely — this is the indicator that she is right at the moment of delivery. Likewise, as the world comes closer and closer to the end of the age, the pain in the world will become greater. These pains will become more intense and more frequent, and as they grow in intensity and frequency, it will be a signal that we are approaching the time when Jesus will return for the Church.

Sparkling Gems From the Greek, Volume 2

Sowing and Reaping

The *more strategic and orderly the sowing process is from beginning to end, the easier the harvest.*

Life in the Combat Zone

Maybe *you* have been trusting God for a desire of your heart to burst forth in your life but have gotten discouraged during the time of waiting between the *seed sown* and the *harvest reaped.* I want to encourage you not to quit before you've received what you've been expecting. You can rest assured that if you won't give up, God *certainly* won't fail to perform His Word for you!

Sparkling Gems From the Greek, Volume 2

Fear may try to keep you from trying to sow again, but you must think of yourself like a farmer. He doesn't stop farming because he's had one or even several bad years of farming. He keeps planting that seed in anticipation of a bumper crop because one good bumper crop can make up for all those bad years of failure!

Life in the Combat Zone

Scripture exhorts us to sow our financial seeds into good deeds!

Sparkling Gems From the Greek, Volume 2

It's exciting to plant seeds of faith, and it's *really* exciting when the harvest comes — that moment when your faith finally turns into sight! But in order to reach that point, you must hold tight to what God has told you and remember that your seed — whether it's financial seed or seeds of uninterrupted, useful deeds toward others — has a set season when it will produce, *if* you do not disrupt the process. As long as you *stay the course*, it is guaranteed that you will reap what you have planted.

Sparkling Gems From the Greek, Volume 2

Speaking for God

In the past, an oracle was a person or place where divine communication occurred, and seekers had to travel great distances to the remote locations where these oracles could be found. But today *every* believer has become an oracle because he is indwelled by the Holy Spirit. That means wherever we are, we can be a channel or mouthpiece through whom the Holy Spirit can speak. But to be an instrument the Holy Spirit can use, we must surrender and give ourselves as living sacrifices to God, yielding to the Holy Spirit so God can use us to help bring answers, direction, and assistance to others.

Apostles and Prophets

The Body of Christ is in need of quality spiritual leaders who are willing to pick up the torch and boldly declare the Word of God to an end-time generation as the absolute, dependable, infallible, reliable, unchanging Word of God.

*How To Keep Your Head on Straight
in a World Gone Crazy*

If the Church does not raise its prophetic voice to speak as God's spokesman in these times, other voices will fill the vacuum.

Last-Days Survival Guide

Those who speak for God must clearly understand that their highest priority is to come into His presence in order to hear both the message and every nuance of what God wants to communicate to His people. More than just intellectually communicating information, those who speak for the Lord must capture not only *information*, but also His *heart* that needs to be conveyed to His people — and they must do it with conviction and passion.

Apostles and Prophets

In this late hour at the end of this age, it is of paramount importance that spiritual leaders accept responsibility to speak truth and to call the Church back to the authoritative voice of the Scriptures.

**How To Keep Your Head on Straight
in a World Gone Crazy**

When you are called upon to do something new — something that seems bigger than you or outside of your capabilities, yet you *know* it is your assignment — that is the moment for you to push aside those feelings of deficiency and turn to the sufficiency of the Holy Spirit. Prepare as well as you can, but when the time comes for you to stand, to speak, to sing, to witness, or to testify — lean upon the Holy Spirit and His power.

Unlikely

Spirit (and Mystery) of Iniquity

The last-days spirit of iniquity is at work — and a steadily growing mutiny against God and His Word is rapidly spreading across the planet. A dark spiritual force is in full swing against the holiness of God and the voice of Scripture.

Last-Days Survival Guide

It's true that believers of *every* generation have had to deal with issues of moral degradation and societal ills in the world around them, but in these last of the last days, it seems as if *all* restraints have been thrown off and society is galloping along on a collision course with disaster — and the closer we get to the end, the deeper this lost world will sink into deception and depravity.

Last-Days Survival Guide

Nations that once thrived because of their adherence to biblical values have slipped into so much deception that the rule of the Christian faith is in jeopardy, and this decline is the result of the "mystery of iniquity" at work (*see* 2 Thessalonians 2:7), luring the world to a position of mutiny against God and grooming it for a new world leader — the Antichrist.

Signs You'll See Just Before Jesus Comes

Spiritual Disease

It only takes a few visible spiritual leaders getting off track to bring the infection of spiritual disease into the Church.

How To Keep Your Head on Straight in a World Gone Crazy

Never forget that physical infections begin at the microscopic level with a relatively small number of contagions — and that many infections are often easily treatable if they are addressed in their early stages — but, if those same infections are left untreated, they can quickly grow out of control and lead to serious physical complications or even death.

How To Keep Your Head on Straight
in a World Gone Crazy

To stop spiritual infection from metastasizing inside a congregation, the person spreading the disease must be willing to "undergo treatment" by submitting to spiritual authority and correction. If the church has become diseased due to a long-term toxic condition, then the spiritually infected person may also be required to submit to a stricter discipline, and in extreme cases, it may be that the only way to bring correction to the situation is to remove the person who is the source of infection.

No Room for Compromise

If the multiplication of a spiritual infection is not stopped by the power of the Spirit, it will spread from one believer to another to another until it finally affects not just a few, but entire congregations. But just as a physical infection can be stopped in its early stages from fully developing, God calls for spiritual leadership in the Church to urgently *stop* the spread of infectious teaching.

How To Keep Your Head on Straight
in a World Gone Crazy

Spiritual Fire

The amount of spiritual fire you have burning at your core is directly related to how much of God's Word is planted in your heart.

Last-Days Survival Guide

The Early Church was literally ablaze with the fiery power of the Holy Spirit. And as we allow the Spirit of God the freedom to move among us, His gifts will also manifest in *our* midst. The Holy Spirit is always ready to do the supernatural work that the human heart craves.

A Life Ablaze

People often make the tragic mistake of thinking that just because they have been successful in the past, they will continue to be successful in the future. But I have known many ministers of the Gospel who once experienced great success in the ministry and then slowly allowed their fire to go out. Whether they fell into sin or just became lethargic and complacent, the result was they lost the cutting edge they once possessed in their ministries.

Sparkling Gems From the Greek, Volume 1

In order to avoid being taken captive by the infectious deceptions that pretenders will try to peddle, we must keep our minds renewed daily with the Word of God, stay connected in a vibrant church with spiritual fire that accurately teaches the Scriptures, and stay filled with the Holy Spirit.

Last-Days Survival Guide

When our hearts are open to the work of the Holy Spirit, He will set them ablaze with His passion to fulfill the plans and purposes of God. It will be like throwing one log after another on the fire as that Holy Ghost fire keeps us burning stronger and stronger, year after year, without abatement or diminishing till we finish our race or till Jesus returns!

A Life Ablaze

Spiritual Gifts

Many who were reared in traditional churches have been taught that it is wrong to *seek* spiritual gifts. But if these spiritual gifts are from God, why would it be wrong to seek them? If they really are God-given manifestations of the Holy Spirit, shouldn't we earnestly desire for them to work among us?

Why We Need the Gifts of the Holy Spirit

God said it's right for you to want the gifts of the Holy Spirit! In fact, He wants you to *burn* with zeal and intensely long for the working of the Holy Spirit in your midst.

A Life Ablaze

If you will yield to the gifts of the Holy Spirit, these gifts that lie resident within you will flow from you to bring His help to those in need right when it's needed. They are intended to help people — so make the decision to become skilled at yielding to the Holy Spirit's promptings and allowing His gifts to flow through you to those who are in need of a divine touch from Heaven.

Last-Days Survival Guide

The New Testament makes it clear that the Holy Spirit is loaded with spiritual gifts that He wants to manifest in the life of a local church. These gifts from the Holy Spirit are intentionally given to the Body of Christ for specific purposes, so they are vital and needed in *every* congregation. Some churches, however, have gone so long without making room for the manifestation of these gifts that they don't even know *how* to make room for them anymore.

Why We Need the Gifts of the Holy Spirit

When the Holy Spirit is allowed to move, He speaks, He acts, and He unleashes phenomenal amounts of supernatural power that utterly transform what human reasoning, effort, and talent can never touch.

A Life Ablaze

The writers of the New Testament wrote about the operation and administration of spiritual gifts *four* times more than the subject of water baptism and almost *four* times more than the subject of Communion. This should speak volumes about the importance placed on the gifts of the Holy Spirit and the prominent role these gifts should have in the life of every believer and every congregation.

Why We Need the Gifts of the Holy Spirit

God wants *every* Christian to function in spiritual gifts. *Not one believer* is to miss out on receiving and operating in this vital part of his or her spiritual inheritance.

A Life Ablaze

Most congregations today do not need to worry that they have too many spiritual gifts in operation. Most are asking for *more* of these gifts to be manifested, *not* less, and it is impossible to have too much of anything that comes from the Holy Spirit.

Why We Need the Gifts of the Holy Spirit

Spiritual Maturity

True spiritual maturity takes time to develop in our lives!

The Holy Spirit and You

Spiritual maturity isn't measured by the number of meetings you've attended, how many speakers you've heard, how many books you've read, or how many tapes you've listened to in the past year. You have to take the Word of God you've heard and find a way to make it work in your life. God is looking for people who actually *do* what they've heard preached!

Sparkling Gems From the Greek, Volume 1

Many Christians try to act like they are on a very advanced spiritual level, but too often, they don't even know the ABCs of their Christian faith — and that lack of knowledge causes them to make critical mistakes.

Build Your Foundation

We are not called just to win masses to Christ and then leave them behind as spiritual infants. Rather, our God-given task is to help people walk out of immaturity while leading them onward into spiritual maturity.

Sparkling Gems From the Greek, Volume 2

How we treat others is a mark of our maturity or *lack* of maturity.

Life in the Combat Zone

Remember that you can't go on to the next grade spiritually until you *pass* the first grade! You have to understand the basic fundamentals before you can go on to the more profound and deep truths of God, for only when the basics are established in your life will you be able to spiritually advance.

Build Your Foundation

Spiritual Riches

There is a different kind of richness believers can experience — one that can't be measured in worldly wealth. It is a richness of the Holy Spirit's presence, a richness of patience, a richness of strength to endure, a richness of faith, a richness of love among the saints, and a richness in spiritual rewards for remaining steadfast in the face of adversity.

A Light in Darkness

It is a fact that when the Word of God really comes to feel at home in you, dwelling lavishly inside your heart, it enriches you with the wisdom, the gifts, and the power you need. You become so filled with the riches of God that you automatically find yourself admonishing and encouraging other people in their faith. And when you are filled with the Word to this extent, those inward spiritual riches will easily flow out of you to bring life to everyone around you.

Sparkling Gems From the Greek, Volume 1

We must never forget that some of the poorest churches in history have been *spiritually rich* and some of the wealthiest churches have been *spiritually destitute*. Church buildings may be adorned with gold, silver, and treasures, but they are often vacant of the true riches of the Holy Spirit. In God's eyes, many financially prosperous churches are actually spiritually famished.

A Light in Darkness

When we are joined to others in the Church, the vast repository of riches we each respectively carry is divinely connected to others who are *also* repositories of spiritual riches and power, and once supernaturally joined to each other, the combined spiritual riches and power becomes beyond anything our minds can begin to fathom.

Apostles and Prophets

Jesus identifies with believers who patiently endure tribulations because of their faith. Those who suffer scandal, false accusations, slander, loss of jobs and income, discrimination, and death for Christ's sake prove the fervency of their love for Him. Jesus will demonstrate His love for *them* by publicly crowning them with honor and life for eternity. Those who experience the loss of their material goods, reputation, and potential livelihood because of their uncompromising commitment to Christ are highly esteemed by Him as being truly rich.

A Light in Darkness

If you are a child of God, you don't have to lie, steal, fight, murder, or kill to be rich. You are already "rich" beyond your wildest imagination! Even though you may not have tapped into your riches yet, those resources are nonetheless at your disposal — and they will make you feel like you're *filthy stinking rich*!

Sparkling Gems From the Greek, Volume 1

Temporal goods can be accumulated by those who are impoverished spiritually. However, true riches — that which is not measured in monetary or material wealth — are reserved for those who prize faithfulness to Christ above all else, even if it means the loss of all worldly goods. Pursue eternal riches, which cannot be stolen or plundered by man, and the eternal favor that God alone can bestow.

A Light in Darkness

Don't settle for spiritual poverty! You have every right to expect an abundance of manifested promises, power, and spiritual gifts in your life. These spiritual riches are yours by virtue of your relationship with Jesus. The day you were placed in Him, they legally became yours! In God's eyes, you are a *spiritual plutocrat* — so loaded with spiritual assets and treasures that you'll never be able to fully explore or exhaust all of them in your lifetime!

Sparkling Gems From the Greek, Volume 1

Spiritual Warfare

Preaching God's Word is the highest form of spiritual warfare, for the mighty two-edged sword that is the Word of God has the greatest power available in this life to banish the forces of darkness from any environment.

A Light in Darkness

A large portion of spiritual warfare is mental preparation. If you are mentally prepared and alert to the way the enemy operates and to the potential of attack, you have already eliminated half the battle.

Dressed To Kill

The devil wants to wage warfare against you — and if you allow evil images into your head through your eyes, you will open the gates for the enemy to attack you in your mind. What you look at has consequences, so be careful about what you allow in through your eyes.

Last-Days Survival Guide

The devil does not want you to make spiritual progress in your life, and he will try to stop you dead in your tracks! If nothing else, these attacks prove that you are making headway in your spiritual life and are becoming a threat to the security of the kingdom of darkness. Otherwise, these unseen enemies would leave you alone.

Dressed To Kill

We're not fighting for the sake of *fighting* — we are fighting for the purpose of *winning!*

Life in the Combat Zone

Satan will try to wage warfare against us after we have experienced the new birth. He will try to afflict us with past bondages, afflictions, or poverty. He will use every kind of demonic weapon he can to pull us back under his control, but we have been given divinely empowered weapons to resist the enemy's attacks and maintain the blessings of our salvation.

Dressed To Kill

These are days to exercise great caution and to learn how to block any inroads the devil would try to use to find access into our lives personally and into the lives of all God's people at this crucial hour.

How To Keep Your Head on Straight in a World Gone Crazy

If spiritual warfare is not taught properly, it can be devastating, for this subject has a unique way of captivating people's attention so completely that they eventually think of nothing but spiritual warfare. This is a favorite trick of the devil to make believers magnify his power to a greater degree than it deserves. If this trick works, imbalanced, devil-minded believers begin to imagine that the devil is behind everything that occurs, thus becoming paralyzed and incapable of functioning normally in any capacity of life. In this way, the enemy eliminates them from future usefulness in the Kingdom of God. Unfortunately, this has been the outcome in the lives of too many people who have focused on the issue of spiritual warfare in years past.

Dressed To Kill

Spiritual Weapons

You may live in a fleshly body that has all kinds of limitations, but you can go forth with spiritual weapons to do warfare in the Spirit. Regardless of what you look like in the natural realm, you can, nonetheless, be a holy terror to the devil in the spiritual realm. Take hold of the loinbelt of truth, the shoes of peace, the breastplate of righteousness, the shield of faith, the helmet of salvation, and the sword of the Spirit, which is the Word of God, for when you're clothed in the whole armor of God, you can win the victory over the kingdom of darkness every time!

Sparkling Gems From the Greek, Volume 1

The whole armor of God that worked so effectively for these early believers is the identical set of spiritual armor worn by the Church of Jesus Christ today. Just as these early Christians were fully equipped with the whole armor of God for the troubles of their day, we have the whole armor of God to live victoriously for Jesus Christ in our day.

Dressed To Kill

Your unbroken, ongoing fellowship with God is your absolute guarantee that you are constantly and habitually dressed in the whole armor of God.

Dressed To Kill

Everything a Roman soldier needed to successfully combat his adversary was at his disposal. Likewise, we have been given the whole armor of God — *everything* we need to successfully combat opposing forces. *Nothing is lacking!* Every piece of armor has great significance for us in our battle against an unseen enemy. God has provided everything you need to successfully stand up to the devil, to resist him, and to defeat him.

Sparkling Gems From the Greek, Volume 1

There is no reason for you to live your life slumped over in defeat. You are equipped to beat the living daylights out of any foe that would dare assault you! You can walk *boldly* and *confidently* — with your shoulders thrown back and your head lifted high — because you are dressed in the whole armor of God!

Dressed To Kill

Stormy Seasons

Jesus warned that rain, floods, and winds *will* come in life, but if a person has built his life upon the solid foundation of God's Word, he can survive any storm, because all that he is and possesses is built on that immovable rock.

Last-Days Survival Guide

As a believer consistently ingests the Word of God into his heart — and as he *keeps* it working in his heart, meditating on its truth and allowing those truths to renew his mind — the life and power in that Word will *equip* him for any rough weather ahead. He'll become *thoroughly furnished* to go the whole distance and be divinely equipped to make it through any stormy weather that comes his way.

Last-Days Survival Guide

If we'll listen to what the Holy Spirit says, we'll be able to sail victoriously through this stormy season and not be overcome by the evil that Scripture says would inevitably emerge and become widespread in society as the age approaches its end.

Last-Days Survival Guide

The stormy season of the very last of the last days is when we are needed most — and we have the power of the Holy Spirit to empower us to face any challenge and to conquer any foe.

Last-Days Survival Guide

Strength

The Bible promises that those who "wait upon the Lord" (*see* Isaiah 40:31) will have *power* instead of faintness, *strength* instead of weakness, and that they will soar like an eagle, they will run and not be weary, and they will walk and not faint. It promises that whoever "waits upon the Lord" can live long and live strong all the way to the conclusion of their lives!

*Fallen Angels, Giants, Monsters,
and the World Before the Flood*

If you will draw near to God's table and eat the heavenly bread He has set before you, Christ will personally provide the manna you need — *a divine touch* — to strengthen and replenish your spirit so you can finish your race and complete your divine assignment. *He will provide the manna you need to stay strong for the journey!*

Sparkling Gems From the Greek, Volume 2

When Jesus' disciples and friends couldn't be depended on in His hour of need, God provided an angel to *empower*, *recharge*, and *impart strength* to Jesus, and to *renew His vitality* with the strength needed to victoriously face the most difficult hour in His life. God will do the same for you!

Paid in Full

The Bible provides *freedom* for the mind, *strength* and resolve for the will, *healing* for the body, *vision* for a bright future, and *light* for the path ahead.

A Life Ablaze

Strife

The flesh always wants to react when someone hurts or wrongs us, but reacting to carnality with more carnality only escalates the situation into a full-fledged manifestation of strife, creating an atmosphere for every evil work.

You Can Get Over It

Don't forget — Satan was kicked out of Heaven because of his unique ability to create confusion, discord, and strife. Heaven is as perfect as an environment can be. Yet in that perfect environment, the devil was still able to affect one-third of the angels with his slanderous allegations against God. Angels who had worshiped together for eons of time stood opposed to each other over issues the devil had conjured up in their minds.

Paid in Full

You need to know that when a spirit of strife operates inside you, inside your home, inside your business, or inside your church, it won't be too long until people who used to love each other are standing in opposition to each other. That is the way the spirit of strife operates, and that is the fruit it produces.

Sparkling Gems From the Greek, Volume 1

My family and I resolved we would have a "no strife" policy in our home and ministry. We learned that strife-filled attitudes can open the door to *painful, chaotic confusion* that results in hurtful consequences. It's far better not to allow strife to rear its ugly head than to give in to it, let it mushroom to its full-blown, ugly conclusion, and then have to repair the damage left in its wake.

Unlikely

The devil continually seeks to interject thoughts into our minds to cause us to misinterpret the actions of another in order to create walls of division. When he succeeds in this strategy, the enemy divides us from the very people we need.

Paid in Full

Don't let Satan sink his hook in you through offense! Instead, follow in the footsteps of Jesus and go the way of the Cross. It may seem painfully difficult at the moment, but I guarantee you that it isn't as painful as a heart full of bitterness, resentment, and strife!

You Can Get Over It

Stronghold

A mental stronghold acts like a prison. Those same walls that keep other people from getting in will also keep a person from breaking out and becoming all that God meant for him to be. Like the steel bars of a prison, mental strongholds hold a person captive, making him believe the lie that he will fail, that no one wants him, that he isn't worth anything, and so on.

Dressed To Kill

There is no better mental protection against the enemy's strategies than to fill your brain with God's Word! It will strengthen you and keep your mind free from unbelief and lying strongholds.

Sparkling Gems From the Greek, Volume 1

There's power in the proclamation of the Gospel to snatch a person right out of a lifetime of bondage and plant his feet firmly on the right path. On that path is everything that person could ever need: light for his feet, freedom for his mind, strength and resolve for his will, and vision for a bright future. *That's* what God's Word can do! It is therefore no wonder that Satan tries to stop the preaching, teaching, and ministry of the Word! Mental, emotional, and spiritual strongholds are *demolished* when the Word of God is proclaimed!

Sparkling Gems From the Greek, Volume 2

It's time for you to let the enemy of your soul know that you're not going to bite his bait anymore, so he may as well go fishing somewhere else. You're no longer going to be a sucker! You have just been informed that there is a deadly hook inside that bait that is designed to hook you, pull you into the devil's net, and turn you into dead meat for the devil to chomp on for a long time. *But he has hooked you with that bait for the last time!*

Sparkling Gems From the Greek, Volume 1

Success

You have to *want* success in order to get it. It doesn't float on clouds, and it takes hard work to achieve it. Because most people are willing to do only average work, they reap average results. To achieve super results, one must do super work, be deeply committed to the task, and be willing to do whatever is necessary to realize goals and aspirations.

Sparkling Gems From the Greek, Volume 1

Success for one's life often happens through a series of small breakthroughs — and sometimes through even more subtle changes that can be almost undetectable at times.

Unlikely

It may be a hard fact to face but ultimately we are all responsible for our success or our lack of success. We all possess the same promises, the same faith, the same power, the same Spirit, and the same Jesus who sits at the right hand of God to make intercession for us, but the main thing that determines who succeeds and who doesn't succeed is *attitude.*

Sparkling Gems From the Greek, Volume 1

When the Bible is applied to your life, it has the supernatural ability to make you a success in life. It doesn't matter how many failures you have experienced or how many times you have faltered. If you are willing to believe, embrace, and act on the Scriptures, it will release all the power needed to set your faltering life back on the road to success.

Last-Days Survival Guide

Success doesn't come without *sustained commitment.*

Sparkling Gems From the Greek, Volume 2

We live in a world that loves to take it easy. We want instant results — and we want them *right now.* Technology has made almost everything instantly accessible. Our entire Western lifestyle is centered around making things as easy, fast, effortless, and painless as possible. A newer generation is so accustomed to getting everything they want that they don't understand there is a price to pay for true success. If anyone wants to achieve something great and significant, he or she will have to put a lot of hard work and effort into making it happen.

Sparkling Gems From the Greek, Volume 1

Surrender

When you let go of things you count dear and choose to give everything you have to Jesus, you always receive back far more than you could ever ask or imagine.

Paid in Full

Just beyond our common struggle of self-surrender is where we discover the greatest power of God. Getting there can be difficult, but once we put our flesh under and surrender to the Holy Spirit, resurrection power is soon released in our lives.

A Light in Darkness

Saying *yes* to the Lord requires surrender. I'm talking about a moment when you are willing to lay down all your own plans and yield to what the Holy Spirit has revealed to you about God's will for your life. Some people pass this test, whereas others do not. However, those who surrender, yield, and obey experience the joy, power, and victory of the Spirit. They live an enriched life filled both with opportunities to be seized and obstacles to be overcome in order to attain victory and to complete the assignment!

Sparkling Gems From the Greek, Volume 2

Dying to *self* is an act of surrender we must perform *daily*.

Christmas — The Rest of the Story

By asking us to release or surrender our dreams to God, He is never trying to take something from us; He wants to give us something wonderful. But to receive what He desires to give, we first have to *release* what we were holding on to and *surrender* to what He wants to do in and through us.

Sparkling Gems From the Greek, Volume 2

Sword of the Spirit

The Word of God is a mighty sword wielded by the Holy Spirit! He uses that divine "sword of the Spirit" to slice open lost men's hearts, attack the works of Satan, and perform divine surgery on every category of people who are afflicted in any way.

A Life Ablaze

A genuine rhema — a word or verse that the Holy Spirit quickens in your heart at a specific time and for a specific purpose in your life — is so strong and powerful that it is as if God has put a supernatural sword in your hand. With that sword in hand, you have a powerful weapon with which to repel Satan's attacks against you.

Dressed To Kill

Praise God for all the knowledge you've gained, but now it's time to turn your intellectual knowledge of God's Word into the sword of the Spirit. Then you must raise it high and brandish it against the onslaughts the enemy has been trying to bring against you! And it's time for you to turn your knowledge about faith into a shield that withstands every demonic attack!

Sparkling Gems From the Greek, Volume 1

When the Holy Spirit reaches into that reservoir of Scripture inside of you and quickens one of those verses to your memory — you are ready to wield that verse like a mighty sword as it rises up from your inner man to your mind and then is spoken forth through your mouth! And as it proceeds from your mouth, a second deadly edge is miraculously added to it! At that very moment, that Word becomes a "two-edged" or a "two-mouthed" sword!

Dressed To Kill

T

Teachers

A significant portion of a fivefold ministry teacher's task should be focused on *translating* and *explaining* the meaning of the Scriptures. Of course, inspiration is important, but the God-given task of a teacher has more to do with exploration and study than a momentary gust of inspiration. One of their chief tasks is to delve as deeply as possible into the original Hebrew and Greek so they can communicate the essence of its meaning in common language so people can understand. This may sound daunting, but with all the Greek and Hebrew study tools readily available today, this is possible even for those who do not read original biblical languages.

Apostles and Prophets

In the Body of Christ, a minister's job as a teacher of the Bible is to establish sound beliefs for some and strengthen sound beliefs for others. We are also called upon to uproot and stop the dangerous spread of misconception and error that have unfortunately taken root in some churches and in the lives of believers — error that has wreaked much havoc and harm in people's lives.

Unlikely

There are some teachings, like good leftovers, that are always tasty and enjoyable — and a common staple around the dinner table. But there also comes a time when you want to eat something new. The good news is that the Kingdom of Heaven is full of wonderful *established* teaching — and it is also overabounding with *new*, fabulous teaching that you've never heard or tried before. A good teacher — like a good food-preparer — will bring out *new* and *old* recipes for a family to enjoy! Good "leftovers" are always enjoyable, but your spiritual taste buds will eventually cry out to eat something new!

Sparkling Gems From the Greek, Volume 2

True fivefold ministry teachers must study, pray, and prepare — and once preparation is complete, they must depend on the anointing and inspiration of the Holy Spirit as they speak from their spirits and souls — processing, elaborating, and incorporating human experience to convey what God has shown them in the Scriptures. The teacher must fill his inner being with the Word of God and let it affect him completely, for only then can he step into the pulpit and publicly deliver a word from God with authority and power.

Apostles and Prophets

Teaching

It is imperative that we diligently pray for skilled, solid Bible teachers to be raised up who will feed the pure Word of God to those whose hearts are crying out for it.

How To Keep Your Head on Straight
in a World Gone Crazy

When one preaches or teaches a message that he hasn't first internalized, it is like a chef who heartily recommends a dish he has never even tasted. Such a chef may know all about the cuisine he is recommending; he may possess all the right ingredients to produce that dish; and he may even know how to cook and prepare it for others. But if he has never actually tasted that dish himself, everything he knows about it is merely head knowledge. He cannot truly speak about that food with authority because he hasn't had a tangible, firsthand experience with it.

Apostles and Prophets

Jesus constantly adapted His style of teaching to various audiences *without* mitigating the truth.

How To Keep Your Head on Straight in a World Gone Crazy

Much preaching and teaching today lacks the power of the Holy Spirit, because feeling the pressure to produce spiritual meal after spiritual meal, ministers rush to their Bibles and take out scriptures, like recipes pulled from a cookbook, to cook up something new and different. Trying to keep up with the schedule, they rush from the kitchen to the table to serve meals they have never tasted themselves, and because they never took the time to digest these truths on their own, they merely dish out sermons that may be interesting but are rarely life-transforming.

Apostles and Prophets

Team

If you will open your eyes and look around, you'll find that God has graciously surrounded you with the very people you need. They are just waiting for your invitation to help you nurture your God-given dreams, visions, and projects and bring them to fulfillment.

Sparkling Gems From the Greek, Volume 1

God intended for you to be a part of a team! If you try to act like you can do everything on your own, you're going to find it quite humiliating when you fail miserably in front of everyone. Trying to tackle a huge project all by yourself is the surest way to end up embarrassed in front of others. When you fail and fall flat on your face, you'll regret that you didn't say, "I think someone else can do this job better than I can. This is simply not where I'm most gifted. Who can help me out with this project?"

Sparkling Gems From the Greek, Volume 1

I wouldn't be able to do what God has told me to do if I had to do it by myself. The vision is too big and demanding. That's why God didn't stop after He called me. He also called others to stand with me, pray with me, and stay for the long haul, working beside me "on the under-rowers' bench." Their call is just as real as my call. They will answer for their part just as I will answer for mine. And when rewards are given, they will be rewarded for how they helped "row the boat" and keep this ministry moving forward to reach millions of souls.

Sparkling Gems From the Greek, Volume 1

Television

Even though we have an array of Christian TV channels available in our own home, I do not allow every program on Christian television to be broadcast into the privacy of our living room. I am very selective about what is allowed entrance into our lives under the label of "Christian," because I understand that a little poison ingested over a long period of time, even if it is mixed with good food, can produce ill effects.

How To Keep Your Head on Straight
in a World Gone Crazy

Can you honestly say that the Holy Spirit is pleased by the things you are subjecting Him to that you watch in movies, on TV, on digital devices, or on the Internet? Can you imagine asking Jesus to sit on the sofa next to you to watch the things you are watching, or would you be embarrassed to ask Him to join you?

Last-Days Survival Guide

Your mind is too sacred to let the world of television or social media fill it with trash and unbelief. What do you accomplish by watching television hour after hour anyway? All that does is waste a great deal of your precious time while pouring worldly thoughts, pictures, and philosophies into your soul — and then afterward, it requires a deliberate commitment of time and effort to deprogram all the garbage you've allowed ungodly, carnal people to feed your mind!

The Point of No Return

Temple

Since the outpouring of the Holy Spirit on the day of Pentecost, God has been progressively constructing a new Temple where His Spirit can dwell and work mightily. And in this new Temple, each born-again believer is singularly *a living stone* that God is using and placing side-by-side with other living stones to progressively construct the Temple He has always longed to indwell.

Apostles and Prophets

When you were saved, the ultimate miracle was performed inside your heart, as the Holy Spirit took your spirit, which had been dead in trespasses and sin, and raised it to new life. His work inside you was so glorious that when it was all finished, He declared you to be His own workmanship — and at that moment, your spirit became *a marvelous temple of God!*

Sparkling Gems From the Greek, Volume 1

To Greek-speakers, the word *temple* immediately gave the impression of a grand temple with vaulted ceilings and marble, granite, gold, silver, and highly decorated ornamentations. Such pagan temples were prevalent in inestimable numbers at that time in the Greek and Roman worlds. So regardless of whether or not one was Jewish or Greek, they each comprehended the word *temple* as Paul used it in his letters. Both Jews and Greeks used the word *temple* to describe in their respective cultures *a temple, a house for God (or a so-called god)*, or *a shrine.*

Apostles and Prophets

If everything is calculated from the biblical record that David and his leaders contributed for the building of a Temple for the One True God in Jerusalem, we can roughly estimate that the cost for the Temple's construction in today's currency would be approximately $183,056,935,252. (That's more than one hundred and eighty-three *billion*, fifty-six *million*, nine hundred and thirty-five *thousand* dollars!) The Temple itself was approximately 6,000 square feet, so if you take the total construction cost of $183,056,935,252 and divide it by 6,000 square feet, you will see that the cost for the Temple in Jerusalem was about $30,509,489 per square foot (more than thirty *million*, five hundred and nine *thousand* dollars per square foot!). This is why it can confidently be said that the Temple in Jerusalem was categorically the most expensive building to be constructed in human history.

Apostles and Prophets

What an honor to be the dwelling place of the Holy Spirit! Just stop and think about it — Almighty God designed for Himself a home in your heart! What greater honor is there than this? If you need a self-image booster, stop and meditate on that fact. *All the riches and treasures of Jesus Christ permanently reside within you.*

The Holy Spirit and You

An inexplicable, mystifying supernatural event occurred when the massive, fortified veil that stood before the Holy of Holies was suddenly split in half supernaturally, from the top all the way to the bottom. Many agree that the dimensions of the veil were 60-feet high, 30-feet wide, and four inches thick. The sound of that veil splitting must have been deafening as it ripped and tore, starting from the top some 60 feet into the air and going all the way down to the floor. God's invisible hands reached from eternity to grab hold of that veil separating Him from man, to rip it to shreds and to permanently discard it from having any place between God and man.

Apostles and Prophets

Temptation

Sometimes the smartest thing you can do is *get up* and *get out* of a situation as fast as you can — just as Joseph fled with haste to escape the seductive advances of Potiphar's wife. If you're in a setting where you're being tempted, or you feel yourself being lured to do something contrary to the Word of God — *get out of there!* It's time for you to get your feet moving and resist sin by saying *goodbye* as you walk out and let the door slam behind you! A weak person won't have the strength to say *no* and walk away — but a wise person will say, *"Enough is enough!"* and walk away.

Sparkling Gems From the Greek, Volume 2

Whenever you're feeling maligned and mistreated, it's a prime opportunity for the devil to tempt you to become bitter, angry, hard-hearted, and resentful of those who have treated you unjustly. If you yield to that temptation, your wrong response won't do anything to improve your situation, but it *will* produce negative consequences in your own life.

Paid in Full

The devil will always try to convince you that you are a tiny, powerless being with no authority to withstand his lies. If you take his bait, you'll have a very difficult time walking away from the temptations that assail your mind. Instead, you can choose to say, "These silly temptations are nothing special that human beings haven't faced many times. There is nothing powerful or special about them, and I will walk away from these emotions." As you do, you'll find the mental drama from those negative thoughts will become negligible! Always make the decision to believe that you and the Holy Spirit are bigger and stronger than any problem that will ever come your way.

Sparkling Gems From the Greek, Volume 2

Jesus has faced every temptation that any human being has ever encountered in life. This means He has experienced every temptation *you* face. Although He was personally tempted in all ways just as we are, Jesus was without sin. This means He is qualified to intercede on our behalf.

Paid in Full

Be unbending and unyielding in the way you resist the devil so he knows he is up against a serious contender. If you'll take this kind of stand against him, he will tuck his tail and run like a criminal who knows the day of prosecution is upon him. Once you start resisting him, he'll flee from you in terror!

Unlikely

It is important to learn how to recognize those times when the devil is trying to inject a seed of division into your heart. You see, he wants to drive a wedge between you and the people you love. Rather than let him get away with this evil tactic, you must make a decision to resist every temptation to get angry and offended — and by resisting these thoughts, you will resist the devil and protect your relationships.

Paid in Full

God had called His people *out of* darkness *into* His marvelous light, and He knows that skirting around the edges of darkness is *not* the way for His children to flourish in His light.

No Room for Compromise

Testimony

When you open your heart and share these holy things with someone else, you are opening the door to your most private treasures. When you begin to share details, secrets, insights, and wisdom that you've learned through the hard knocks of life and from the Spirit of God, it is a precious gift you are giving. You should never underestimate the tremendous value God places on the experience and wisdom you've gained. These are *holy* things.

Sparkling Gems From the Greek, Volume 1

The word "witness" is historically connected to the idea of suffering. If a person was called to be a witness, he was required to be faithful to the truth, regardless of any possible acts of retribution that might be carried against him by those who opposed his witness or wished to suppress the truth. Therefore, when an individual was summoned to be a "witness," it was inherently understood that it could place him or his loved ones in jeopardy. It was an honor that required the highest level of integrity and commitment, as well as a willingness to sacrifice oneself or one's status to uphold the truth. It was a very real possibility that a person could pay a high personal price for being a faithful witness.

No Room for Compromise

You are preaching the Gospel every day of your life by the way you live and conduct yourself. It is true that public pulpit ministry is a very special gift and honor that some are called to do. But the truth is, *you* preach every day that you get up and faithfully go to work! You preach when you choose to dress modestly or when you speak kindly to your fellow employees, believers, or friends. All these things reflect on the message of the Gospel.

Sparkling Gems From the Greek, Volume 1

If you have damaged your testimony for some reason in front of non-Christians — perhaps as a result of a lack of integrity or bad behavior — with God's grace, even this can be turned around, if you are willing to do whatever is necessary to achieve it. God's grace will help you to even redeem a damaged testimony. It may require that you apologize to someone, admit you were wrong, or perhaps make a correction in some area of your life, but if you are willing to swallow your pride and to do what is right, God will miraculously enable you to buy back a lot of missed opportunities and recover a testimony that had been lost.

Sparkling Gems From the Greek, Volume 2

Tests

Tests are a necessary part of life that allow you to move onward and upward in your spiritual walk. The finest porcelain product must be fired to bring out its richest colors and prove its trustworthiness before it is put on display or sent out to serve. If this is how a human artist tenderly works to create a high-quality product, think of how wonderful Jesus, *your Great Refiner*, is! He doesn't test you to hurt you; rather, He wants to glaze truth onto your heart and bring out a richness of color that you otherwise would not know.

Sparkling Gems From the Greek, Volume 2

Don't be surprised if Jesus asks you to do something that seems impossible to your natural mind. When He tells you that He expects you to take a leap of faith and accomplish what others say can't be done, His request may expose the fact that you need to work a little more on your faith! What a blessing that Jesus would ask us to do things that reveal who we really are — for only then will we really discover the areas of our faith that need improvement!

Sparkling Gems From the Greek, Volume 1

God never tests you to learn new information about you. He doesn't need a "test" to find out something new because He already knows it all. Rather, He is trying to show you something about *you* — to make you more self-assured and confident as you go forward to do His will. Every test you are going through is being done for your own self-discovery — lessons learned *if you go through those tests correctly* to give you confidence as you proceed to do the will of God for your life.

Sparkling Gems From the Greek, Volume 2

If you test a dream, vision, an angelic visitation — or any new revelation you're hearing — it doesn't necessarily mean you are doubtful of the supernatural or that you are opposing God — it simply means you want to make sure what you're hearing is really from the Lord and not some other source.

Testing the Supernatural

If you and I build our lives hastily, cheaply, or with the wrong motives, a situation or test will eventually arise that will reveal the truth of what we've been building. So rather than waste our precious time on works that have no eternal value, let's ask God to speak to our hearts to show us what we need to correct *before* a fire comes to teach us the hard way!

Sparkling Gems From the Greek, Volume 2

Thankfulness

Thankfulness is the voice of faith!

How To Receive Answers From Heaven

Even if things seem to be going wrong all around us, we can stop to count our blessings! We may feel besieged by need at the present moment, but the fact is, we each have many reasons *to be thankful.*

Last-Days Survival Guide

God not only expects you to be bold in prayer; He expects you to thank Him for being good to you! It simply isn't right to ask boldly for something without expressing thanksgiving. If you've ever generously given to someone who never took the time to thank you for the sacrifice you made for him or her, you know how shocking ingratitude can be. In a similar way, you must be careful to thank God for being so good to you!

Sparkling Gems From the Greek, Volume 1

We all want to be appreciated. I like to be thanked when I work hard, just as we all do. This is a natural, normal desire. If we'd all treat each other with good manners in the Body of Christ, it would solve a world of problems and remedy a lot of hurt feelings. But people are people, and sometimes they forget to say thank you. It's absolutely true that people should be more thoughtful and appreciative, but the bottom line is this: Ultimately, it doesn't matter whether or not those around us ever show us appreciation for what we do. *If the boat is going to move, we must row the boat!*

Sparkling Gems From the Greek, Volume 1

The truth is, *everything* is a *blessing* from Heaven for which we should be *grateful, thankful,* and *appreciative.*

Last-Days Survival Guide

Theater

In every part of the Roman Empire, theatrical stages were filled with actors and entertainers who performed music, mime, comedy, and tragedy. Theaters were also used for public speeches; however, in time the honorable talent of giving public speeches degenerated into public opportunities to mock, disdain, disparage, ridicule, and scoff at public figures or segments of society who were looked down upon or not accepted.

A Light in Darkness

By the time of the New Testament, not only had the eloquence of Greek plays disappeared for the theater, but the ridicule of Christians had become acceptable entertainment. As the crowds sank deeper into depravity, attendance at the theater increased, requiring larger and more elaborate structures to be built. The theater became a symbol of Rome's claim to sophistication and civilization — but in reality, the crude and depraved practices perpetrated in theaters throughout the Roman Empire were far from civilized.

A Light in Darkness

Thorn in the Flesh

Due to his revelations and boldness to preach them, Satan was so alarmed by the progress Paul was making with the Gospel that the enemy launched a full-scale attack to impede that progress. Satan didn't want Paul to be recognized or magnified to a greater extent, so the devil attempted to ruin him, to destroy him, and to discredit the message he preached. Paul said he was afflicted with a "thorn in the flesh" and plainly stated that this thorn in the flesh was given to him by a "messenger of *Satan*" — a special force that had been dispatched to keep Paul from gaining additional status and prestige and to prevent him from taking the Gospel further and higher into the world scene.

Apostles and Prophets

Paul's thorn in the flesh wasn't sickness or any other physical malady; it was the *people* who opposed and irritated him and continually caused him problems!

Sparkling Gems From the Greek, Volume 1

Satan wanted Paul's head on a stake!

Apostles and Prophets

Time

Because the time that is left is short, we must use the time that remains wisely!

Last-Days Survival Guide

The ability to properly manage your time and to establish sound, balanced priorities is one of the most critical keys to experiencing a stable, fruitful life as a believer and a leader. Prioritize your time by carefully identifying the things that are most essential to your life, and once you've determined your top priorities, focus on those areas and let other, less important pursuits fall into place beneath what you truly value most.

Sparkling Gems From the Greek, Volume 2

If you work *with* time, it won't work against you.

Dream Thieves

We generally make time to do what we want to do in life. In other words, if it's important to us, we'll find time for it.

The Holy Spirit and You

If we've lost precious opportunities in any area — including time lost with our families — we can *reverse* that condition. Through our recommitment to ourselves and to the Lord, we can buy back time that has been lost, wasted, or forfeited — and with the Holy Spirit's help, we can accomplish in *a short time* what we thought was forever lost. We really can *redeem time* and get back on course!

Last-Days Survival Guide

Spending time alone can be very healthy and may be what you need right now to help you evaluate honestly what God has called you to do in this life.

The Will of God — The Key to Your Success

Don't be discouraged if it takes time for your dream to become a reality in your life! God never gets in a hurry, because godly character is more important to Him than gifts, talents, or temporary success in the eyes of other people. He wants to use you, but He also wants you to be ready to be used!

Sparkling Gems From the Greek, Volume 1

Learn to appreciate the stage of life you're in right now. You are on *God's* schedule; He's not on *yours*.

Unlikely

Our God is a Redeemer, and He has the amazing ability to redeem what has been lost and to restore both time and opportunities that were lost along the way.

Last-Days Survival Guide

As committed Christians, we must determine to live with our eyes wide open to the times we live in and to the events that are occurring around us.

Last-Days Survival Guide

Tithe

If your spending habits are so out of control that you don't tithe and cannot give to other works that the Holy Spirit prompts you to support, then you're failing a test that God uses to determine whether you're ready to be promoted into higher realms of spiritual power, responsibility, and authority. Since God *is* looking at how you manage your money, do you think He finds you faithful and therefore ready for a big promotion — or do you think God finds you lacking and therefore not ready for the next step up in His good plan for you?

Sparkling Gems From the Greek, Volume 2

God's promise is that the moment we open our hand to give the tithe on all the increase God brings, He will open

His mouth to rebuke the devil. For those who give, God literally promises that He will tell the devil, "Move off of those people because they are tithers!"

A Life Ablaze

Be unmoved in your commitment to support the work of God, regardless of what is happening in the economy. Every time you write a check for the furtherance of God's Kingdom, *God is watching.* He sees each time you cut back on something else but refuse to skimp on your tithes and offerings. *God sees it all, and He takes note of your unwavering commitment to support His work.* And as a result, God will provide for you in ways that your natural resources could never provide. *God will multiply your seed back to you in ways you could never expect or anticipate.*

Sparkling Gems From the Greek, Volume 2

If you've been having financial difficulty or other problems in your life, the issue may be that you have unintentionally removed yourself from the sphere of God's blessing and, as a result, you are experiencing the effects of the enemy's access into your life. You need to understand that this kind of difficulty could be self-imposed because of a wrong heart or wrong action. If you have chosen not to give God the tithe, which biblically belongs to Him, you have removed yourself from the place of divine blessing.

A Life Ablaze

Titles

Titles are very important, as they define relationships, for example the words "Daddy" and "Mother" define the unique relationship between a child and a parent. The word "boss" defines a relationship between an employee and his employer, a relationship much different than the one that exists between the employee and his fellow employees. In a nation, the words "Mr. President" define the relationship between a nation and its leader. Likewise, the word "pastor" defines a relationship between a congregation and their pastor. Titles are so important to provide clarity to relationships and define who people are in our lives that a world without titles would be a world with confusion, because titles give rank, order, and definition to relationships.

Apostles and Prophets

Jesus told the disciples, "Ye call me Master and Lord: and ye say well; for so I am" (John 13:13). He affirmed that it was correct that the disciples called Him by the title "Master," for that title defined *who He was* to them and *who they were* to Him. Although they were in one spiritual family, they were not equal in terms of mastery and authority. Every time they called Jesus "Master," they were recognizing who Jesus was and who they were. Jesus was the One with *a masterful grip* on the Scriptures, and they were the learners who were to follow, obey, and explicitly do what He told them to do. Every time they called him Teacher, Rabbi, or Master, it reaffirmed His leadership position where they were concerned — and their submissive position as learners in the relationship.

Apostles and Prophets

Transformation

As you align yourself with God, you become more like Him. His plan is not just to bless you, nor does He want you to do it His way just to prove your obedience to Him. He wants to *transform* you from the inside out and make you into the image of Jesus Christ.

Dream Thieves

Many believers come right to the edge of real change, only to turn away at the last minute in defeat. They think they're ready to tackle their wrong thought patterns, wrong believing, and wrong attitudes, but just when they are on the verge of victory, they draw back at the thought of what it will cost them to experience true transformation.

Sparkling Gems From the Greek, Volume 2

We must be willing to remove the veil from our eyes and to take an honest look in the mirror in order to truthfully acknowledge the condition of our present stage. Only after we have truthfully seen and acknowledged what we are can we make a sincere decision to change. A truthful recognition of the facts is required so the Lord can correct us, change us, transform us, and prepare us to move upward into the next glorious phase for our lives. We can try to hide our heads in the sand and pretend that everything in our lives is glorious when it is not, but that does *not* make everything glorious. In fact, denial of the truth will just keep us stuck in the same hard place for a longer period of time. To move into the next phase of our life in

God, we must be willing to lift the veil from our eyes and acknowledge that we need to be *transformed*!

Sparkling Gems From the Greek, Volume 1

When we see Jesus face to face, we will all finally be transformed into His image, free from all imperfections just as He is. But until then, Jesus will keep working as the Great Refiner, washing us with the water of His Word and allowing the Holy Spirit's fire to burn away the dross and make us the light He has called us to be in this world!

A Light in Darkness

Transgenderism

In the ancient cult of Cybele, males served as eunuch-priests. To qualify, males were required to emasculate themselves and then, from that point on, dress in feminine garments in order to be more closely identified with Cybele and deemed worthy to be called her "priestesses." Once their male organs had been removed, these neutered "priestesses" were considered a "third gender" — neither male nor female. The transformation of these men was so dramatic that they took female names, and their physical appearance became so feminine that they were frequently mistaken for genetically born women when they ventured beyond the temple grounds.

A Light in Darkness

The preposterous notion that a person's gender can be changed is a recurrent message that continually bombards modern society through its educational institutions and many forms of media. The intention is to wear people down until the shock factor wears off and they begin to adjust to the idea that changing a person's gender isn't so bad or so physically and emotionally damaging after all.

How To Keep Your Head on Straight
in a World Gone Crazy

Time-tested truths, long-held moral standards, and even scientific evidence are being tossed aside by a last-days generation who possess almost no fixed principles — especially when it comes to the issues of human sexuality.

How To Keep Your Head on Straight
in a World Gone Crazy

Transhumanism

Today the emergence of a new kind of human and new type of animal is regretfully becoming an unthinkable reality because of transhumanism and genetic engineering. Transhumanists are avidly working to produce a new kind of human being and are very forthright about their future intentions. The foundational belief of transhumanism is that human beings are weak and poor — both physically and morally — and for humans to become better and to overcome aging, disability, disease, and mental limitations there must be a convergence between humans and technology to create *transhumans* that will be less-weak and have greater abilities. The thrust of transhumanists is to see humans and technology converge, and already a convergence has occurred that has assisted in helping some disabled people regain certain lost physical features and functions. After interfacing with computers and other forms of technology, some of these individuals have genuinely regained lost function — but the long-term goal of transhumanists is to take this idea further until a greater convergence of bodies, minds, and emotions is reached.

Fallen Angels, Giants, Monsters,
and the World Before the Flood

Some transhumanists see so far into the future (but maybe it's not really so far in the future) that they envision a time when mankind as we know it will enter into a posthuman period. This may sound like the stuff of science-fiction, but well-known, large companies are already developing computer chips that can be implanted into the brain or under the skin to merge humans with artificial intelligence. Hence, we're living in a time when one can not only be transgender, but he can also become transhuman.

Fallen Angels, Giants, Monsters,
and the World Before the Flood

Trouble

Escaping trouble was never promised in Scripture, but experiencing the overcoming power and presence of God *is* promised to those who trust Him as they hold fast to His revealed will for their lives. Times may be difficult, but those who stay on track and refuse to budge from their divinely assigned place will encounter the presence of God's power to sustain and undergird them, no matter what they face.

The Will of God — The Key to Your Success

Often when problems erupt in our lives, we yearn to escape the difficulties that surround us and dream about running away to some new location. However, in most cases, there *is* no escape. It is a fantasy to think we can run and hide from the issues that face us. Jesus firmly encouraged them to face their challenges head on, no matter how difficult the situation became. This should come as no surprise, considering He faced incredible persecution throughout His ministry — enduring even the Cross and the grave.

No Room for Compromise

Don't get too upset if troubles come against you. It doesn't mean you have a lack of faith; it just means you live in a world where the devil operates and hassles people. The fact that you *do* have faith means you never have to be overcome by these attacks of the enemy!

Sparkling Gems From the Greek, Volume 1

No matter how difficult the circumstances become, Christians are not called to defect from the place God has ordained them to be planted. *They are called to stand!*

Life in the Combat Zone

Trust

Sometimes people are paralyzed by not knowing answers to issues of the past while God is endeavoring to simply give them the grace to move forward. Someday God will show all of us how we could have done some things differently. So don't be disturbed if you don't always know the reason for everything that happens or what should have been done differently.

Unlikely

Regardless of the difficult circumstances you may find yourself in, it is imperative that you know in your heart if you're surrendered to God and trusting Him in your difficulty, *He is in control of your situation.* You may not emotionally feel like He's in charge — especially if things don't seem to be turning around yet — but you can trust that God knows what is happening in your life. He has not forgotten about you, and He remembers what He promised you.

The Will of God — The Key to Your Success

When Jesus was surrounded by liars who unjustly accused Him and called for His death, He didn't wither and collapse emotionally, nor did He beg or negotiate His way out of the situation. He knew who He was and what He had come to do, and He held fast to His trust in the Father. He knew that His life was in God's hands, not man's.

Paid in Full

The Bible clearly teaches that people who trust in *anything* other than Christ will go to hell after death. It's that simple, so never let yourself forget that the only ones who go to Heaven are those who have wholly and completely put their trust in Christ alone.

Build Your Foundation

Trustworthy

God is watching *you*. So what do you think He has discovered by observing you? Do you stick with projects even when things become difficult? Have you proven yourself to be a person of integrity that is trustworthy? Has God discovered He can trust you with a bigger assignment?

Christmas — The Rest of the Story

Faithful, trustworthy, reliable, dependable, true, and unfailing people are so rare that God *thoroughly* and *exhaustively searches* to find them. But once He finds through observation that a particular believer is committed to do His will and to do it with excellence, He knows that He has found a faithful person He can depend on to lead and carry out a new and important assignment.

Sparkling Gems From the Greek, Volume 2

Without question, God's selection of Joseph to be Jesus' earthly father was not an accident, nor was it the result of a random choice. He watched Joseph for quite a long time, and He knew all these things about his character. God had seen that Joseph was trustworthy with his talents, his business, and his money. He had watched him behave mercifully toward Mary instead of being judgmental. He knew that Joseph would be a spiritual leader in his family and that he was spiritually tuned to the voice of His Spirit. Joseph had a track record of prompt obedience and showed that he was even willing to sacrifice everything to do whatever God asked of him.

Christmas — The Rest of the Story

Truth

When biblical truth is proclaimed in its purity, it acts in the same way that a lamp provides light for a darkened room in the natural realm, and God's truth that is embraced shines light into every sphere of life, bringing understanding and enlightenment and eradicating the ignorance that governs darkened minds.

How To Keep Your Head on Straight
in a World Gone Crazy

One reason that truth is rejected is the inappropriate way it is sometimes packaged. When truth comes bundled with harsh tones of judgment, criticism, and condemnation, it can cause the recipient to put up a wall of defense as a safeguard against the attack. But when truth comes wrapped in patience, tenderness, and love — it is much easier to receive. Truth in itself isn't as hard to hear as the *wrong way* in which it is sometimes spoken.

Sparkling Gems From the Greek, Volume 2

When you understand what the Bible is and the power it contains, you'll want to commit your life to sharing it in its fullest and purest form — nothing added, nothing modified.

How To Keep Your Head on Straight
in a World Gone Crazy

There are large numbers of present-day believers who, like infants, have put a lot of spiritual poison into their spiritual mouths that isn't safe for consumption. As a result, this mixing of truth with incorrect teachings not only weakens their foundation and minimizes their ability to produce fruit that is eternal, but it can also pull them so far off course that it eventually results in spiritual shipwreck in various areas of their lives.

Build Your Foundation

There is pressure today to dilute the faith to be more accommodating to the lost world, but it is not *our* faith, it is the Lord's, and we do not have the right to adapt the faith — only to *keep* it. We must protect the faith, guard it, and hold tight to it, even if it requires giving our lives for it.

How To Keep Your Head on Straight in a World Gone Crazy

Turbulence

In this modern age, society is degenerating at an ever-increasing rate. Laws are being implemented that are antagonistic toward people of faith, and Christians are increasingly labeled as *intolerant* because they refuse to endorse the activities of a morally bankrupt world. Therefore, it is important for us to stay continually aware that Christ is still seated on His throne in Heaven, ruling over the affairs of mankind. No matter how turbulent the waters around us may seem, Christ has never moved from His highly exalted seat of authority, and a day of reckoning is coming soon for all mankind.

No Room for Compromise

Rest assured — Satan will certainly try to attack you with unexpected turbulence from time to time — and His attacks against you will probably escalate whenever you're right on the edge of a break-through. But that event will provide an opportunity for Jesus to demonstrate His power and authority, so you need to see each demonic attack against you as an opportunity to rise up, take authority, and demonstrate who you are in Jesus Christ!

Sparkling Gems From the Greek, Volume 1

U

Understanding

Bend your mind to the Word. Make your mind work hard and consider what the Scriptures have to say to you. As you do your part, a supernatural understanding will begin to emerge, and God will drive a thought into your mind that will put it all together for you and give you *understanding*.

Life in the Combat Zone

The Greek word for "understanding" describes *a coming together of all the parts*. This means, if we will use our minds, God will speak to us and bring all the difficult, hard-to-understand pieces of information in our head together like the pieces of a jigsaw puzzle. And when He brings all those pieces together — we'll be able to see clearly what He has to say to us, and *THAT is understanding!*

Life in the Combat Zone

Truthfully, God gave us our brains so we could use them, and we need to learn how to use them well — but there are some things the mind alone will *never* perceive. If you have been seeking answers that your mind can't find, why not go to the ultimate Source of divine revelation! God holds all the answers you seek, and as you sincerely ask in faith and genuinely open your heart so the Holy Spirit can speak to you, He will tell you everything He wants you to know!

Sparkling Gems From the Greek, Volume 1

Unforgiveness

It doesn't matter where a person is from, where he lives, what his culture is like, or what level of society he belongs to — unforgiveness grows in human hearts everywhere. It's *universal*.

You Can Get Over It

Satan watches for that opportune moment when a person is tired, weary, or exasperated. Then he waits until someone does something that person doesn't understand or agree with. Suddenly it is as if the devil shoots a fiery arrow of rage straight into the person's emotions! Before long, strife, bitterness, unforgiveness, and division begin to mount, and friends who once stood side by side and cherished each other now stand facing each other as hostile rivals.

Paid in Full

Unforgiveness is used by Satan to put us six feet under the ground. It not only works death in our physical bodies, but it kills our spiritual life and makes us spiritually lifeless.

You Can Get Over It

We are often tempted to blame our *bad attitudes, bitterness, resentments, or feelings of unforgiveness* on other people. But the truth is, we are responsible for our own emotions and reactions! If a person does something that has the potential to offend us, God holds *us* responsible for whether or not that offense takes root in our minds. We can choose to let it sink into our souls and take root, or we can opt to let it bypass us. We are not able to control what others do or say to us, but we *are* able to control what goes on *inside* us!

Sparkling Gems From the Greek, Volume 1

Unforgiveness must be dealt with clear down to the roots; otherwise, it will keep springing up again and again. Its roots go down deep into the human soul, and only *genuine repentance* can rip those roots out so they stop growing back over and over again.

You Can Get Over It

Unholiness

Unthankfulness always leads to unholiness and to thinking and actions that are *ill-mannered, impure, unclean, lewd, indecent, crude, coarse, vulgar, offensive,* and *rude.*

Last-Days Survival Guide

When society loses a fear of God and develops a casual attitude toward Him and His holy instructions, it is only a matter of time before it will begin to conduct itself in ways that violate God's moral code — and people will do it *blatantly*, with no fear of accountability for their actions. This total disregard for God's holiness can cause a person, a generation, or a nation to become *impure, ill-mannered, unclean, lewd, indecent, crude, coarse, vulgar, offensive,* and *rude.*

Last-Days Survival Guide

When people lose their fear of God, they begin to *tolerate* what was once intolerable and ultimately *do* what they once condemned as wrong and displeasing to Him.

Last-Days Survival Guide

An evening of watching television reveals that *impure, ill-mannered, improper, unclean, indecent, coarse, vulgar, offensive crude, lewd,* and *rude* behaviors are infiltrating every sphere of society. Immoral conduct is now found in children's cartoons as part of a public-relations campaign to change the way children perceive what was once considered abnormal and perverse behavior. What was once *vulgar* and *immoral* now fills the world of entertainment at every age-group level.

Last-Days Survival Guide

When God is put to the side in society, it will begin a slippery, downward slide into *unholiness.*

Last-Days Survival Guide

Unity

When the Body of Christ focuses on doctrinal differences, we remain divided — but when we gaze upon Christ, often minor differences evaporate in His glory and we are divinely melded into a supernatural unity that is indeed *remarkable*. Although, I do recognize some doctrinal differences are very important, and I am not negating this reality.

Apostles and Prophets

Unity doesn't mean we blindly agree with each other like mindless robots. Likewise, silence and compliance don't necessarily spell unity.

Sparkling Gems From the Greek, Volume 2

It is simply a fact that phenomenal results are reaped when people become cemented together by a common goal and produce *unity*. When this kind of chemistry is at work among your team members in your church, ministry, business, or organization, that team becomes a mighty force that helps you reach the goals and visions God has placed in your heart.

Sparkling Gems From the Greek, Volume 1

What would life be like if everyone was exactly like you? There would be gaping holes and terrible deficiencies all around us. Rather than allow differences in personalities to rub us the wrong way, we need to let the Holy Spirit teach us to see the benefit that each person we meet has to offer!

Sparkling Gems From the Greek, Volume 2

Even among my most cherished friends in ministry, sometimes we see things differently and have various opinions about certain minor doctrinal matters. Yet I experience amazing unity with them because our focus is not on our differences — it's on the lordship of Christ over the Church. And when we focus on Jesus, these differences fade and melt away and God's Spirit miraculously blends our hearts and minds together in worship of Him. We are reminded of our unified effort to carry out the all-essential Great Commission in the earth.

Apostles and Prophets

What a pity to let our differences go on separating us when the things that distinguish us from each other could be helping us. The truth is, we need a whole spectrum of personalities in order for us to be complete and to success-fully perform in life.

Sparkling Gems From the Greek, Volume 2

My own ministry has been powerfully enriched because I am a part of a "symphony orchestra" of ministers in the city of Moscow. The unified front of this group has made an impact that could never have been as great if each of us had tried to accomplish the same goals individually. Over the years, we have spoken to each other in ways that have positively changed our attitudes, doctrines, and practices. Do we always agree on finer points of doctrine? No! But we're the family of God, and we act like it. After all, we don't always agree with our natural family members either — but we're all still family, tied together by blood and birth. The same thing is true in the family of God.

Sparkling Gems From the Greek, Volume 2

Unsaved

If you have friends or family who are unsaved and blinded to the Gospel or who have wandered from the Truth, now more than ever before, it's time to fervently pray for God to open their spiritual eyes so they can see the truth for themselves and be transformed by the power of Jesus Christ.

Last-Days Survival Guide

Think of people you know who need to receive Jesus as their Savior — as well as Christians who have strayed and who need to rededicate their lives to the Lord. Do you love them enough to sit down with them and tell them the truth, explaining how serious their spiritual condition is according to the Word of God? If you were unsaved — or living in a backslidden state — wouldn't you hope someone would care about *you* enough to tell you the truth?

Repentance

As you share Jesus Christ with your family and friends, don't overlook the fact that the Holy Spirit is speaking to their hearts at the same time you are speaking to their ears. The Spirit of God will use you and your witness to stir hunger deep in their hearts, and long after you are done talking, God will still be dealing with them. Later, when they come to Jesus, they will thank you for loving them enough to care for their souls!

Paid in Full

Unthankfulness

Jesus said that an *unthankful* attitude is evil!

Last-Days Survival Guide

Don't fall into this mindset of unthankfulness. It is a trap the devil wants you to fall into because he knows where it will lead you — it will darken your mind and, ultimately, your *life*. You must resist it and determine to continually maintain an attitude of thankfulness, regardless of the circumstances surrounding you at the moment.

Last-Days Survival Guide

History shows that *unthankful* people are generally *not* God-fearing people.

Last-Days Survival Guide

Western nations are being groomed to live under a system of entitlement and benefits at the government's and taxpayers' expense. It's as if there has been a cultivated dependency mindset that has bridged generations, making the cycle of entitlement more entrenched into people's way of thinking as it has been perpetuated for years on end. All of this is a result of an attitude of *unthankfulness* and *entitlement*, which produces a narcissistic mindset that continually says, "What's in this for *me*?" As much as these people possess — and as much as will be heaped on them in the form of benefits they didn't have to labor for — they don't feel thankful, because they feel *entitled* to it all.

Last-Days Survival Guide

It is spiritually criminal to be unthankful for what we have in life, even if it seems like we have *little* compared to someone else's blessings.

Last-Days Survival Guide

Unwavering

Those who are *single-minded* are in a solid, convinced position and hold tightly to what God has told them. Heart, soul, and mouth — all are in agreement with that which God has promised. Although they still have imperfections that seem glaring to them personally, this one quality of being *single-minded* and *unwavering* is enough to bring the manifestation of what God has promised them, regardless of their other flaws.

Sparkling Gems From the Greek, Volume 2

Like Abraham and others who have seen the impossible come to pass, you must be steadfast and stable in your stance of faith — not *moving*, not *budging*, and not *wavering*. You must resolve to stand in faith and give glory to God, because what is impossible with men is possible with God!

Sparkling Gems From the Greek, Volume 2

Early Christians were bombarded daily with opportunities to deny their faith. Yet even in the face of these immense external pressures, there was a core of steadfast individuals in this church who *refused* to waver in their commitment to Christ. This company of believers simply would not cave in to the nonstop badgering and intimidation of the pagan population or government authorities.

No Room for Compromise

Satan will always attempt to sidetrack you and me and anyone else whom God calls to do a job. The enemy will try to use discouragement and a host of other tactics to move us off course from our God-assigned place of service. That's why it's imperative that we make up our minds to be a *permanent fixture* in that place where God has called us to serve. You and I must be thoroughly dedicated to fulfill our assignment and follow through until the task is done the way the Lord expects it to be done.

Sparkling Gems From the Greek, Volume 2

Used by God

God wants to use you in a significant way — and your ability to be used by Him doesn't depend on your education, your money, or your status in society. It doesn't depend on where you came from. Your effectiveness in life depends only on your heart and your availability. If you'll say *yes* to God — if you'll allow Him to position you in the place He has ordained you to be and then determine to *stay* at your post, no matter what — victory *will* come to you.

The Will of God — The Key to Your Success

You have a voice within your sphere of influence, perhaps even beyond what you have yet conceived, so what are your gifts, abilities, and opportunities that the Lord has placed within you and at your disposal? How might God want to use you to reach those around you? I urge you to let God show you how to help establish His truth as the eternal compass in people's hearts in this day — even if it is in one heart at a time.

How To Keep Your Head on Straight
in a World Gone Crazy

You will become a person God can use to help people in need only when you get your eyes off yourself and start focusing on those around you.

Last-Days Survival Guide

All kinds of vessels and people are needed in God's house. Just imagine how dysfunctional a house would be if all the vessels in it were made of gold, silver, precious stones, or highly priced porcelain. You couldn't function in such a house! In fact, you would probably be afraid to even move about in a house where everything was made of precious materials. For a house to function normally, it needs regular pots and pans. The utensils in the kitchen may not receive the same adulation as the more elegant objects displayed in the living room showcase, but kitchen utensils are indispensable for the proper functioning of a household. Just try cooking bacon and eggs in porcelain vases or with utensils made of gold and silver, and you'll be quickly reminded how important regular ol' pots and pans are!

Sparkling Gems From the Greek, Volume 2

For God to be able to use you to effectively help others, you need to tell fear farewell *forever*.

Last-Days Survival Guide

I know many well-known spiritual leaders who are alive today. They are my personal friends. I could use some of them as modern-day examples of how God uses normal, common, flawed human beings. Rather than go into detail about them, let me assure you that God is still in the business of using people made of dust, and perhaps no illustration of this truth is clearer to me personally than the fact that God has chosen to use me.

Promotion

God *hasn't* primarily specialized in using kings, queens, royalty, politicians, scientists, philosophers, writers, movie stars, or celebrities to advance His Kingdom. From the onset of time, God has reached into the hearts of *ordinary* men and women. These are the ones who most often accomplish mighty feats through His grace and power. So if God isn't looking for the upper crust of society, He must be looking to "the lower crust" — in other words, *to the ordinary, usual, regular, routine, run-of-the-mill, standard, typical kind of people.* This means that if you come from a normal, average background — you are possibly the very one God wants to use!

Sparkling Gems From the Greek, Volume 1

Victors

We are *at all times,* and *in every place,* and *in every way* always triumphant in Christ!

Last-Days Survival Guide

God sends us to invade the enemy's territory to plunder him! Regardless of what type of season you and I are living in right now, Christ's power enables us to overcome every obstacle, barrier, and difficulty and to victoriously share in Christ's triumph over the enemy.

Last-Days Survival Guide

We are not *victims* — we are *victors!*

Last-Days Survival Guide

With the Word of God in our hearts and the Holy Spirit's power working in us — we are supernaturally equipped for any circumstance that tries to rise against us. We may face situations we've never faced before, and we may need wisdom unlike any wisdom we've ever needed, but if we will rely on the Word of God and the Spirit of God, we will have everything we need to triumph in Christ!

Signs You'll See Just Before Jesus Comes

Christ has called us to rise up as mighty, Spirit-filled victors!

Last-Days Survival Guide

We were not born at this time in God's prophetic timeline by accident, so rather than fret because the world seems to be going haywire, we need to embrace the anointing God has made available for each of us who are part of this last-days generation — and regardless of what we see, hear, or feel, these truths remain: Jesus *is* Lord, His Kingdom and Word *will* prevail, and *nothing* will ever change that!

Last-Days Survival Guide

If we will reinforce ourselves with the Word of God, avail ourselves to the power of the Holy Spirit, use the weapons of warfare given to us, and learn to lean on others who are in the fight with us — we can live as *triumphant victors.*

Last-Days Survival Guide

Victory

As you take your steps of faith, the bleachers of Heaven are *filled* with people who faced great challenges, refused to deviate from God's plan, and eventually won. They faced the impossible, they accomplished the unthinkable, and they are proof that you can make it too — and they're all cheering you on to victory! Just listen with the ears of faith, and you'll hear them shouting, *"Go for it! You can do it! Your faith will carry you through!"*

The Will of God — The Key to Your Success

There is no reason for you to live your life slumped over in defeat. You are equipped to beat the living daylights out of any foe that would dare assault you! You can walk boldly and confidently — with your shoulders thrown back and your head lifted high — because you are dressed in the whole armor of God!

Dressed To Kill

By serving Jesus Christ, you have joined the greatest Champion in the universe. There is no power that can equal or surpass His power. There is no might on planet earth to compare with His awesome might. And just think — when you become a child of God, you become a joint heir with Him! Everything He possesses — including His power and His victory — becomes yours!

Sparkling Gems From the Greek, Volume 1

You must determine to *never* let defeat determine your theology.

The Will of God — The Key to Your Success

Jesus completely destroyed Satan's power over you through His death and resurrection. Satan was utterly smashed, crushed, and bruised by Jesus' victorious resurrection from the dead. Now your mission is to reinforce the victory already won and to demonstrate just how miserably defeated Satan already is!

Dressed To Kill

It doesn't matter what the devil does — God is able to turn it around and make it work for your good. Even though

God did not authorize the assault waged against you and would never do such things to you. But by the time God is done using that attack as a stepping-stone to get you to a place of greater victory, the devil will be sorry he ever attacked you!

The Will of God — The Key to Your Success

The victory is already yours! Your healing, your miracle, your financial blessing — all of these are already yours! Jesus accomplished a total, complete, and perfect work on the Cross of Calvary and in His resurrection from the dead!

Dressed To Kill

There have been many moments in my own life when I felt overwhelmed by circumstances and challenges. Usually those are the times when the devil seized the opportunity to whisper, *There is no way out. You have no way to crawl out from where you are. You're trapped with no escape.* However, his words of discouragement and despair have *never* proven to be true! Although it may have taken longer than I anticipated to reach my goal and may have required me to grow to new levels of faith, there was always a way to do whatever Jesus had asked me to do. I ultimately found victory in every challenge.

Sparkling Gems From the Greek, Volume 2

Refuse to cooperate with negativism and make a faith declaration that you are *not* participating in a crisis. Declare that this crisis is going to turn out to be the greatest opportunity you've ever experienced and that you will sail through this event with victory!

The Will of God — The Key to Your Success

Life can be overwhelming at times, so we need to remember that although we may experience momentary afflictions, our victory in Christ is *permanent* and *eternal.* When the shifting tides of life threaten to unnerve us or to displace our footing, we need to recognize the permanent stability of our True Foundation, Jesus Christ. He is our Strong Tower, our Shelter, and our Dwelling Place!

Sparkling Gems From the Greek, Volume 2

Warriors *deserve* rewards. Good athletes *earn* recognition. Farmers have *every right* to eat their crops. And if *you* are living and fighting by faith to see a certain victory in your life, you can claim God's promise that a day is coming when you will eat the sweet fruit of victory!

Sparkling Gems From the Greek, Volume 1

There is absolutely no impasse you cannot get through or conquer if you are really determined to achieve your God-given assignment. Don't stop until you know you've finished the job! *God is with you and you can do it!*

The Will of God — The Key to Your Success

With the Word of God as your guide, the Holy Spirit as your Teacher, and the support of brothers and sisters in the Christian community, you can rise above anything the enemy has waged against you — and you can live the rest of your life victoriously.

Last-Days Survival Guide

Never forget — the only place that rightfully belongs to the devil is the small space of ground right under your feet! (*See* Romans 16:20.)

Sparkling Gems From the Greek, Volume 1

Violence

This present "civilized," "sophisticated," and "technologically advanced" generation is the most "wholly given to violence" generation in human history. Violence is glorified on television, on the Internet, in music, and in video games. Violence is the hottest-selling ticket at the box office, and children across the world *play to kill* with video games that realistically emulate murder. The long-term result is evident, as actual acts of violence are increasing in every part of society today. If we will listen to the Holy Spirit, we will hear His voice pleading with us to turn off violence in our homes — through *all* forms of media.

Last-Days Survival Guide

We are in the midst of a morality-altering period, and as a result, moral filth and violence are overflowing through every avenue and medium — in television, movies, music, Internet, gaming, print, and even educational institutions.

Signs You'll See Just Before Jesus Comes

Entertainment with violence has only increased in popularity. Great masses of people are finding pleasure in thrilling movies and TV shows filled with carnage. Just as the ancient Romans had a taste for blood, modern society pays money to sit and be entertained by murder, barbarism, and bloodshed.

Last-Days Survival Guide

The slower, kinder, safer world many of us grew up in is nearly gone, and with every new day it seems like society is being inundated with violence. People are increasingly intrigued by images of violence, and statistics at the time of this writing even show that it is seeping more and more into mainstream media. Anyone with spiritual eyes opened can see that violence is on the rise.

Fallen Angels, Giants, Monsters,
and the World Before the Flood

The Holy Spirit prophesied that in the last of the last days, violence would become *even more* widespread and commonplace in society, and this present generation has seen so much brutality as entertainment on screens in front of them that they have become numb to its hideousness.

Last-Days Survival Guide

Vision

Maintaining a clear-cut, unambiguous, and indisputable vision is vital for your life. That trail may occasionally lead you through dense forests, dry places, and even occasional danger, but if you stay on track, the vision God placed in your heart will ultimately lead you to His destination for your life.

The Will of God — The Key to Your Success

Your dream — your God-given vision, your word from the Lord — is unique. God has a special plan for you that is for you alone and no one else. In fact, you are so special and unique that God had His hand on your life even before the foundation of the world!

Dream Thieves

Prayer is essential to fulfilling your vision. Not only is it the only way you're going to discover the specific boundaries and perimeters of your vision, but it's the only way you will discover *how, when, where,* and *with whom* you are to proceed.

The Point of No Return

There is something about seeing — visualizing, dreaming, and imagining — what God has promised us that causes faith to rise up in our hearts and sustain us in difficult times. We should never underestimate the power of the images and dreams God places in our hearts and minds.

Dream Thieves

Voting

Believers in New Testament times had no option to vote. I'm sure if they had been given the right to vote, they would have rushed to the polling booths to cast their votes. But the only vote they could cast was in prayer — so they prayed! Since their governmental leaders were entrenched in power and there was nothing they could do to change it, these early believers took their role in prayer very seriously. And ultimately the power of those prayers brought about change far greater than any election day could ever produce!

Sparkling Gems From the Greek, Volume 2

A democratic system allows people to vote, and we must exercise this cherished right. But once the election is over, we have to face the fact that the men and women who have been placed in positions of power are there because of the democratic system that elected them. They represent the choice of the people who put them there. If we are unsatisfied with the outcome, our opportunity is coming again a few years down the road to change the situation.

Sparkling Gems From the Greek, Volume 2

Waiting

You may be tempted to feel like you've wasted years waiting for your calling or your dream to come to pass. The devil may try to beguile you into thinking your bold confessions of faith are mere fantasies that are never going to happen. But God's Word promises He will reward you for all you've sacrificed and invested along the way. He has heard every faith declaration you have made, and He will reward you and reimburse you for all the time, energy, commitment, and money you've given over the years!

Sparkling Gems From the Greek, Volume 1

If you use your time wisely, there will be no wasted time in your life, but if you just sit around and complain that it's taking too long to get where you want to go, you *will* waste time. Sitting and complaining doesn't make anything happen faster — and it often further delays the manifestation of the answer you've been waiting for.

Sparkling Gems From the Greek, Volume 1

Perhaps you know people who once intensely longed to do the will of God and who firmly believed in what God had called them to do. But when it didn't turn out the way they expected or when they hit a few unforeseen bumps along the way, they said, "Forget this faith thing! It doesn't work!" Did they back away from what God had called them to do or from what He had revealed to them? Isn't it sad to see what happens to people like this — people who had so much potential and who could have achieved so much if they had just held on a little longer?

Sparkling Gems From the Greek, Volume 1

Wandering Stars

Jude 13 addresses the topic of *wandering stars* — a phrase used to describe unaccountable "free-floating" ministers who may have started out authentically, but somewhere along the way their course was disrupted and they strayed off track. Even though they started as God's spokesmen and messengers and may still be emanating a measure of authentic light, they began to "wander" off track and thus they have veered into a dangerous spiritual place. Because they veered from God-appointed relationships that were meant to provide protection and accountability — or because they outright rejected those relationships — Jude 13 says they became "wandering stars," that is, free-floaters with no accountability.

Apostles and Prophets

Just as natural stars have an appointed orbit, God also has a predetermined course for each of His God-appointed messengers to follow throughout his or her life and ministry. In the same way that stars cross the paths of other stars in the heavens above, each minster's course will cross the paths of others that God intends for him or her to fellowship with, interact with, and be influenced by. And like natural stars that have a predetermined orbit from which they do not veer, it is vital for any spiritual leader to know those he is called to orbit with in his or her life and ministry. He or she must determine not to get out of sync with that God-appointed orbit and to not veer from those God-appointed relationships.

Apostles and Prophets

A real danger exists if any fivefold ministry gift becomes a "free floater" with no relationships who have authority to speak into his or her life. This kind of "free-floating," places both that person and those who follow him or her in jeopardy.

Apostles and Prophets

Will of God

The will of God for *your* life has been in you since the moment you surrendered to Christ. You may not have grasped it yet, but that marvelous divine plan is lying inside you — waiting to explode into your mind so you can lay hold of it and begin to walk it out.

The Will of God — The Key to Your Success

You are not here by accident. God has a plan for your life. He separated you from your mother's womb to fulfill that assignment. If you don't know that yet, ask the Holy Spirit to begin to open your eyes to see why you are here and what you are to do with your life. Your life will begin to take on real purpose only when you know what you are supposed to do and you begin to follow that plan.

Sparkling Gems From the Greek, Volume 2

When we finally discover a portion of God's will for us, His plan begins to awaken in our hearts. We come to understand what *job* to take, what *business* to start, what *ministry* God has called us to fulfill, and so forth. But if we don't hold fast to our God-given vision, tightly embracing what He has shown us, "dream thieves" will see to it that we slowly let our dream slip away. We must seize that dream — *wrap our arms of faith around it, hold it down, grasp it tightly, and place all our weight on top of it.* If we don't, the dream thieves of life will come to steal the wonderful plan God has for our lives. And if they succeed, they will steal our uniqueness and our individual purpose in the magnificent plan of God — and nothing would be more tragic than this.

Dream Thieves

Knowing the will of God and deliberately positioning yourself *in* the will of God is the combination that produces the key to success. Just knowing the will of God won't bring you success — you have to know it *and* be in it through your conscious choice to obey what He has asked you to do.

The Will of God — The Key to Your Success

When you align your life with God's plan for you, what happens is nothing short of miraculous. It doesn't mean you won't have challenges, because the devil will most certainly try to sidetrack you along the way, but if you'll stick with the plan of God and refuse to budge from it, God will release supernatural power and provision to help you.

The Will of God — The Key to Your Success

If you want to achieve God's will for your life, you must live your life every day as the apostle Paul did — with an attitude of holy boldness and Holy Ghost-imparted determination. This alone will take you through the obstacles and attacks of the enemy, ultimately bringing you to the place God desires for your life.

Dream Thieves

In the center of God's will, you are unstoppable. It doesn't matter what the devil or life tries to throw at you, there is simply nothing and no pressure that can stop you from fulfilling God's call!

The Will of God — The Key to Your Success

Wind

Change happens when winds blow — and when the Holy Spirit moves, He brings change like wind. Just as energy is produced by wind — when the Holy Spirit moves in this manner, He supplies us with supernatural energy and empowers us to do what we could not naturally do on our own!

Sparkling Gems From the Greek, Volume 2

Just as wind moves ships, empowers engines, drives wind-mills, and disperses pollution from the earth — when the Holy Spirit moved on the Day of Pentecost, He released *power* strong enough to transform 120 disciples into a mighty force for God!

Sparkling Gems From the Greek, Volume 2

When the wind of the Spirit blows upon a near-dead church, it can blow life back into that congregation again.

Sparkling Gems From the Greek, Volume 2

When all of our organizing is done and is nearly perfect, yet we still lack power, it is the wind of the Holy Spirit that can blow strongly upon us and cause a vision or organization to come alive with the life of God.

Sparkling Gems From the Greek, Volume 2

If you are someone who desires a "quiet" relationship with God, I must warn you that when the Holy Spirit's wind blows, it is rarely a quiet affair. It is usually noisy and attention-attracting — a powerful force that sweeps downward from Heaven like the roaring of the sea!

Sparkling Gems From the Greek, Volume 2

Wineskins

During the time of the New Testament, wineskins were watertight containers, usually crafted from pliable goat-skin, that were used to hold wine as it aged. When new wine was put in a wineskin, it would continue to ferment, and this process produced gas as a byproduct, which would cause the wineskin to expand and stretch. However, if new wine was poured into an old wineskin that had already been stretched on multiple occasions and was no longer flexible, the subsequent expansion of the gas could cause the material to burst, destroying the bag and spilling the wine.

The Will of God — The Key to Your Success

In my own life, I've had to intentionally determine to stay pliable in God's hands and not to get stuck doing something a certain way just because it's the way we've always done it. It takes great commitment for a church, ministry, or person to remain pliable. I'm thankful for the many assignments God has given me that have never allowed me to remain stagnant very long. *I never want Jesus to call me an old wineskin!*

Unlikely

How would you describe yourself — as a dry, stretched-out old wineskin, or as a new wineskin that is open and flexible to receive the flow of the Holy Spirit? What evidence in your life confirms that you are spiritually flexible?

The Will of God — The Key to Your Success

Winning

If we stick with our assigned tasks and keep moving forward — even if it's one step at a time — we will always win! And after we've pressed beyond our struggles into victory, we'll always be thankful we didn't give up!

Sparkling Gems From the Greek, Volume 2

For you and me to come out winners as God has destined us to be, we'll need to learn how to move quickly and hear accurately as the Holy Spirit gives us strategies to dodge the enemy's attacks and combat the evil influences that are trying to affect so many in society right now.

Last-Days Survival Guide

If you're going through a difficult time, you may be tempted to obsess over the questions, *How did this happen? What did I do wrong? Why did God allow this to take place? How did I let Satan get in and do this to me?* But your questions won't change your situation. What's important is that you deal with the devil's attack bravely, endure hardness if you must, and come out of that combat zone a winner!

Life in the Combat Zone

God has called you and has empowered you with His Word and His Spirit to live victoriously for Him and to fulfill His purpose for your life in these days, so embrace the honor of being in His plan and be who He needs you to be in every moment of this season!

Signs You'll See Just Before Jesus Comes

It's never a question of *if* we will win this battle — it's only a question of *when* we'll win!

Last-Days Survival Guide

Wisdom

Like a father holding his child on his lap, our heavenly Father longs for us to press up close to him so we can receive his love and hear his words that have the power to cleanse and change our souls, and as we position ourselves near to Him, God opens his hand to reveal what we need to know and understand about the situations we are facing.

How To Receive Answers From Heaven

You need to treat education like it is important, but you also need to understand that having an education is *not* the equivalent of having wisdom. Education gives you information and facts; but wisdom gives you principles, solutions, and answers. Wisdom gives you special insight that helps you know what to do. Wisdom contains the principles that will lead you out of a baffling situation and into a place where things begin to work again! Wisdom guides you to do what is right.

Sparkling Gems From the Greek, Volume 1

Timing is important. Moving slower on a project may take more time initially — but in the end, it will produce more stable, serious, and lasting results. Make the wise choice to move slow and steady, gather all the facts you can, analyze the accumulated information, and then seek the Lord in prayer, listening for what He might have to say to you through those facts. Only then make announcements concerning your plans. To move ahead too quickly — without taking these steps — can prove to be a harmful mistake!

Sparkling Gems From the Greek, Volume 2

People who are indoctrinated in biblical truths are out in front of the rest of the crowd when it comes to wisdom and common sense. They are easily able to look at a given situation, doctrine, or statement and say, "That's crazy!"

or, "That's right!" because their inner man and mind are so exercised by God's eternal truths that have inwardly and mentally developed them.

Build Your Foundation

God isn't offended when you ask Him for clarification — He *encourages* you to ask! When He answers, you may not enjoy what He has to tell you, or you may not be mature enough to really understand it yet, but God *likes* it when you ask Him for His wisdom. So ask in faith to receive a *bountiful, liberal, extravagant* dose of *divine insight and guidance* for the path right up ahead!

Sparkling Gems From the Greek, Volume 2

The good news is the Holy Spirit has come to teach us everything we need to know, and an unlimited supply of wisdom and revelation is available regarding God's plan for our lives and how we fit into His greater plan for man — *if* we'll listen to the Holy Spirit, cooperate with Him, and allow Him to do what He was sent to do for us.

The Holy Spirit and You

Go boldly before Jesus' throne with full assurance that He will hear you, answer you, and give you the power and wisdom you need to press through every difficult situation in your life.

Paid in Full

Witnessing

We live in an age when people want to be comforted and told everything is going to be all right. But the truth is, some things are *not* going to be all right unless a change is made. We must love people enough to be graciously honest with them, regardless of how painful it is for them to hear the truth. Especially regarding people's salvation, we must speak the truth and not be fearful of their response. If we are not forthright with unbelievers regarding their spiritual condition, they could spend an eternity separated from God.

Sparkling Gems From the Greek, Volume 2

As we present truth to people who are non-Christians or to those who are wayward Christians, we don't need to be ugly or harsh, but neither do we need to water down the truth or act apologetically regarding what the Bible teaches.

Repentance

Like a diligent farmer who works his field — plowing through hardened soil and sweltering heat during the hottest time of the year — we cannot neglect our responsibility to sow. Even if the task is difficult, we must never forget that our place is to be in the field.

Life in the Combat Zone

God uses people, and you may find that He orchestrates a meeting between you and a person who ends up sitting next to you. You don't have to be a theologian to tell someone why you love Jesus and what He has done in your life. But it would be wise for you to ponder what you would say if someone asked you a reason for the hope that is in you.

Sparkling Gems From the Greek, Volume 2

Your mission field is right down your street or on the other side of your city in a neighborhood where the culture and customs are different than your own. Your mission field is to every person whose skin color is different than yours. You are to take the Gospel to *every* culture, civilization, and ethnic group in the community where you live.

Sparkling Gems From the Greek, Volume 1

It is interesting to note that *the most violent weather of the year always coincides with the perfect time to plant seed*, and this is often true in the spirit realm as well.

Life in the Combat Zone

We must never forget that people are watching us! They see our walk, they hear our talk, and they notice what we say and what we do. We must live our lives wisely and prudently, especially for the sake of the non-Christians who are observing what we say and how we act.

Sparkling Gems From the Greek, Volume 2

Women

In the Garden of Eden, a woman operating under deception disobeyed and thus aided the fall of mankind, but in the garden of the resurrection, a woman empowered by revelation obeyed and carried the news of man's redemption and restoration!

Paid in Full

A mere suggestion by Paul that there was no distinction between "male and female" was one of the most revolutionary statements ever written at that moment in history. It makes it altogether strange when modern critics charge Paul with being "anti-women," when, in truth, Paul — inspired by the Holy Spirit — wrote the most liberating words that had ever been written about women. Paul's actual practices in ministry also provided women more freedom than had ever been granted in the ancient world up to that time.

Apostles and Prophets

In telling the disciples about her experience with the risen Lord, Mary Magdalene became the first woman preacher of the Gospel!

Paid in Full

Prior to Christ, women sitting in a meeting with men would have never happened because the boundary lines between males and females in both the Jewish- and Greek-speaking worlds generally did not permit it. However, in Christ, those restrictive distinctions *were* and *are* obliterated. But to imagine that men and women would sit side by side and participate together in public meetings was preposterous in that ancient culture — yet it happened *in Christ*.

Apostles and Prophets

Word of God

I urge you to make God's Word the highest priority of your life. Put it before your eyes every morning — let it fill your eyes, flood your mind, touch your emotions, and become your guide — and in doing this, your life will be strengthened and changed.

Last-Days Survival Guide

When we willfully take the Word of God into our lives and allow it to do its supernatural work in us, that Word acts like a divine blade, slicing right to the heart of the matter. It does what no spouse, friend, pastor, teacher, psychologist, or psychiatrist could ever do — dividing asunder the soul and the spirit and correctly discerning the thoughts and intents of the heart.

Dressed To Kill

Like a lighted match put to kindling, when the fire of God's Word is lit in the heart, it sets the heart *on fire*.

A Life Ablaze

The truth is, there is nothing more powerful than the Word of God, and it has the answer to every question you will ever ask, and it contains the power to meet every need in your life. The Word promises that if you will obey it, it will produce health for your body. It is the answer to every human need!

Sparkling Gems From the Greek, Volume 2

The Word of God carries *creative, restorative power* that can deliver us from every power of darkness and infuse our lives with the music and aroma of Heaven. Literally everything you need is in God's Word — and if you will simply unlock it and release what's in it, it will supply answers to every problem you face and provision for every one of your needs.

Last-Days Survival Guide

Whenever, wherever, at any moment, or at any time a person makes the decision to build his life on the Word of God and to allow its light to shine into the deepest parts of his being to expose the dark areas that need to be changed — that Word will release the power required for the necessary change. It will lift up that person even if he has been knocked flat on his back in life, and it will *set him back up on his feet again*. The Word of God will release so much power into that person's life that it will *put him back on level ground*!

Sparkling Gems From the Greek, Volume 2

When the Word of God takes up residency in you and becomes a vital part of your life, it will *enrich* you with spiritual wisdom and insight. It will put victory in your heart, start a song in your mouth, and turn you into a *spiritual billionaire*!

Sparkling Gems From the Greek, Volume 1

God's Word is God's power!

Sparkling Gems From the Greek, Volume 2

Workmanship

When we were saved, God put forth all His best efforts and creative power to marvelously fashion and create us in Jesus Christ. God wielded His fullest, greatest, and most creative power when we were born again. We weren't just mildly saved; rather, God took us into His hands and marvelously made us new in Jesus Christ as He released His most powerful creative forces and made us a workmanship that would be worthy to bear His name.

Sparkling Gems From the Greek, Volume 1

You were born to be remarkable! No one else in the world is just like you. Your genetic makeup belongs only to you. Your fingerprints are unlike any others in the entire world. Your blood type, your chemistry, your eye color — all of these are so unique and so special that there isn't any other human being on the face of the earth exactly like you. You are truly one of a kind!

Dream Thieves

The Holy Spirit performed the ultimate miracle when He came to dwell in our hearts. He came to occupy our spirits, which were dead in trespasses and sins and then He quickened us together with Christ. In that miraculous moment, He created us to be like God in righteousness and true holiness. The work inside us was so glorious and perfect that when it was all finished, He declared we were His workmanship created in Christ Jesus. From start to finish, we were apprehended by Him, regenerated by Him, and molded and fashioned to be a magnificent temple, fit for the Spirit of God Himself to make His permanent habitation.

Sparkling Gems From the Greek, Volume 2

In Christ, you became *a masterpiece* that Christ has *skillfully* and *artfully* created. Christ's *creative, artistic, intelligent* genius went into your making!

Christmas — The Rest of the Story

Works

We don't do good works in order to *get* saved. We do good works because we *are* saved. It's a natural byproduct of salvation to want to do good for others, go to church, serve others, and give tithes and offerings.

Build Your Foundation

What God may view as "dead works" in your life could actually be *good* works in that it is a good thing that you do those works, but if you're trusting in those good works to save you, you have misplaced your trust. Trusting in Christ's sacrificial death and His precious blood is the only guarantee that you will go to Heaven.

Build Your Foundation

When we became new creatures in Christ, we received a new nature, the very nature of God, and that new nature gives us the desire to do good works. So if we're saved, we will do good works, but we don't do those good works to obtain salvation; those good works become the proof that we *are* saved.

Build Your Foundation

Even good works do *not* merit you any rights to salvation. If you are trusting in your works or your outward actions to be "good enough" to obtain salvation, you are in serious trouble. The only way you go to Heaven after this earthly life is over is to trust in Christ and His blood alone.

Build Your Foundation

Worldliness

Worldliness tries to wrap its arms around all of us. Not one of us is exempt from its seductive pull. Take a moment to honestly evaluate yourself to see what things you tolerate in your life today that you would never have tolerated ten years ago. If we don't deal with these areas as the Holy Spirit leads us, over time we will become more conformed to the world than to Jesus Christ.

The Holy Spirit and You

Today Jesus is still crying out for the Church to repent of worldliness and carnality, and as is true in each generation, we have a choice to harden our hearts and turn a deaf ear to the Holy Spirit, or to allow Him to deal deeply with us and produce true repentance in our hearts and souls. Although Christ is always ready to transform His Church, no transformation can occur unless we are willing to hear what His Spirit is saying to us. And once we do hear that divine message, we must be willing to respond with humble obedience.

A Light in Darkness

The Holy Spirit is *not* a passive Partner. He aggressively and actively pursues you. He fiercely wants more of you. When you give part of yourself to something or someone else's control, the Holy Spirit wants to seize that part of your life and bring it back under His divine control. He even has malice toward your preoccupation with things in this natural realm. Make your relationship with the Holy Spirit your top priority. Don't give Him a reason to feel betrayed by or envious of other things in your life that have taken His place.

Sparkling Gems From the Greek, Volume 1

Worry

Nothing is too big or small to talk to the Lord about!

How To Receive Answers From Heaven

I learned long ago that fretting, worrying, and being troubled never adds one cent toward meeting needs or takes us closer to our goals. That doesn't mean I wasn't *tempted* at times to fret or feel worried, but I have learned over the years that God is well aware of every need we face and of every cent that is required. And He is *far* ahead of us — working in ways we can't even imagine — to make sure everything we need comes to us on time.

Sparkling Gems From the Greek, Volume 2

We are not designed to carry the burden of worry, fretting, and anxiety. This load is simply too much for the human body and the central nervous system to tolerate. In fact, the medical world confirms a major source of sickness is stress and pressure. Man was simply not fashioned to carry pressures, stresses, anxieties, and worries; this is the reason his body breaks down when it undergoes these negative influences for too long.

How To Receive Answers From Heaven

Worship

A day is coming in the near future when all those who have been washed in the blood of the Lamb will join around His majestic throne to worship and give honor to Jesus Christ.

A Light in Darkness

When a person or a congregation worships God from the heart — when the attitude is one of humility and intimate adoration and not of mere performance — that worship creates an atmosphere so powerful that God responds by basically saying, *"I want to be a part of what is happening!"* Then He manifests His presence and enthrones Himself on top of that person or congregation.

A Life Ablaze

During heart-felt worship, the glorious presence of God becomes heavy with *everything* that is needed — His *goodness*, His *miracles*, and His *deliverance*. It is heavy with the *gifts of His Spirit.* It is heavy with *power* to change and transform those who are present.

A Life Ablaze

With our hands, we touch people, we work, and we make money. In fact, nearly everything we do in life, we do with our hands. This is why Paul told us to "lift up holy hands" when we pray and worship (1 Timothy 2:8). So when we lift our hands to God, it is the same as lifting our entire lives before Him, because our hands represent our lives.

Paid in Full

Worship is vital because it brings worshipers into a place where their hearts are open to the Holy Spirit and He can reveal what they otherwise would have difficulty seeing or hearing. In that place of worship, the Holy Spirit can also ignite His people's hearts with fresh fire so they can carry His presence with them through every aspect of their daily lives.

A Life Ablaze

The New Testament basically gives us only one rule to follow in regard to this question of what is acceptable and appropriate in worship. That rule is found in First Corinthians 14:40, where the apostle Paul tells us, "Let all things be done decently and in order." This throws open the door to all kinds of worship! It can be quiet, loud, soft, or bold. The important thing is that the time of worship would not be something thrown together at the last minute with no thought or organization. After all, we're talking about believers coming together to worship the Almighty God!

Sparkling Gems From the Greek, Volume 1

X

'X' Marks the Spot

The body of *every individual believer* has become the residence of the Holy Spirit. That means you are a treasure hunter's greatest dream. "X" marks the spot for where the hidden treasure lies, but this time you don't have to go searching for the hidden treasure because the "X" is written on *you*. You really are the hiding place for God's greatest treasure — the Holy Spirit!

Apostles and Prophets

What an honor to be the dwelling place of the Holy Spirit! Just stop and think about it — Almighty God designed for Himself a home in your heart! What greater honor is there than this? If you need a self-image booster, stop and meditate on that fact. *All the riches and treasures of Jesus Christ permanently reside within you.*

The Holy Spirit and You

Because of the vast riches of the Holy Spirit inside you, you are a spiritual plutocrat!

Why We Need the Gifts of the Holy Spirit

The devil works nonstop to sow seeds of strife and division in the Church because he understands the spiritual treasure and power in us and that it becomes amplified when we are *joined together*. The devil knows that once we are connected, God's treasure and power in us *meld together* and enable the Church to emerge as a force so powerful that the gates of hell cannot stand against it.

Apostles and Prophets

Y

Yielding to the Holy Spirit

Far too many Christians today have come to lean on their own understanding and intellectual abilities at the expense of consulting the Holy Spirit for His guidance in their lives. They assume they already know what He wants them to do — and because they don't depend on and yield to the leadership of the Holy Spirit the way the Early Church did, they miss opportunity after opportunity to see His power released in their lives.

The Holy Spirit and You

If we will be sensitive to the Holy Spirit and listen to His voice, we will hear Him speak to us when we do something that grieves the heart of God. In that moment, we have a choice: We can harden our hearts and turn a deaf ear to God's Spirit, or we can allow the Holy Spirit to deal deeply with us and produce a desire in us to never transgress in that particular way again. God is willing to work in us and with us, but we must have hearts that want to positively respond to His dealings.

Sparkling Gems From the Greek, Volume 2

Satan may try to stop you from doing the will of God, but he cannot prevail against you if you will yield to the Lord and stand fast on what He has told you to do. In those moments of intense opposition, you will find that God supplies you with more than enough grace to match whatever the enemy is trying to do. It's yours for the asking!

The Will of God — The Key to Your Success

Youth

There are no age restrictions in God's army. He is looking only to find *yielded vessels* to accept into His ranks. Even young people can be used as mighty fighters if they have the breath of the Almighty on their lives!

Life in the Combat Zone

If you are a father or mother of this next generation, make it a matter of serious prayer and determine to wake up to the awesome responsibility God has charged you with to lead and provide a godly influence for your children and the younger generations in your life. You have the potential of changing young lives as you lead others through your authentic and godly example.

Sparkling Gems From the Greek, Volume 2

As God's people, we must be alert to the fact that Satan is loosing hordes of seducing spirits with doctrines of demons in these last days to lead an entire younger generation into delusion — and Satan has launched a covert operation to seize minds — *especially young minds* — to lead them off track.

How To Keep Your Head on Straight
in a World Gone Crazy

Z

Zeal

As years pass, the zeal a church once possessed for the things of God can slowly ebb away. Knowledge may increase among the congregation, but the believers' fiery passion for Jesus is diminished. Undoubtedly, as a church grows, so do schedules, routines, habits, customs, and traditions — and as this happens, often a subtle backsliding can occur as the people become so busy serving Jesus that they lose their intimacy with Him. This can begin to take hold in any church. In such cases, they also experience a loss of joy in their services, since joy is impossible to maintain without a vital connection to the Savior.

A Light in Darkness

The Holy Spirit will often send another believer to fortify you and help you renew your passion and zeal when you're out of touch in your walk with God. That friend in Christ will help reconnect you with the power of God's Word and the fire of the Holy Spirit. That godly friend may be exactly what's needed to help stir up the fire in your heart and to help propel you to fulfill your destiny.

Dream Thieves

ABOUT THE AUTHOR

Rick Renner is a highly respected Bible teacher and leader in the international Christian community. He is the author of a long list of books, including the bestsellers *Dressed To Kill* and *Sparkling Gems From the Greek 1* and *2*, which have sold millions of copies in multiple languages worldwide. Rick's understanding of the Greek language and biblical history opens up the Scriptures in a unique way that enables his audience to gain wisdom and insight while learning something brand new from the Word of God. Rick and his wife Denise have cumulatively authored more than 40 books that have been distributed worldwide.

Rick is the overseer of the Good News Association of Churches, founder of the Moscow Good News Church, pastor of the Internet Good News Church, and founder of Media Mir. He is the president of GNC (Good News Channel) — the largest Russian-speaking Christian satellite network in the world, which broadcasts the Gospel 24/7 to countless viewers worldwide via multiple satellites and the Internet. Rick is the founder of RENNER Ministries in Broken Arrow, Oklahoma, and host to his TV program, also seen around the world in multiple languages. Rick leads this amazing work with Denise — his wife and lifelong ministry partner — along with their sons and committed leadership team.

CONTACT RENNER MINISTRIES

For further information
about RENNER Ministries,
please contact the office nearest you,
or visit the ministry website at:
www.renner.org

**ALL USA
CORRESPONDENCE:**
RENNER Ministries
1814 W. Tacoma St.
Broken Arrow, OK 74012
(918) 496-3213
Or 1-800-RICK-593
Email: renner@renner.org
Website: www.renner.org

MOSCOW OFFICE:
RENNER Ministries
P. O. Box 789
101000, Moscow, Russia
+7 (495) 727-1467
Email: blagayavestonline@ignc.org
Website: www.ignc.org

RIGA OFFICE:
RENNER Ministries
Unijas 99
Riga LV-1084, Latvia
+371 67802150
Email: church@goodnews.lv
Website: www.goodnews.lv

OXFORD OFFICE:
RENNER Ministries
Box 7, 266 Banbury Road
Oxford OX2 7DL, United Kingdom
+44 1865 521024
Email: europe@renner.org

facebook.com/rickrenner • facebook.com/rennerdenise

youtube.com/rennerministries • youtube.com/deniserenner

instagram.com/rickrrenner • instagram.com/rennerministries_
instagram.com/rennerdenise

BOOKS BY RICK RENNER

*Digital version available for Kindle, Nook, and iBook.
Note: Books by Rick Renner are available for purchase at:
www.renner.org

SPARKLING GEMS FROM THE GREEK 1

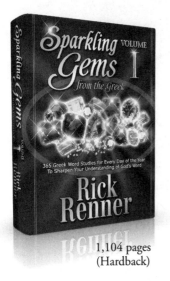

Rick Renner's *Sparkling Gems From the Greek 1* has gained widespread recognition for its unique illumination of the New Testament through more than 1,000 Greek word studies in a 365-day devotional format. *Sparkling Gems 1* remains a beloved resource that has spiritually strengthened believers worldwide. As many have testified, the wealth of truths within its pages never grows old. Year after year, *Sparkling Gems 1* continues to deepen readers' understanding of the Bible.

To order, visit us online at: **www.renner.org**

1,104 pages
(Hardback)

SPARKLING GEMS FROM THE GREEK 2

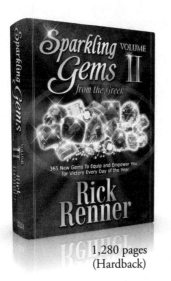

Rick infuses into *Sparkling Gems From the Greek 2* the added strength and richness of many more years of his own personal study and growth in God — expanding this devotional series to impact the reader's heart on a deeper level than ever before. This remarkable study tool helps unlock new hidden treasures from God's Word that will draw readers into an ever more passionate pursuit of Him.

To order, visit us online at: **www.renner.org**

1,280 pages
(Hardback)

DRESSED TO KILL
A Biblical Approach
to Spiritual Warfare and Armor

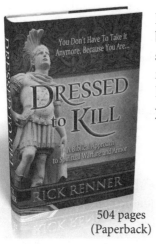

504 pages
(Paperback)

Rick Renner's book *Dressed To Kill* is considered by many to be a true classic on the subject of spiritual warfare. The original version, which sold more than 400,000 copies, is a curriculum staple in Bible schools worldwide. In this beautiful volume, you will find:

- 504 pages of reedited text in paperback

- 16 pages of full-color illustrations

- Questions at the end of each chapter to guide you into deeper study

In *Dressed To Kill*, Rick explains with exacting detail the purpose and function of each piece of Roman armor. In the process, he describes the significance of our *spiritual* armor not only to withstand the onslaughts of the enemy, but also to overturn the tendencies of the carnal mind. Furthermore, Rick delivers a clear, scriptural presentation on the biblical definition of spiritual warfare — what it is and what it is not.

When you walk with God in deliberate, continual fellowship, He will enrobe you with Himself. Armed with the knowledge of who you are in Him, you will be dressed and dangerous to the works of darkness, unflinching in the face of conflict, and fully equipped to take the offensive and gain mastery over any opposition from your spiritual foe. You don't have to accept defeat anymore once you are *dressed to kill*!

CHRISTMAS
THE REST OF THE STORY

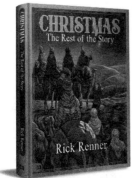

In this storybook of biblical history, Rick takes you on the "magical" journey of Christ's coming to earth in a way you've probably never heard it before. Featuring full-color, original illustrations, *Christmas — The Rest of the Story* gives the spellbinding account of God's masterful plan to redeem mankind, and vividly portrays the wonder of the Savior's birth and His "ordinary" life marked by God's *extraordinary* plan.

304 pages
(Hardback)

If you want to be taken back in your imagination to this earth-shaking course of events that changed the history of the whole world, this book is a *must-have* not just for the Christmas season, but for all time. *Topics include:*

- Why God chose Mary and Joseph.

- The significance of the *manger* and *swaddling clothes.*

- Why angels viewed *God in the flesh* with such wonderment.

- Why King Herod was so troubled by this historical birth.

- How we can prepare for Christ's *next* coming.

Christmas — The Rest of the Story is sure to be a favorite in your family for generations to come! Jesus' birth is truly *the greatest story on earth* — perhaps never more uniquely told than in the pages of this book.

To order, visit us online at: **www.renner.org**

Book Resellers: Contact Harrison House at 800-722-6774 or visit **www.HarrisonHouse.com** for quantity discounts.

APOSTLES AND PROPHETS

THEIR ROLES IN THE PAST, THE PRESENT, AND THE LAST DAYS

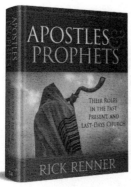

804 pages
(Paperback)

Did the offices of the apostle and prophet pass away with the last of Jesus' disciples? *They did not!*

In his book ***Apostles and Prophets — Their Roles in the Past, the Present, and the Last Days***, Rick Renner biblically defines and historically traces these ministry gifts from the time of the Early Church to TODAY!

Containing 20 pages of vivid illustrations that narrate Old and New Testament history as you have perhaps never seen it, this book answers such questions as:

- Why is the Church referred to in Scripture as a *vineyard*, a *body*, and a *temple* or *building*?

- What is Christ's real intention and masterful plan for His last-days Church?

- Does every member of the Church have a priestly ministry to fulfill?

- Shouldn't *every* believer be prophetic?

- What is an apostle — and what is a *false* apostle?

- What signs must accompany the ministry of a true apostle?

- What is a prophet — and what is a *false* prophet?

- What signs must accompany the ministry of a true prophet?

To order, visit us online at: **www.renner.org**

Book Resellers: Contact Harrison House at 800-722-6774 or visit **www.HarrisonHouse.com** for quantity discounts.

YOU CAN GET OVER IT
How To Confront, Forgive, and Move On

256 pages
(Paperback)

There's no doubt that at some point in your life, someone has wronged you. You may even be in a painful situation right now. But you don't have to let anyone's actions against you pollute your attitude toward God and prevent His good plan for your future. If someone has committed an offense against you, God will deal with that person. What matters now is that you stop unforgiveness and bitterness before they begin producing their deadly fruit in your life.

In this book *You Can Get Over It: How To Confront, Forgive, and Move On*, Rick Renner helps you find your way out of the emotional prison that has tried to hold you captive. Jesus understands every frustration, emotion, and temptation you have, and with His help, you can learn to let go of the offense and strife the enemy is trying to use to ensnare you.

God wants to help *you* so that the pain and trouble of bitterness don't immobilize you any longer. Let God speak to you through these pages so that you can walk free into the future He has planned for your life. No matter what the offense, *He has truly made a way for you to get over it!*

To order, visit us online at: **www.renner.org**

Book Resellers: Contact Harrison House at 800-722-6774 or visit **www.HarrisonHouse.com** for quantity discounts.

MY PEACE-FILLED DAY
A SPARKLING GEMS FROM THE GREEK
GUIDED DEVOTIONAL JOURNAL

256 pages
(Paperback)

Do you feel like you're on a merry-go-round of stress and anxiety that just won't stop? Do you feel like the circumstances around you are shouting *loudly* as you search for peace and calm?

Help is here! You *can* live in peace — fearless and free!

In *My Peace-Filled Day: A Sparkling Gems From the Greek Guided Devotional Journal*, Rick Renner shares 31 teachings, expounding from his thorough knowledge of the Greek language, to help you take hold of the God-given peace that belongs to you. As you devote yourself to the scriptural truths in each devotional — and journal your answers to thought-provoking questions — the power of God will melt away the fears, anxieties, and cares of this world until His peace takes centerstage in your life.

Don't let the turmoil of this world swirl you into an emotional frenzy. As you encounter God on every page of this devotional journal, you will find yourself living the peace-filled life your loving Heavenly Father wants for you!

To order, visit us online at: **www.renner.org**

Book Resellers: Contact Harrison House at 800-722-6774 or visit **www.HarrisonHouse.com** for quantity discounts.

IGNITING A POWERFUL PRAYER LIFE

A Sparkling Gems From the Greek
Guided Devotional Journal

256 pages
(Paperback)

Igniting a Powerful Prayer Life: A Sparkling Gems From the Greek Guided Devotional Journal can take you from feeling overwhelmed by the signs of the times to enjoying a serene sense of wholeness and well-being as you walk and live in God's presence.

You are not impotent against the struggles of broken families and relationships, decaying morality, rumors of wars, and unstable economies! The Father longs for you to release His power in your sphere through prayer. You only need to know how.

In *Igniting a Powerful Prayer Life*, Rick Renner uses scriptural principles and spiritual wisdom that can set ablaze in your heart a passion for potent prayer. Each lesson in this 31-day journal also includes a prayer and a confession to put the Word in your mouth and stimulate a fervent, effectual prayer life.

Topics and word studies include:

- Unleashing new prayer dimensions.

- Praying with boldness and confidence.

- Moving from fear to faith and from defeat to victory.

- Experiencing Jesus as our personal Intercessor.

Don't stand by and let the enemy oppress or destroy you *or* your family. Use this guided journal to ignite your prayer life and set your world *on fire* with the power of God!

To order, visit us online at: **www.renner.org**

Book Resellers: Contact Harrison House at 800-722-6774 or visit **www.HarrisonHouse.com** for quantity discounts.

MY SPIRIT-EMPOWERED DAY

A SPARKLING GEMS FROM THE GREEK
GUIDED DEVOTIONAL JOURNAL

240 pages
(Paperback)

When faced with life's difficulties, do you long for a personal coach to guide you? Do you feel inadequate, even powerless, to achieve what God has asked you to do?

You can experience the same inseparable union with the Holy Spirit that empowered Jesus during His earthly ministry! With the Holy Spirit's help, *you* can participate for yourself with His mission to be your ultimate Comforter, Advocate, Counselor, and Friend.

In *My Spirit-Empowered Day: A Sparkling Gems From the Greek Guided Devotional Journal*, Rick Renner shows you how to escape a powerless Christian life. This interactive journal includes thought-provoking questions that will engage your heart and mind to go deeper with the Holy Spirit.

Through 31 insightful devotional entries, Rick unveils from the Greek text the purpose of the Holy Spirit in a Christian's life. Rick's teaching will help you understand the workings of the Holy Spirit, discover how to receive divine guidance, and exercise spiritual power and authority.

Experience a life of close fellowship with the Holy Spirit and see your life flourish under His favor!

FALLEN ANGELS, GIANTS, MONSTERS, AND THE WORLD BEFORE THE FLOOD

HOW THE EVENTS OF NOAH'S ARK AND THE FLOOD ARE RELEVANT TO THE END OF THE AGE

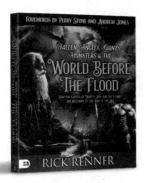

480 pages
(Paperback)

In his newest book *Fallen Angels, Giants, Monsters, and the World Before the Flood — How the Events of Noah's Ark and the Flood Are Relevant to the End of the Age* — which includes more than 300 photos and illustrations — Rick Renner answers long-held questions about the fascinating story of Noah's Ark.

Presenting Scripture as well as the recordings of early writers, such as Irenaeus, Josephus, Origen, Tertullian, and many others, Rick explains such details as the population explosion on the earth just before the Flood; the likely reason the writings of Enoch survived the Flood; who "the sons of God" and "the daughters of men" in Genesis were; why God ultimately saved only Noah and his family of eight; what happened when they finally exited the Ark; Jesus' own prophecy that certain elements of Noah's day would happen again; *and much, much more!*

Using findings from his own expedition of the remains of Noah's Ark in the Ararat mountains — along with other empirical evidence of the Ark's present location — Rick fascinates readers in this book and helps the Bible *come alive* concerning this favorite childhood story from the Bible!

God has had a plan from the beginning concerning Jesus as "the Seed born of a woman" who would destroy the works Satan wrought in the Fall of man. And just as God has faithfully executed that plan in the past, He will continue to carry it out until Christ's rapture of His Church *and beyond.*

To order, visit us online at: **www.renner.org**

Book resellers: Contact Harrison House at 800-722-6774 or visit **www.HarrisonHouse.com** for quantity discounts.

Equipping Believers to Walk in the Abundant Life

John 10:10b

Connect with us for fresh content and news about

forthcoming books from your favorite authors...

Facebook @ HarrisonHousePublishers

Instagram @ HarrisonHousePublishing

www.harrisonhouse.com